"Dr. Jeynes' family and achievement gap research is in great demand among federal government policy makers and it is easy to see why. Both Republicans and Democrats enjoy making him a featured speaker and consultant, and take specific actions based on his research. The numbers he presents and the recommendations he makes are compelling and immensely practical. His research will invariably influence government public policy makers for decades to come."

Shayam Menon, Former Public Policy Government Official, U.S. Department of Education and Private Attorney in Washington, D.C.

"Dr. Jeynes presents the most comprehensive work to date on parent involvement. With many insights, he examines the history of the field and how modern research shows the best ways for parents to stimulate their children's school achievement and character development. Teachers, parents, and policy makers will find this book of great interest and practical importance."

Herb Walberg, Hoover Institute, Stanford University

"As a bilingual teacher, this book is exceptionally valuable in helping me to draw parents into the educational process and empower parents with the most vital ways in which they can become involved in the lives of their children. Most important of all, these ways are very different from what I would have expected, and I am amazed by the great results I've seen in my classroom."

Sinnie Chen, Bilingual Education Teacher, San Francisco, California

Parental Involvement and Academic Success

Providing an objective assessment of the influence of parental involvement and what aspects of parental participation can best maximize the educational outcomes of students, this volume is structured to guide readers to a thorough understanding of the history, practice, theories, and impact of parental involvement. Unique among books on the topic, *Parental Involvement and Academic Success*:

- uses meta-analysis to enable readers to understand what the overall body of research on a given topic indicates at both the elementary- and secondary-school levels
- examines research results in terms of their practical implications
- focuses significantly on the influence of parental involvement on minority students' academic success
- addresses salient topics including parental involvement and issues of diversity; the influence of family structure on educational outcomes, whether parental involvement compensates for the effects of divorce (or single parenthood), and what can be done to enhance parental involvement

Offering vital insight into how different types of students benefit from parental engagement and what types of parental involvement help the most, this book is highly relevant for courses devoted to or which include treatment of the topic, as well as for teachers, parents, and academics who want to inspire students to achieve higher levels and fulfill their greatest potential and believe that parental engagement plays a vital role in reaching that goal.

William H. Jeynes is professor of education at California State University, Long Beach. He graduated first in his class at Harvard University and also graduated from the University of Chicago. He has spoken for the White House and various U.S. Government Departments. He has spoken for both the G. W. Bush and Obama administrations. He has spoken for foreign and UN leaders, Harvard University, Cambridge University, and the Harvard Family Research Project. His 4 point proposal given to the Acting President of Korea was passed and became the foundation for their economic and family policy to arise from the Asian Economic Crisis of 1997–1998. His work has appeared in most of the nation's finest newspapers and in Ivy League journals. He has approximately 100 publications.

Parental Involvement and Academic Success

William H. Jeynes

Routledge
Taylor & Francis Group

NEW YORK AND LONDON

First published 2011
by Routledge
270 Madison Avenue, New York, NY 10016

Simultaneously published in the UK
by Routledge
2 Park Square, Milton Park, Abingdon, Oxon OX14 4RN

Routledge is an imprint of the Taylor & Francis Group, an informa business

© 2011 Taylor & Francis

Typeset in Minion and GillSans by Swales & Willis Ltd, Exeter, Devon
Printed and bound in the United States of America
on acid-free paper by Walsworth Publishing Company, Marceline, MO

Library of Congress Cataloging in Publication Data
Jeynes, William H., 1957-
    Parental involvement and academic success / William H. Jeynes.
    p. cm.
    Includes bibliographical references.
    1. Education—Parent participation. 2. Academic achievement.
    3. Motivation in education. I. Title.
    LB1048.5.J49 2010
    371.19'2—dc22
    2010010219

ISBN13: 978-0-415-99053-0 (hbk)
ISBN13: 978-0-415-99054-7 (pbk)
ISBN13: 978-0-203-84344-4 (ebk)

Contents

Foreword

This is a momentous time in the field of parent and family involvement. On the federal front, President Obama has called for a "new era of mutual responsibility in education—one where we all come together for the sake of our children's success; an era where each of us does our part to make that success a reality—parents and teachers, leaders in Washington, and citizens all across America" (campaign speech, 2008). The current Secretary of Education, Arne Duncan, has repeatedly discussed the importance of families' involvement in their children's education. Parent advocacy groups such as the National PTA and Parents for Public Schools have joined forces with researchers and practitioners to lobby Congress to insert more robust language on family and community engagement into the reauthorization of the Elementary and Secondary Education Act, commonly referred to as No Child Left Behind. Several states across the nation have enacted laws directing school districts, boards of education or schools to implement family engagement policies. Many urban school districts, notably New York City, Boston, Denver, Hartford, Baltimore and Philadelphia, have created senior level positions responsible for the coordination of district family and community engagement initiatives.

As the level of interest in parental involvement policy and practice has risen, so has the level of questioning about the effectiveness and real value of families' engagement in their children's education. The most common questions that pervade the discourse include: What do we *really* know about the impact of parental involvement? Is there any research that *summarizes* the impact of their engagement on children's learning and development? Which *types* of involvement make the most difference when it comes to supporting children's educational success? How does parental involvement differ in type, level and scope as children grow and develop?

Parental Involvement and Academic Success is a comprehensive, detailed, and user-friendly resource for anyone interested in exploring the answers to the aforementioned questions and in acquiring a deep understanding of the research and its implications for practice. Jeynes provides a straightforward analysis of what we now know about the relationship between family engagement and children's academic success as well as the new opportunities for continued research. This is a must-read for advocates, students, researchers, policy makers, and practitioners interested in advancing the field of parental and community engagement.

Karen L. Mapp, Ed.D.
Lecturer on Education, Program Director for the Educational Policy
and Management Master's Program,
Harvard Graduate School of Education
Member of the National Family and Community
Engagement Working Group

Preface

Parental Involvement and Academic Success is a one-of-a-kind book designed to give teachers, parents, researchers, and students greater insight into what the overall body of research states about the association between parental involvement and student academic outcomes. An abundant number of studies have been done examining this association. Should someone choose to read each of these studies individually that person would find the amount of information overwhelming and the findings sometimes ostensibly contradictory. At some point this person would, for the cause of his or her own "sanity," cry out for a study that summarizes the existing body of literature and puts it in historical and contemporary context so that a practical and useful guide for parental involvement would emerge. It is my hope that this book will provide that guide and direction.

Parental Involvement and Academic Success offers the most complete quantitative analysis of parental involvement that is available. It includes several meta-analyses (the statistical combining of all of the studies that have been done on a particular topic to determine what the overall body of research indicates) that examine the effects of parental involvement at both the elementary- and secondary-school levels. It also includes meta-analyses that examine the effects of parental involvement on minority students specifically and the efficacy of school-based parental involvement programs. This analysis is supplemented by the examination of a nationwide data set. In addition, the book examines the historical development of parental involvement and the growth of research on this topic. In perhaps its most revolutionary contribution, the book examines various different components of parental involvement in order to give guidance to teachers, parents, students, and academics regarding what aspects of parental involvement are most important. These results, in particular, are quite surprising. Beyond this, the findings are especially beneficial because they are not based on theoretical speculation, but on the statistical combining of all of the studies that have been done on parental involvement to determine what he overall body of research indicates.

Parental Involvement and Academic Success examines both the research and theoretical aspects of parental involvement, and addresses salient topics including parental involvement and issues of diversity; parental involvement and family structure's influence on educational outcomes; the question of whether parental involvement compensates for the effects of divorce (or single parenthood); success and what can be done to enhance parental involvement; and what do we know and what do we still need to know? As a whole, this book gives greater direction to teachers, parents, and academics who desire to inspire students to achieve higher levels and fulfill their greatest potential, and who believe that parental engagement plays a vital role in reaching that goal.

Acknowledgments

I am very thankful to many individuals who played a large role in making this work possible. I want to thank numerous people in the academic world at Harvard University and the University of Chicago for helping me give birth to this project and in guiding me through the early stages of writing many of these chapters. I especially want to thank the late Bob Jewell for his encouragement in writing on parenting and family topics. I also want to thank Larry Hedges for teaching me how to conduct a meta-analysis, when I was his graduate student. I also want to thank a number of academics whose input into this project helped shape the direction of the book. These individuals include Wendy Naylor, Claude Goldenberg, and Dick Carpenter. I also want to thank several dear friends whose encouragement with respect to this project touched me deeply. Among these dear friends are Wayne Ruhland, Chris Ullman, Rick Smith, Dan Johnston, Larry and Vada DeWerd, Jessica Choi, Sylva Lee, and Randi Johnson. Thank you so much for your support!

I am incredibly blessed to have been married 24 years to my wife Hyelee, whose support has been exemplary. Without her prayers and support, this work never could have been completed. I am blessed and honored to have three wonderful boys, whom I thank for their love and inspiration. I also want to thank God for giving me the strength and providence to complete this project. I am very grateful for His encouragement and strength.

Chapter 1

The History of Parents' Involvement as a Concept

Parental involvement is hardly a new practice. Some of America's earliest European settlers, especially the Puritans, were strong believers in the primacy of parental involvement (McClellan & Reese, 1988). Of course, the Puritans generally did not use the word "parental involvement." However, their family orientation, evening joint reading sessions, and their emphasis on teaching each parent's role all demonstrated a high level of parental involvement (Hiner, 1988; McClellan & Reese, 1988). Understanding that parental involvement is not a new concept is important to comprehend if one is to properly contextualize the parent, school, and community partnership movement that is growing in the United States. The chief researchers and theorists in this movement are not trailblazers introducing a concept that hitherto has been foreign to American ideology (Jeynes, 2005c). Rather, these individuals are calling Americans back to a practice that has been interwoven into the fabric of American life for centuries, but due to the demands of modern society, diverse concepts of family life, and a plethora of other factors have been overlooked or deemphasized (Jeynes, 2007a). If one is to join the effort to call parents back to close participation in their children's schooling and other elements of their lives, one should avoid reinventing the wheel. Instead, the ideal place to begin this trek is to examine past American practices of parental involvement (Jeynes, 2005c). Although the nation has changed over the years, there are particular requirements in a close parent–child relationship that change little or not at all that are necessary for parental involvement to transpire and enrich the lives of children.

The Puritans and the Pilgrims

Two major reasons why parental involvement was so ostensible in Puritan homes included their educational emphasis and their belief that a strong bond between the home, the church, and the family was a prerequisite for children's academic success (Gangel & Benson, 1983; Hiner, 1988; McClellan & Reese, 1988).

The Educational Emphasis of the Puritans and Pilgrims

The Puritans placed a good deal of emphasis on education. They believed that the Bible even commanded people to be educated, given the biblical declaration, "You shall know the truth and the truth will set you free" (Holy Bible, John 8:32). The Puritans influenced the early American education system more than any of the other settlers from Europe. They founded the nation's first secondary school (Boston Latin) and its first college (Harvard), as well as passed the first compulsory education laws (Fraser, 2001; Rippa, 1997). Their emphasis on parental involvement also influenced American educational practices for centuries (Gangel & Benson, 1983; Hiner, 1988; McClellan & Reese, 1988).

William Bradford, the primary governor in the early years the Puritan Massachusetts settlement, was a strong believer in supporting "an intelligent gospel" (Bartlett, 1978). Bradford, like many of the Puritan leaders of the period, possessed a large number of books in his library for the time (400) (Bartlett, 1978). The fact that the Puritans kept records of the number of volumes owned by the leaders demonstrates their emphasis on literacy. Even though the Pilgrims were economically poorer than the Puritans, Bartlett (1978, p. 11) states, "Like the Puritans, the Pilgrims honored education." They considered the Bible the most important book that one could own, and virtually every Puritan home possessed at least one copy (Bartlett, 1978).

The early curriculum of the New England settlers focused on reading, writing, arithmetic, and religious instruction (Pulliam & Van Patten, 1999). Over time, the education system of these settlers became more defined. In 1642 the Massachusetts legislature passed a law requiring that the head of every household teach all the children in one's home, both male and female (Hiner, 1988). This law is often referred to as the Massachusetts Compulsory School Law. There was a special emphasis on helping children to read and understand the principles of religion and the capital laws of the country (Cubberley, 1934). Cubberley (1920, p. 354) noted the significance of the 1642 law when he stated that, "for the first time in the English-speaking world, a legislative body representing the State ordered that all children should be taught to read."

Charles Chauncy (1655, p. 3), an early leader in Massachusetts, asserted that education was necessary in order to prevent children from becoming intellectually "naked." The Puritans placed a great deal of emphasis on literacy, especially with the long-term goal of reading and understanding the Bible. Although the Puritans naturally did not believe that literacy was essential to experiencing salvation, it surely facilitated it. To this end, the Puritans in Massachusetts became the center of the printing industry in the New World (Cremin, 1976). The first printing press in the colonies was set up in Cambridge in 1638 (Smith, 1973). The Puritans' emphasis on utilizing the printing press was consistent with their emphasis on literacy.

Max Weber in his book, *The Protestant Ethic and the Spirit of Capitalism*, traces the American Protestant work ethic all the way back to the Pilgrims and the Puritans (Weber, 1958). Weber averred that Calvinism, as exemplified in the Puritans and Pilgrims, had a profound effect on the American work ethic. In this perspective spirituality, education, and hard work were inextricably connected. The Puritans and Pilgrims were strong advocates of diligence applied to educational pursuits. In their view, the parents were primarily responsible for ensuring that this diligence emerged in the lives of their children (Gangel & Benson, 1983; Hiner, 1988; McClellan & Reese, 1988).

The Puritan and Pilgrim Emphasis on the Strong Bonds between Home, School, and Church

The Puritans and Pilgrims believed that children could reach their highest potential in school if the family, church, and school all worked together in partnership, in what one might call a "holy triad" (Gangel & Benson, 1983; Hiner, 1988; McClellan & Reese, 1988). Traditionally, Puritan teachers visited the homes of their students before the school year began to build a relationship with the family and to obtain insight into the strengths and weaknesses of the child and learn just how they could help the child maximize his or her potential (Gangel & Benson, 1983; Gordam, 1961; Jeynes, 2003a, 2005b, 2006, 2007a; Morgan, 1986). In the mind of the Puritans, the home, school, and church each provided a vital function that contributed to the overall welfare and educational development of the child.

The Home

The Puritans, as a whole, believed that the home was the central place of education (McClellan & Reese, 1988). They surmised that if the home environment were not in order, even if the child attended the finest church and school, the child would not develop into a properly educated individual. The colonists believed that the home was where the spiritual training given at church and the academic training given at school were applied to everyday living (McClellan & Reese, 1988). The child's experience at home was therefore to be a type of spiritual, academic, and job-related apprenticeship. To the extent that this was true, the educational tutelage that a child received at home was child-centered.

The Puritans and Pilgrims asserted that it was ultimately the responsibility of the parents to make sure that their children were educated. Frequently, Puritan parents trained their children in the home during the early elementary school years and then sent their children to a Latin grammar school to prepare them for higher education (Pulliam & Van Patten, 1999).

During the colonial period, particularly among the Puritans, the father was much more involved in the raising of the children than we commonly see in contemporary Western society (Mcclellan & Reese, 1988). Part of this paternal involvement radiated from the Christian concept of the Trinity the Heavenly Father, the Son, and the Holy Spirit. Many colonists believed that children formed a loving and holy image of the Heavenly Father based on seeing these attributes manifested in their earthly father (Eavey, 1964; McClellan & Reese, 1988; Willison, 1966). Consequently, they concluded that the father had a very special role in rearing the children, particularly in raising the boys. The colonists understood that boys obtained a true concept of what it meant to be a godly man from their father. In the eyes of the colonists, therefore, the more time a boy spent with his father, the better off he would be. As soon as a boy reached school age, when he was not in school, he would often follow his father like a shadow. If the father worked in the fields, the boy would work there with him. If the father owned a shop, the boy would often work with him there as well. Likewise, the girls would often follow their mothers in much the same way. The girls, thereby would learn cooking skills, sewing skills, and learn the ins and outs of what it meant to be a godly woman (McClellan & Reese, 1988). If the mother ran the village market, they would learn how to do this job by their mother's example.

Most Puritan and Pilgrim families would have what they called family devotionals in which they would study the Bible and pray together as a family. This family time would serve the purposes of encouraging spiritual growth, family unity, increasing the children's reading skills, and implanting within the children seeds of spiritual wisdom (Hiner, 1988). To the colonists, fostering the growth of human knowledge was salient. They surmised, however, that unless an individual was imbedded in spiritual wisdom, the increased knowledge could be injudiciously used and could create much harm. Parental involvement was also important because children were expected to mature quickly. Some people therefore have an inaccurate stereotype of Puritans, believing that they treated children as little adults (Smith, 1973). In reality, Puritans did not possess this belief (Smith, 1973).

However, due to the necessity of the agricultural age, a shorter life span, and the need to help parents out with caring for large families, Puritans did maintain higher expectations of children than is present in contemporary American society (Smith, 1973). The Puritans practiced a balance between parental discipline and encouragement when they raised their children. Cotton Mather said, "We are not wise for our children, if we do not greatly encourage them" (Mather, 1708, p. 30).

The Church and the School

The church's purpose in schooling was to train the colonists regarding the teachings of the Bible and how to be loving and righteous individuals. The church was where people came to procure wisdom. The church was also the administration center for the vast majority of educational undertakings.

The school was responsible for fostering the academic development of the child. The Puritans believed that the most venerable function of the school was to promote the development of virtuous individuals (Clarke, 1730). John Clarke, a leading educator, expressed views that were quite representative of New England educators at the time. He believed that a school master must ". . . in the first place be a man of virtue. For . . . it be the main end of education to make virtuous men" (Clarke, 1730, p. 93). Academically, the greatest emphasis was placed on reading, so that children could read the Bible as soon as possible.

The Puritans believed that for educational purposes, the family was the most primary of these institutions (Hiner, 1988). Therefore, it was absolutely imperative for teachers to involve parents in the schooling of their children (Hiner, 1988; Morgan, 1986). The Puritans believed that this was impossible unless both the teachers and the parents worked together (Hiner, 1988; Morgan, 1986). Due to the significant influence of the Puritans, the Puritan emphasis on parental involvement and the "holy triad" were embraced by many of the colonies and eventually a large portion of the nation (Greaves, 1969; Hiner, 1988; Morgan, 1986).

Other Pre-Revolutionary War Parental Involvement Practices

Education in Maryland and the Southern states was regarded as more of a family matter than even in New England. One should note that essentially all of the early settlers on the East Coast believed that it was primarily the responsibility of the family to educate children. The New England settlers viewed schools as supplemental, but essential in education. On the other hand, settlers in Maryland and other southern locations, outside of Jamestown, maintained that as long as the family ensured that education was taking place, schools really were not necessary. As a consequence of possessing this orientation, most families in these areas either taught their children themselves or hired tutors to do the instruction (Urban & Wagoner, 2000). Pennsylvanian settlers maintained a perspective somewhere in between those in New England and those south of the Mason-Dixon line. They were strong proponents of parental involvement, whether instruction took place in the home or in the school (Eavey, 1964). In 1683 Pennsylvania passed a law that mandated parents to teach their children to read at a level sufficient to be able to read the Bible (Eavey, 1964).

From the earliest years of many of the major European settlements in America, parental involvement was regarded as indispensable to efficacious instruction. The Puritan practice of having teachers visit the homes of their elementary school students remained a common American practice until the middle of the twentieth century (Gangel & Benson, 1983; Gordam, 1961; Jeynes, 2007a; Morgan, 1986). So prominent and vital was this practice in the United States that several East Asian countries adopted it when American educators and missionaries helped these nations develop their own systems of education in the mid-to-late-1800s (Amano, 1990; Big List of Korean Universities, 2002; Hood, 2001; Keenleyside & Thomas, 1937; Levine & White, 1986; Sah-Myung, 1983

Shimizu, 1992). For many American settlers not only was parental involvement indispensable, but it was the cornerstone of efficacious instruction.

Parental Involvement in the Late Eighteenth and Nineteenth Centuries—the Early Years Following the Revolutionary War

The United States was very fortunate to have many of its early post-Revolutionary War leaders emphasize the importance of parental involvement (Blinderman, 1976; Kliebard, 1969; Webster, 1793, 1834). Benjamin Rush was both an educator and was regarded as the nation's foremost physician (Blinderman, 1976; Lewy, 1996; Urban & Wagoner, 2000). Rush asserted that parents needed to be well educated in order to effectively teach their children (Blinderman, 1976; Rush, 1785, 1786). On this basis Rush argued that education for females was vital for the successful instruction of America's youth (Blinderman, 1976; Rush, 1785, 1786). Rush thought that parental involvement was especially important in order to foster proper moral development in children, which most educators of the era believed stood as the most vital component of education (Blinderman, 1976; Rush, 1785, 1786). Noah Webster, whom many nicknamed America's schoolmaster, maintained similar views to Rush's, averring that parental involvement was key to maximizing a child's development both morally and academically (Webster, 1793, 1834).

In the early 1800s, DeWitt Clinton and Joseph Lancaster emerged as two of the most prominent educators in the country (Bourne, 1870; Cornog, 1998; Cubberley, 1920; Fitzpatrick, 1969). DeWitt Clinton was president of the New York Free School Society, a system of private schools that offered schooling on a sliding financial scale so that a myriad of children could be schooled at no charge (Bourne, 1870; Cornog, 1998; Cubberley, 1920; Fitzpatrick, 1969). Joseph Lancaster, originally from England, created the most popular paradigm for operating these schools (Bourne, 1870; Cornog, 1998). Both Clinton and Lancaster believed that if parents and schools worked as partners, they could have an effect on the moral development of children in particular (Bourne, 1870; Cornog, 1998; Kaestle, 1973). Clinton apparently thought this partnership was effective because after decades of serving as head of the New York Free School Society he declared in a speech: "Of the many thousands who have been instructed in our free schools in the City of New York, there is not a single instance known of anyone being convicted of a crime" (in Fitzpatrick, 1969, p. 54).

The Rise of the Common School

The rise of the national common school movement, under the direction of Horace Mann, Henry Barnard, and others had a dramatic impact on American education. However, one should not assume that the American public unanimously welcomed the movement (Downs, 1978; Gutek, 1968). Aside from political division over the public schools, many parents felt that the common schools would usurp their power as the primary providers of education (Downs, 1978; Gutek, 1968). Initially, parents also preferred private neighborhood schools rather than common schools because in the former type of school parents usually knew the teachers ahead of time. In private neighborhood schools parents and teachers were often involved in the same church and were often neighbors (Downs, 1978; Gutek, 1968). However, in the case of common schools, parents often were not acquainted with the teacher until the first day of class. Consequently, many parents felt hesitant entrusting a stranger with the care of their children (Downs, 1978; Gutek, 1968).

One individual, in particular, was particularly helpful to Horace Mann and Henry Barnard in convincing parents that common school teachers could be trusted—a Swiss man named Johann Pestalozzi {1746–1827} (1898, 1916). Pestalozzi emphasized what is often called the maternal role of the schools. In other words, he believed that the teacher should in many respects function like a mother away from home (Pestalozzi, 1898, 1916). The contribution of Pestalozzi was especially appreciated by Mann and other school leaders because Mann was a strong advocate of the belief that educational instruction was, as Yulish (1980, p. 80) states, to be "undertaken by the schools alongside the instruction of the church and the home." Pestalozzi, especially, spent much of his educational career trying to allay the concerns of parents about the realities of schooling (Spring, 1997). That is why Pestalozzi placed so much emphasis on the maternal role of the schools. In his view, if educators alienated parents by dictating to them a major change in curriculum, teachers and principals would lose the trust of parents. Consequently, parents would show a disinclination for working together with teachers (Downs, 1978; Lilley, 1967; Ulich, 1957, 1968). According to Pestalozzi, educators should seek to be sensitive to parents and only then could they hope to maximize parental trust and activity (Downs, 1978; Lilley, 1967; Ulich, 1957, 1968).

Johann Pestalozzi authored a book entitled *Leonard and Gertrude*, in which he described the practice of education during his time. It is a story of how extending the maternal influence of the home to the school can lead to positive moral change. Ulich (1968, p. 230) describes the book this way:

> It pictures the rottenness of the life in a poor Swiss village, where Gertrude, the pious wife of a mason . . . is the only source of educational wisdom and inspiration . . . Observing how Gertrude brings up her children he and his friends realize the interdependence between family spirit and the spirit of the community, of religion and education and also of physical welfare and human dignity.

Pestalozzi (1898, 1916) affirmed that it was the maternal nature of the mother that made the home a wonderful place of refuge for most children (Pestalozzi,

1898, 1916). He asserted that to the extent that teachers could also demonstrate this kind of maternal influence in the schoolroom, the school could emerge as a place of refuge for children. Pestalozzi thought that in such a place of acceptance and security, a child could learn at an advanced pace (Pestalozzi, 1898, 1916). He desired to make the school room a pleasant place in which children could function, just as in their homes. The classroom, in Pestalozzi's view, should be a place of perpetual activity, even as the children's homes are (Spring, 1997).

Johann Pestalozzi urged schools to recognize the centrality of the maternal role of the educator. As Gerald Gutek (1968, pp. 61–62) states, "Pestalozzi was deeply impressed by the mother's crucial role in the kindling of love." Gutek (pp. 24–25) also notes, "In developing educational theory Pestalozzi affirmed the crucial importance of the home circle as the origin of all education." Pestalozzi believed that the more effectively teachers incorporated maternal qualities, the better teachers they would be.

In Pestalozzi's view, children learned best in the home because the home was a place of love. Gutek (1968, p. 62) adds, "If a child is given love and care by the mother, the child's idea of benevolence will be activated. If he continues to experience tender loving care, the child will grow into a person who is capable of giving and receiving love." Pestalozzi believed that parents had an especially ameliorative role in teaching moral education (Downs, 1978). To him moral education was at the heart of his educational rubric (Downs, 1978).

John Griscom, a respected American educator, traveled to Europe and encouraged American educators to adopt the Pestalozzian approach in the United States (Spring, 1997). Horace Mann and other common school leaders adopted many of Pestalozzi's suggestions. As a result, numerous Americans developed a fondness for the Pestalozzian schools that enabled the school to prosper (Spring, 1997). The Pestalozzian method calmed many of the fears of people by humanizing certain aspects of school life. The teacher was designed to be a type of "mother away from home." As a result of Pestalozzi's assurances, many people no longer regarded the public school as a place where one leaves children with strangers, but as a place with a mother away from home. Many Americans thought that a "maternal" public school would provide a wonderful bridge between the home and the school (Spring, 1997). Pestalozzi served as both a theorist and practitioner who, through his emphasis on the teacher functioning as a mother away from home, enabled the citizenry to have a new level of trust in the public schools. Pestalozzi portrayed the public school teacher as a partner for parents in the schooling of children (Pestalozzi, 1801). One of Pestalozzi's main concerns was to foster parental support of the schools (Pestalozzi, 1801). In order to accomplish this goal, Pestalozzi would often assure parents that his aims for educating their children were the same as theirs (Downs, 1978; Lilley, 1967; Ulich, 1957, 1968).

In Pestalozzi's view schools operated most effectively when they honored the general wishes of the parents and reinforced the family's values (Pestalozzi, 1801). The teacher was to partner with a parent to supply the children with some of the moral training that children from previous generations had acquired mostly at home (Pestalozzi, 1801). Horace Mann also claimed that the schools had a responsibility to uphold the moral values of parents and society at large (Mann, 1849). Mann (1849) believed that it was especially vital for schools to partner with parents in moral education, which he believed to be the most important function of school instruction. Mann was concerned about the potential of teachers emphasizing only academics, at the expense of partnering with parents to teach moral education. Mann stated,

> The more I see of our present civilization and of the only remedies for its evils, the more I dread intellectual eminence when separated from virtue. We are in a sick world, for whose maladies, the knowledge of truth, and obedience to it, are the only healing.
>
> (Mann in Filler, 1965)

Mann believed that only parents and teachers working together could this be facilitated.

Friedrich Froebel and the Kindergarten

Friedrich Froebel's founding of the kindergarten was also an important event in the historical development of parental involvement. Although industrial progress was changing society, Froebel believed that this transformation was also causing a growing number of components in society to become more interconnected. Consequently, parents and teachers needed to work harmoniously to reach common goals (Downs 1978, Lilley, 1967). Froebel believed that it was very important for the school not to dictate to the parents what the orientation of early childhood schools would be (Downs, 1978; Lilley, 1967; Ulich, 1957, 1968). Froebel did not so much exhort parents to become involved, rather, like most educators of his day, he assumed they would (Downs, 1978; Lilley, 1967; Ulich, 1957, 1968).

Froebel contended that the level of parental involvement had a considerable impact on child development (Downs, 1978; Lilley, 1967; Ulich, 1957, 1968). Froebel frequently observed that there existed a considerable variation in school children's academic abilities, even at a young age (Downs, 1978; Lilley, 1967). Moreover, he noted that this variation increased as children grew older (Downs, 1978; Lilley, 1967). Froebel opined that these variations were due to more than simply differences in intelligence levels. Froebel asserted that maturity, self-discipline, and personal virtue accounted for most of these factors, although he intimated that he realized individual experiences played a role as well (Downs, 1978; Lilley, 1967). From Froebel's perspective, parental example and investment into the lives of their children stood as the primary factor that expedited maturation in these qualities (Downs, 1978; Lilley, 1967). Froebel envisioned the kindergarten as a supplement to the personal parental investment into their children (Downs, 1978; Lilley 1967). Therefore, Froebel viewed the kindergarten as a conduit through which children could grow as a garden and become caring, moral, and self-disciplined individuals who would be ready for school (Ulich, 1957). Froebel believed that, to the extent that kindergarten teachers supported parental values and worked cooperatively with them, family members would possess a greater tendency to participate in school-related activities.

The Role of Parental Involvement Declines—Seeds of Decline in the Common School Movement

Although the rise of the common schools increased the partnership between parents and teachers in many respects, urbanization and the beginnings of industrialization were causing the balance of power in that relationship to change (Barth, 1980; Bender, 1975; Cubberley, 1920; Cremin, 1977; Rury, 2002; White, 1989). The family was retreating somewhat from its earlier role of participating in the education of children. Americans were increasingly aware of this trend and had some mixed emotions about the school taking on a larger role in the education of children. Some people thought that the school was usurping some of the roles of education that were best left in the home (Downs, 1978; Gutek, 1968). Previously, Americans patently viewed the parent as the primary partner in this relationship (Downs, 1978; Gutek, 1968). However, as the common schools matured into the mid-to-late1800s the principal role of the parent was not as ostensible. Urbanization was increasing, the beginnings of industrialization were taking place, and as a result of this process, parents participated less than before in their children's education.

Although Horace Mann and other common school leaders emphasized the importance of parental involvement and partnering with the student's family, Mann also emphasized the need for parents to regard teachers as professions at a level Americans had never before witnessed (Mann, M. P, 1907, Mann, 1957; Tharp, 1953). Mann supported legislation that expanded the role of the state in securing the educational and psychological welfare of children (Gatto, 2001). The legislation contributed to a growing distrust that numerous Americans possessed for the chief architects of the common school movement (Gatto, 2001).

Concurrently, Mann also advocated that teacher preparation become more standardized, via the proliferation of teacher training institutes and the parallel program of core curriculum (Mann, 1907; Messerli, 1972; Tharp, 1953). Mann wanted teachers to regard themselves as professionals and for parents to regard them in the same way (Mann, 1907; Messerli, 1972; Tharp, 1953). Mann emphasized the fact that teachers needed to be very competent at their profession (Mann, M., 1907, Mann, 1957; Tharp, 1953). Mann believed that teachers could be trained to be efficacious. He believed that teachers could be trained to maintain a good mastery over their subject matter and teach effectively (Mann, 1907; Messerli, 1972; Tharp, 1953). Mann claimed that if schools had a common curriculum, educational leaders could establish teacher institutes that could train teachers to be effective no matter at what common school they taught (Mann, M., 1907, Mann, 1957; Tharp, 1953). Horace Mann developed a very sophisticated vision for the common schools and was an adroit organizer. Mann viewed schools as an organization and in adopting this paradigm, teaching became more and more of a profession.

Mann inaugurated many actions that made schools into more of an organization and teachers into more of a profession within that organization. First, Mann espoused a high degree of collaboration among schools so that they could help each other succeed (Mann, 1839). Second, he enforced the dissemination of school inspectors to help guarantee that schools were meeting certain standards (Mann, 1845). Third, he instructed that school boards could function as overseers to help ensure that teachers would set a good moral example (Mann, 1846, 1849; Mann, M., 1907; Messerli, 1972; Tharp, 1953).

Under Mann, teachers became professionals and started to regard themselves as such (Lindle, 1990; Peressini, 1998; Tyack, 1974). Although most would portray this as a positive historical development, as schools entered the twentieth century, it did pose certain quandaries for the parental involvement movement. That is, many teachers were reluctant to partner with parents because teachers viewed themselves as professionals who knew significantly more about education than parents did (Lindle, 1990; Peressini, 1998). Although many teachers recognized the value of parental involvement as a concept, often they viewed the actual process of partnering with parents as parental meddling (Lindle, 1990, 1990; Peressini, 1998).

One might wonder why parents were raising considerably stronger objections to the public schools than they ever had to the proliferation of private schools. There are two reasons why parents were at variance with public schools especially. First, because the government sponsored public, i.e. common schools, parents thought that the government was taking education out of the hands of the community (Downs, 1978; Gutek, 1968). Second, public schools were different than the private schools in that in many cases the parents were not familiar with the teachers (Downs, 1978; Gutek, 1968) Usually, when children attended private schools, the local church operated the school and therefore parents and teachers were either neighbors or fellow parishioners. To many parents schools were becoming increasingly impersonal and the job of instruction was being given to professionals rather than parents (Downs, 1978; Gutek, 1968). To a large extent, this debate still remains with us today.

The Role of Industrialization and the Dewey Era

Although the common school movement and the changes taking place in society planted the seeds of decreased parental involvement in the nineteenth century, the overwhelming number of American parents were nevertheless still active participants in their children's education (Gangel & Benson, 1983; Gordam, 1961; Morgan, 1986).

As industrialization settled into the American landscape parental involvement became more difficult (Husband & O'Loughlin, 2004; Jacob, 1997; Rury, 2002). When the United States was principally an agricultural country, work for both fathers and mothers took place principally around the home. However, as the United States expanded its industrial base, many fathers, in particular, worked outside the home (Husband & O'Loughlin, 2004; Jacob, 1997; Rury, 2002). This was a major step to parental involvement becoming more difficult (Husband & O'Loughlin, 2004; Jacob, 1997; Rury, 2002).

The influence of industrialization accelerated with the emergence of educational philosopher, John Dewey (1859–1952). Dewey (1915, 1990) not only observed that industrialization did have an effect, he averred that it *should* have an effect (Lawson & Lean, 1964). Dewey claimed that two realities were especially becoming clear as a result of the industrial revolution. First, people in society were becoming more specialized. Dewey (1915, 1990) not only argued that industrial development was transforming the United States into a more specialized society, but that each person now had a function (Lawson & Lean, 1964). For example, on an auto assembly line one person was in charge of installing the transmission, another was in charge of constructing the steering column. Dewey (1915, 1964, 1990) asserted that these economic orientation changes were also sociological ones and that schools now needed to become the educational specialists in society. Before the Industrial Revolution, people generally viewed parents as those primarily responsible for educating their children (Blinderman, 1976; Lawson & Lean, 1964). Schools were to support and supplement the efforts of parents (Gangel & Benson, 1983; Gordam, 1961; Morgan, 1986). Now, however, with the onset the industrial age, schools were the educational specialists, according to Dewey (Dewey, 1990; Lawson & Lean, 1964).

Second, the Industrial Revolution was eroding the cohesiveness and the primacy of the family (Dewey, 1964). In Dewey's view, this trend was happening all around the world (Dewey, 1964). Therefore, it was the school's responsibility to increase the puissance of its role and execute some of the same functions previously reserved for the family (Dewey, 1964). Dewey (1964) stated that industrialization was eroding the primacy of the family and that it was the responsibility of the schools to assume some of the responsibilities that had previously been reserved for the family (Dewey, 1964).

Equally significant to Dewey's ideas was the fact that most Americans accepted the validity of these assertions (Dewey, 1964; Martin, 2002). To many, Dewey's contentions were logical and promised relief to families who felt challenged by all the change (Dewey, 1964). The timing of Dewey's statements enhanced people's receptivity to his philosophical orientation (Bagley, 1915; Martin, 2002).

Dewey (1902, 1964, 1978) also asserted that teachers did not have an obligation to support the present values of parents. Rather, he declared that instructors should teach in order to help children to think for themselves (1902, 1964,

1978). Indubitably this perspective often caused consternation among parents, who felt that this exhortation undermined the spirit of partnership that had long existed between parents and teachers (Horne, 1923, 1931, 1932). The forces of industrialization and Dewey's interpretation of those forces had a dramatic impact on American education (Horne, 1923, 1931, 1932).

The Changing Nature of the American Family

Despite the fact that the changes of the late nineteenth and early twentieth century had caused some deterioration in the level of parental involvement, by the early 1960s, most families were strongly involved in their children's education (Gangel & Benson, 1983; Gordam, 1961; Morgan, 1986). However, beginning in 1963 the American divorce rate began to surge, after being in slight decline during the 1948–1962 period (U.S. Census Bureau, 2001). Concurrently, married women were entering the workforce in record number (U.S. Census Bureau, 2001). What this meant is that not only were fathers frequently away from the home, but wives were as well (McLanahan & Sandefur, 1994).

The sharp rise in the divorce rate attracted considerable attention not only because the rate rose for 17 consecutive years, but also because the infamous SAT score decline took place during precisely the same 1963–1980 period (Wirtz, 1977). Although there are some people who claim that these two concurrent trends are merely coincidental, most social scientists believe there is a relationship (Albrecht & Heaton, 1984; Hetherington & Clingempeel, 1992; McLanahan & Sandefur, 1994; Wirtz, 1977). In 1977 the College Board, the architects of the SAT, also concluded that there was a relationship (Wirtz, 1977). For example, just as SAT scores started a sudden and precipitous decline beginning in 1963, so did the stability of the intact family. Divorce rates, which had been in a gradual decline from 1948–1962, suddenly started to surge in precisely 1963 (U.S. Census Bureau, 2001). Ironically, just as SAT scores declined seventeen consecutive years before bottoming out in 1980, divorce rates rose seventeen consecutive years, topping out in 1980 (U.S. Department of Education, 2005). Between 1963 and 1980 the divorce rate rose 117% (U.S. Census Bureau, 2001). Regarding these two trends, The College Board concluded, "There is probably more than coincidence between the decline in SAT scores and the drop in the number of children living in two-parent homes" (Wirtz, 1977, p. 34). Social scientists also believe that the substantial increase in births resulting from premarital pregnancy also contributed to the changing face of the American family (Jeynes, 1999a, 2000b, 2003a, 2003b). Given this confluence of statistics, most social scientists agree that the decline of the family impacted achievement test scores during the 1963–1980 period.

The panel adds,

> Yet if the question is why those scores have been going down, few would respond without recognizing that part of the answer is almost certainly

hidden in these gaps in present knowledge—about the effects of change on the whole meaning of family and youth decline.

(Wirtz, 1977, p. 35)

By the 1970s and 1980s a strong line of research also emerged indicating that the deterioration of the family influences juvenile behavioral outcomes, as well as achievement. Children from non-intact homes are considerably more likely to end up in prison than children from two-parent homes (U.S. Department of Justice, 1983). Children from one-parent homes have a greater tendency to take illegal drugs, alcohol, and cigarettes than children from two-parent homes (CBS News, 1994).

The surge in divorce rates, according to the College Board panel, meant that parents were spending less time teaching their children than before. Ernest Boyer (1985) argues that teachers are discouraged by problems originating with students' families. According to the 1987 *Metropolitan Life Survey of the American Teacher*, teachers listed "having parents spend much more time with their children in support of school and teachers" as the number one step that would "help a lot to improve education." It is noteworthy that 84% of the teachers questioned viewed this as very important (U.S. Department of Education, 1990).

Although there are many single parents who make every effort to care for their children, the absence of the second parent clearly makes raising children more difficult (Albrecht & Heaton, 1984; Hetherington & Clingempeel, 1992; Jeynes, 1999a, 2000b, 2002a; McLanahan & Sandefur, 1994; Zill & Nord, 1994). Helping children with their homework, giving them constant verbal support, and consistently attending parent–teacher conferences are simply more difficult if all of these responsibilities are on one parent (Jeynes, 2005a, 2005b). Often single parents must work in order to make ends meet (McLanahan & Sandefur, 1994). Keeping this fact in mind, meeting these responsibilities can be particularly difficult (McLanahan & Sandefur, 1994). Complicating the challenges faced by overburdened families, teachers often do not adjust their schedules to accommodate families who face obstacles related to single parenting or two parents working (Lindle, 1990).

The heightened concern about family dissolution on children would not have possessed the impact that it did had student academic outcomes not plummeted and juvenile crime and illegal drug usage soared during the same period (Wirtz, 1977). To be sure, one could not justifiably blame the changing nature of the American family for all of these trends (Jeynes, 2002a). Clearly, several other factors played a role (Wirtz, 1977). In the College Board, *On Further Examination*, analysis indicates that demographic changes in the United States were responsible for 38% of the decline (Jeynes, 2009; Wirtz, 1977). In addition, prayer and Bible reading were removed out the schools just before the test score decline and the surge in juvenile crime (Jeynes, 2004). Many theorists believe that when the moral education component (which included teaching on love, self-discipline, the work ethic, and forgiveness) that was associated with this was removed, children's behavior was affected (Jeynes, 2004; Wirtz, 1977). Other social scientists placed onus on schools for diluting the content of their curriculum and the rising use of illegal drugs (as a causal factor in itself apart from how family dissolution might influence it) as likely agents of change (Wirtz, 1977).

Although, most social scientists acknowledge that the deterioration of children's typical family experience could not account for all the SAT score decline, the fact that the rising divorce rate almost mirrored the decline in SAT scores caused many people to re-examine the primacy of parental involvement (D'Andrea, 1983; Durst, Wedemeyer, & Zurcher, 1985; Williams, Wright, & Rosenthal, 1983; Wirtz, 1977).

Reports in the 1970s, 1980s, and early 1990s magnified the concern over parental involvement. First, the College Board announced that SAT scores had fallen more than previously believed, because their analysis indicated that the SAT had become twenty points easier than it was in 1963 (Wirtz, 1977). As criticism of schools and parents reached an apex in the 1980s and early 1990s, in 1995 the College board decided to significantly renorm the SAT scores upward to give the impression that SAT scores were not as low as they appeared (Feinberg, 1995; Young, 1995). Second, the American illiteracy rate, which had stood at a half of 1% and the lowest in the world in the 1960s, rose six-fold to reach 3% by the 1990s and early 2000s (United States Census Bureau, 2001). By 2005 the United States' illiteracy rate had slid to sixty-second in the world, behind a number of third world countries, including Tonga, Mongolia, Guyana, Turkmenistan, and Trinidad and Tobago (GeographyIQ, 2006). Third, *A Nation at Risk* was published, and cited the decline of the family as at least one of the reasons for the decay in educational outcomes for American students (National Commission on Excellence in Education, 1983).

Fourth, the performance of American students on international comparison tests also alarmed researchers, especially because those nations with the lowest divorce rates tended to have the highest levels of performance (Jeynes, 2002a; National Center for Educational Statistics, 1989; U.S. Census Bureau, 2001). The United States, which had the highest divorce rate, had its students finish last on the 1988 International Assessment of Educational Progress (National Center for Educational Statistics, 1989).

The Reemergence of Parental Involvement as a Primary Emphasis in Education

In the 1960s and 1970s, concurrent with the increase in family dissolution, some expressed a renewed interest in examining the effects of family structure on educational outcomes (Carlsmith, 1964, 1973; Duberman, 1975). The turning point came in 1966 with the publication of the Coleman Report that asserted that family factors were considerably more salient than school variables in influencing school outcomes (Coleman, 1988). Head Start, a government educational initiative designed to raise achievement among poor and minority students, placed a prodigious amount of emphasis on parental involvement as a means of raising student grades (Fagan, 2000). A myriad of social scientists launched initiatives designed to assess the effects of family structure on parents and children (e.g. Carlsmith, 1973; Cherlin, 1978; Duberman, 1975).

As the 1980s and 1990s progressed an increasing number of leaders grew concerned about the lack of educational support that many children were receiving from their parents (Hetherington & Jodl, 1994; Popenoe, 1994; Zill, 1994; Zill & Nord, 1994). Educators appeared to confirm the worst fears of researchers by asserting that parents were considerably less likely to attend school functions and be involved in their children's education than in the 1950s and early 1960s (Jeynes, 2002a).

As family configurations became more diverse, researchers realized that they needed to give guidance to parents regarding communication with their children and participation in their lives (McLanahan & Sandefur, 1994; Wallerstein & Blakeslee, 1989). Social scientists realized that they needed to give more guidance to single parents to become involved in their children's education and that although intact family structures facilitated parental involvement, they did not guarantee that it would take place (McLanahan & Sandefur, 1994; Wallerstein & Blakeslee, 1989). Therefore, families with two biological parents needed guidance in this area as well (Epstein, 2001; McLanahan & Sandefur, 1994; Wallerstein & Blakeslee, 1989). Furthermore, teachers faced with a growing complexity of family situations with regard to work and structure also need advice on how to best adapt to a plethora of unique circumstances (Jeynes, 1999a, 2003a, 2003b 2005a, 2007b).

In response to the Coleman Report's findings and other subsequent analyses that confirmed its findings and reaction to the decline of parental involvement since the mid-1960s, a new wave of theorizing and research arose in the 1980s and 1990s to assess the place of parental involvement (Ballantine, 1999; Griffith, 1996; Keith & Lichtman, 1994). The emergence of parental involvement research grew out of three realities. First, single parents needed more guidance on how to become involved in their children's education. Second, although intact family structures facilitated parental involvement it did not guarantee that it would take place (Ballantine, 1999; Griffith, 1996; Keith & Lichtman, 1994; Simons, 1994). Therefore, families with two biological parents needed guidance in this area as well (Ballantine, 1999; Griffith, 1996; Simons, 1994). Third, teachers faced with a growing complexity of family situations with regard to work and structure, also need advice on how to best adapt to a plethora of unique circumstances (Lindle, 1990).

The rise in parental involvement theory and research that materialized in the 1980s and 1990s possessed a firm foundation. The practice of parental involvement had deep roots dating back four centuries, in spite of its decline over the past several decades (Jeynes, 2006a, 2007a, 2010). Child development research also had a long history of lauding supportive parents as a key for producing children who are likely to live up to their potential (Huffman, Mehlinger & Kerivan, 2000).

The emergence of theories and research about parental involvement therefore should be understood in its proper context. As social scientists propound parental involvement theories and research initiatives, one needs to understand that these ideas are really not new. Rather, these efforts are an attempt to exhort Americans to readdress the obvious (Jeynes, 2005a, 2007b). That is, parents should be involved in the lives of their children. However, apparently there is a need to reintroduce this concept to Americans. By and large, American parents acknowledge the need for parental involvement. However, the strains of industrialization and changes in educational philosophy and family dynamics have presented new quandaries (Husband & O'Loughlin, 2004; Jacob, 1997). Therefore, scientists and educators need to provide guidance for these parents. In the next chapter we will examine the maturation of parental involvement research and summarize some of the key findings that may be able to supply some of that guidance.

Teachers Need Help

Increasingly teachers in the 1990s realized that they could not effectively teach children to live up to their fullest potential unless they also partnered with parents (Epstein, 2001; Hoover-Dempsey, Walker, & Jones, 2002). A host of statistics of juvenile crime, academic achievement, and illegal drugs suggested that teaching was more of a challenge than ever before (Epstein, 2001; Hoover-Dempsey et al., 2002; Jeynes, 2002a). The body of research was growing that suggested the primacy of the influence of the family. Research indicated that parenting had a major enduring effect even at the preschool and kindergarten level. For example, there is a strong relationship between the extent to which parents sufficiently prepare children to enter preschool or kindergarten and their likelihood of attending college (Spodek, 2003). In other words, the influence of parental input into the cognitive and emotional development of preschool age children is so paramount that it is a major predictor of college attendance and graduation (Stipek & Seal, 2001). Although this finding is in some ways disconcerting, those who have taught at the preschool, kindergarten, or first grade level are well aware of the considerable variation in the cognitive aptitudes of students even at these very early ages (Spodek, 2003; Stipek & Seal, 2001). Moreover, those individuals who are familiar with the psychological and sociological research on development realize that this finding is in total concert with mainstream theories in child development and the sociology of education (Hoffer, Greeley, & Coleman, 1987; Coleman, Hoffer, & Kilgore, 1982; Erikson, 1964).

Nevertheless, the presence of studies highlighting the salience of the family in influencing student outcomes is a healthy reminder to teachers that they really cannot regard themselves as the educational specialists in much the same way that those on an assembly line can view themselves as specialists. Generally speaking, when educators have tried to run schools like a business they have found that teaching is far different than operating a business (Beckner, 1983; Gump & Barker, 1964). As the twentieth century came to a close, an increasing number of teachers realized that they needed the help of parents in order to help children become all that they can be (Epstein, 2001; Henderson & Mapp, 2002).

Conclusion

The practice of parental involvement has a long illustrious history. The love that parents possess toward their children has for centuries propelled a myriad of parents to make the sacrifices necessary to ensure the academic and psychological success of their children. With the advent of industrialization and changing educational perspectives, the role of the parent in education began to decline. In the last several decades, sociological changes made it increasingly difficult for parents to become as involved in their children's lives as they once were. In the last fifteen years, in particular, social scientists have become more aware of the price children have paid because of the lack of parental participation and have made a renewed call for mothers and fathers to become increasingly involved in their children's education. There is a great deal that one can learn from this historical perspective, both in terms of the successes and missteps of the past. Ultimately, if one learns from these historical trends, the practice of parental involvement can be enhanced to reach its fullest potential.

Chapter 2

The Development of Parental Involvement Research

Parental Involvement research grew as an offspring of other types of family studies that existed previously (Jeynes, 2010). The two primary "parents" of parental involvement research were family structure and family functioning analysis (Jeynes, 2010). As one examines the development of parental involvement research in retrospect, it seems only logical that these two other types of academic inquiry would be the ones to yield parental engagement research. This is true because it is probable that family structure and functioning are the two primary contributors that determine the level of involvement that exists in a given family.

The role of the structural aspect is axiomatic in the sense that clearly parents cannot participate in a child's education if they have passed away, are absent, or were never really in the household to begin with, engagement becomes difficult if not impossible (Jeynes, 2002b, 2003b). The highest expression of family involvement takes place when a mother and father are present to offer their support and assistance (Brooks & Goldstein, 2001; Jeynes, 2003a; Wallerstein & Blakeslee, 1989; White, 1987). To the extent that this is true, it should come as no surprise that the relationship between parental family structure and student outcomes and behaviors can best be expressed in the following way.

Generally, the farther one departs from the two biological parent intact family structure, the greater an impact there is on the academic, psychological, and behavioral outcomes of the children (Jeynes, 2000b, 2002a, 2006b; McLanahan & Sandefur, 1994; Wallerstein & Blakeslee, 1989). Determining the extent of the departure generally depends on two factors: first, the number of family structure transitions that a given child has endured and second, the amount of exposure the child generally has to the parent in terms of accessibility and time (Jeynes, 2000b, 2001a, 2001b, 2001c, 2002a, 2006b; McLanahan & Sandefur, 1994; Wallerstein & Lewis, 1998). Regarding the first point, for example, a child who is from a divorced remarried family structure on average has more depressed levels of achievement, psychological, and behavior measures because the child has not only experienced the challenge of having one's parents divorce but has experienced the additional adjustment of having to adjust to a person who is from outside the household joining in residence with the custodial family members

(Hetherington & Jodl, 1994; Jeynes, 1999b, 2000b, 2002a, 2002b, 2003b, 2006b; Popenoe, 1994). Clearly, such adjustments are not without exception negative experiences for children, but in the overwhelming number of cases they are and it would be an act of great insensitivity to ignore this fact (Jeynes, 1999a, 2000b, 2006b; McLanahan & Sandefur, 1994; Pong, Dronkers, & Hampden-Thompson, 2003; Rodgers & Rose, 2002). In addition to the number of transitions emerging as a major consideration, it is also vital to fathom that children do better in virtually every aspect of their lives if they have greater access to their parents versus when such access is elusive or non-existent (Hetherington & Jodl, 1994; Jeynes, 2002b). This belief has persisted in virtually every society on the planet for centuries and to question its veracity in academic research studies would probably result in engaging in a quarrel that would yield only a tremendous amount of wasted funds on "pugilists" that would best focus their funding on less futile efforts (Jeynes, 2002c). For as long as any historian can recall, humankind has acknowledged, for example, that losing one's father in warfare was a development that had severe consequences for the welfare of children (Jeynes, 2007a). There is an age-old understanding that children originating from such family structures on average experience lower levels of parental involvement than do their counterparts in families with both fathers and mothers present.

How Research on Family Functioning Yielded an Interest in Parental Involvement

It is also ostensible that family functioning also influences the level of parental involvement. Few would deny the fact that although coming from a two-biological-parent intact family is conducive to experiencing high levels of mother and father engagement more so than coming from a single-parent family structure, originating from this environment does not guarantee that mothers and fathers will be involved (Jeynes, 1999a, 2000b, 2003a, 2003b, 2006a, 2007b; Pong et al., 2003; Rodgers & Rose, 2002). There are a variety of functioning variables beyond that of family structure that are indicative of the likelihood of such engagement. From the standpoint of the general public, there are prominent tangible external indicators that suggest that a household is functional or dysfunctional (Jeynes, 2002d; Pong et al., 2003; Rodgers & Rose, 2002). For example, the likelihood that a father or mother is engaged in illegal drug abuse, nicotine addition, alcoholism, promiscuous and disloyal sexual behavior, and similar behaviors, is often indicative of dysfunctional behavior and tends to exert a downward pressure on parental engagement (Jeynes, 2001a, 2001b, 2001c, 2002d). Parents who are engaged in extramarital affairs and who spend at least some of their time under the influence of substances that have a profound affect on the expression of responsible and responsible behavior are likely to be less available to help their children and, in fact, are likely to be less concerned about tending to certain needs of their children because they are focused on fulfilling certain selfish drives (Popenoe, 1994; Wallerstein & Lewis, 1998).

Psychologists and family scientists are naturally interested in examining these overt expressions of the presence of absence of healthy family functioning. They are, however, also interested in examining the underlying factors that are causing such destructive parental behaviors to manifest themselves. In the past these social scientists relied on Freudian concepts to guide their examinations (Crews, 1998; Freud, 1938; Salkind, 2006). In recent years, however, an increasing number of theorists and psychologists have dismissed the majority of Freudian theories, asserting that they may have reflected Freud's own personal psychological problems more than they constituted any coherent theory (Crews, 1998; Doinick, 1998; Salkind, 2006). Since then other sociologists have sought to apply more of a behavioralist perspective to explain family functioning. This orientation yielded some excellent studies that contributed to the wider body of research, but were often rigid and focused on externally measured outcomes that possessed limited utility, because they did not sufficiently represent internal realities that enabled academics to procure insight into the inner workings of human emotions and thought (Jeynes, 2006a).

Since the first seventy years of the twentieth century, academics posited more sophisticated paradigms to help explain the levels of functionality apparent in a copious number of families. Some of these rubrics, like Baumrind's (1971) descriptions of rearing styles, i.e. authoritarian, authoritative, and permissive, examined the family within the largely closed environs of the household. Other paradigms found these examinations too limited, given the illimitable influences of the broader social environment. These social scientists preferred to incorporate the most sophisticated and complete description of societal functioning that was possible. They averred that only within this prodigious model could family functioning truly be understood.

In this context, myriad researchers esteemed the approach of Urie Bronfenbrenner of Cornell University. Bronfenbrenner's (1979) multidimensional and multilevel approach, called Ecological Systems Theory, launched a more inclusive approach that appeared to render previous approaches almost unfathomably simplistic. Bronfenbrenner's paradigm was also attractive because it appeared most faithfully to reflect the prevailing understanding of the general public. The general public never totally embraced Freudian psychology, which appeared to challenge many people's notions of common sense. Freudian concepts such as the Oedipus and Electra complexes seemed aberrant to many in the public and appeared to reduce humans to pure animals with the most baleful and barbaric motivations. Freud's conceptualization of humans seemed totally devoid of integrity and any trace of the divine touch (Bronfenbrenner, 1979). In addition, his obsession with Freudian slips, dreams, and phallic symbols also coalesced into a simplistic and naïve model phenomena that could be the result of a gamut of causal phenomena (Crews, 1998; Doinick, 1998; Fromkon, 1973).

Whatever the public's perceptions of academics might have been, researchers conversant with the family structure and functioning literature realized the need for the research discipline of parental involvement that appeared to highlight the household realities that were most likely to influence children academically and perhaps psychologically as well (Epstein, 2001; Wallerstein & Lewis, 1998).

Ever since the study of family structure has emerged, there has been an understanding overt or unstated, that family engagement is easiest when there an intact two-biological-parent family structure is present (Jeynes, 2003a, 2003b, 2005b, 2007b; Wallerstein & Lewis, 1998). In fact, for decades social scientists did not aggressively study parental involvement for two reasons: 1) a high percentage of parents in the first half of the twentieth century were actively engaged in their children's education and 2) there was an assumption that parental involvement was highly correlated with family structure (Jeynes, 2003a, 2003b, 2005b, 2007b). This latter assumption was not meant in any sense to disparage the efforts of many American single parents across the country. Rather, it emerged out of an understanding that it takes time and commitment to reach a level of involvement with which parents are satisfied (Cherlin, 1978; Jeynes, 2003a, 2003b, 2005a, 2007). The reality is that with only one parent caring for a child there is no other parent available to provide a "relief" to custodial mothers or fathers that every caretaker, no matter how skilled or energetic, needs in order to continue to function at he fullest rested capacity (Bo, 1995; Boehnke, Scott & Scott, 1996).

It is also a reality that in certain highly populated urban areas, in particular, where the cost of living is especially high, it is very difficult for a single parent to provide both a sufficient level of income and be available a plenteous level of time (Borruel, 2002; Davalos, Chavez, & Guardiola, 2005). In such instances the parent generally makes a decision in one direction or the other. That is, they either decide to sacrifice a middle class standard of living in order to be available personally to the child or they decide to pursue a more typical American monetary lifestyle, but at the expense of being available to the child at a level that most of those knowledgeable about children's needs would recommend (Casanova, Garcia-Linares, de la Torre, M., & Carpio, 2005; Jeynes, 2003a, 2003b).

Historical Trends in Family Structure and Parental Involvement

As various educational historians and parental involvement researchers have pointed out, high levels of mother and father participation are hardly new. Such engagement was vivid even going back to the era of the pilgrims and the puritans (Hiner & Hawes, 1985; Jeynes, 2006a, 2007b, 2010). Moreover, caregivers in the settlements and the United States maintained a high level of parental involvement for at least three centuries (Jeynes, 2006a, 2007a, 2010). There are several reasons for this elevated level of participation, but clearly one of them was because it was an integral part of American culture to believe that parents were of central importance in schooling children (Hiner & Hawes, 1985). As much as people in the United States valued the teaching profession, they surmised that the year-round love, nurturing, encouraging and educational support that parents was indispensable for children to succeed (Hiner & Hawes, 1985; Jeynes, 2006a, 2007a, 2010). To the vast majority of Americans, teachers, although important, were active for only a portion of a given year and then not until a youth's fifth year or afterward. In contrast, they surmised that it was the first five years of a child's that were both the most important and foundational to a child's intellectual development. In their view the family involvement at this point was particularly intense and in their minds it is consequently particularly unwise to equate the importance of the role of the teacher and the parent (Hiner & Hawes, 1985; Jeynes, 2005c; 2006a, 2007b, 2010).

In spite of this parental orientation in terms of educational importance, John Dewey convinced the American people that the industrial evolution required a change in educational orientation (Dewey, 1902, 1910, 1915, 1920, 1990; McCluskey, 1958). To Dewey, just as the industrial revolution produced an emphasis on individual specialization, so did it require a new orientation toward educational specialization. From Dewey's perspective, teachers in their professionalism were to be regarded as such by parents and entrusted with the academic development of children. Dewey's approach was no doubt well-meaning, but the result was to relegate the position of parents as instructors to a patent secondary level (Dewey, 1902, 1910, 1915, 1920, 1990; McCluskey, 1958). This development was not only significant in and of itself, but it established a pattern in which over the last number of decades parents have increasingly looked to the schools to perform functions that had in the past been associated with parents (Dunn, 1955; Kay & Fitzgerald, 1997; Jeynes & Littell, 2000; Lamb, 1997).

There were several ways in which Dewey's new industrial model of the schools contributed to the parental abdication of some of the responsibilities that had generally been theirs in the past. First, Dewey's model caused many parents to view teachers as the professionals responsible for the academic development of their children, which parents often believed reduced the time commitments that were necessary on their part. Second, this new paradigm as convenient because it reduced some of the guilt that mothers and fathers felt for accruing a growing number of hours in the workplace and reducing the number of hours they spent at home (Lamb, 1997). Third, increasingly first fathers and eventually mothers began to view themselves as the material providers for children rather than having the overwhelming degree of influence on the emotional development of children. Such a conclusion was also in harmony with Dewey's general belief that: a) parents (and teachers) needed to allow youth to explore the world for themselves free from the predispositions and presuppositions that adults usually encumber upon children (Dewey, 1902, 1910, 1915, 1920, 1990; McCluskey, 1958) and b) schools needed to direct children away room the values of their parents, so that they could develop their own values (Jeynes, 2007a). It as healthier, in Dewey's view, for children to procure their values from their own experiences and those of their peers than it was for their values to be instilled in them from the convictions and beliefs of their parents (Egan, 2002; Jeynes, 2007a). These perspectives that Dewey inculcated into his college students, colleagues, and American society at large changed how many Americans viewed the process of childrearing. Previous to Dewey, most Americans had viewed raising children as primarily the duty of the parent with supplementation on the part of the community (Jeynes, 2000a; 2003a, 2005c, 2007a). Now, an increasing number of the nation's citizenry viewed it as a mutual compact between the parents and the state (Egan, 2002; Jeynes, 2008a; Spring, 1997). And indeed, as time passed a debate emerged as to how much of the responsibility rested with the maternal and paternal facets and how much should be the responsibility of the state.

Just how much of these developments could be attributed to some of the realities of capitalism or even in the worst case, the brutalities of industrial development, and how much could be blamed on emerging socialism of which John Dewey was a part, is difficult to determine. In fact, it may be disturbingly difficult to separate these two trends. That is, historically, cries for socialism have generally followed the excesses of capitalism that emerge when the latter is not morally restrained by love, compassion, and moral responsibility (Etzioni, 1964; Jeynes, 2009; Micklethwart & Woodridge, 2009). Nevertheless, it is also true that the change in parental roles and significance, as perceived in the schools particularly by the 1960s (by which time nearly every teacher had been trained in Deweyism), was likely one of many contributing factors to parents viewing the two-biological-parent intact family as having a less decisive role in rearing well adjusted children (Davis-Kean, 2005; Delgado-Gaitan, 2004; Dunn, 1955; Lamb, 1997).

Parental Involvement Becomes More Difficult in the 1960s

In precisely 1963, after fourteen years of edging downward, the American divorce rate surged (Cherlin, 1978; U.S. Department of Education, 2005). This trend as significant not only in its own right, but also because the changing trends in family structure ultimately made fathers' and mothers' involvement more difficult. More frequently than not, marital dissolution made paternal participation more challenging because 90% of the time that there was parental absence, it was the father who was not available (Hetherington & Jodl, 1994; Wallerstein & Lewis, 1998). Nevertheless, even though it was generally the father who was absent, marital dissolution usually also ultimately made an impact on the levels of mother participation that were possible as well (Pong et al., 2003; Rodgers & Rose, 2002). This is because there were now new financial and time pressures on the mother to financially provide for the family and perform everyday tasks such as working on the house and running various errands that often the family's fathers had done previously. Clearly, as a result of the surge in divorce rates and out-of-wedlock births, youth generally had less access not only to the father but also the mother (Pong et al., 2003; Rodgers & Rose, 2002).

As a consequence of the rising tide of marital dissolutions, it was inevitable that social scientists should not only manifest a new interest in studying family structure, but also examine the axiom that American people had known for centuries that maternal and paternal involvement had a wide array of benefits for children (Jeynes, 2003b, 2005a, 2005b, 2007a, 2007b). Admittedly, there was a certain degree of irony to these undertakings by researchers. Clearly, academics truly convinced themselves that they were breaking new ground by "divulging" relationships that existed between parental family structure and school outcomes, as well as between parental involvement and those same outcomes (Jeynes, 2007b). In reality, American ministers, community leaders, parents, and teachers had been declaring these truths for centuries. The only difference was that academics now had the numbers to support what nearly all Americans already knew via common sense. However, with the rise of marital dissolution and the accompanying decline in the average level of parental involvement, there were now emotional reasons to challenge what nearly all had previously declared was common sense. When one goes through such a trauma as a marital breakup, about the last truth a person wants to acknowledge is that the failure of the marital union has wider implications for others that one loves, especially the children (Wallerstein & Lewis, 1998). Indeed, when one experiences such family trauma, one longs or comforting words of assurance that the ramifications of this decision are isolated and transitory (Pong et al., 2003; Rodgers & Rose, 2002; Wallerstein & Lewis, 1998). Although that may be naturally what one wants to hear, consistent with previous common sense and the prevailing research, such is clearly not the general case. The fact, however, that many Americans experiencing marital dissolution were in no frame of mind to receive the realities of common sense probably made it necessarily for researchers to rediscover the value of family by presenting numbers from their myriad studies that confirmed what had long been held as widespread societal belief: that the parental family structure and the involvement of mothers and fathers in raising children were of crucial importance in raising well-balanced youth (Jeynes, 1999a, 2002a, 2003b, 2005b, 2007b).

How Research on Parental Involvement Grew out of Educational Research

Parental involvement almost inevitably became a major area of research also because of the growing body of educational research that asserted that family factors were actually more salient than school variables in determining and predicting the scholastic outcomes of youth. The Coleman Report emerged as the foremost of the educational reports declaring that family factors together constituted well over half the explanatory power for student achievement in school (U.S. Center for Education Statistics, 1966). As a result of the findings of this study, there were calls from the federal government, parents, and African Americans in many facets of society for a more intensive examination of the influences of both family structure and parental involvement on school outcomes (Cohen, 1973; Jeynes, 2007a; Ravitch, 1974). The infamous New York City teachers' strike that lasted until nearly Thanksgiving of 1968 and came very close to causing the entire 1968–1969 public school year to be canceled was based in part on the call by African Americans for more parental input into school decisions, including the hiring and firing of teachers (Cohen, 1973; Jeynes, 2007a; Ravitch, 1974). Whether parents should insist on the right to hire and fire teachers and whether all the school children in the city of New York should have been blocked from going to school because of this desire is up to the readers to determine. Nevertheless, one truth stands clear: educational research, led by the Coleman Report, had transformed the landscape regarding the debate over the place of mothers and fathers in the schooling of their children (Cohen, 1973; Jeynes, 2007a; Ravitch, 1974).

The Coleman Report raised the specter of the possibility that teachers discouraging, or at least not welcoming, father and mother participation, and the lack of the nation's support for the two-parent biological family, had contributed to the burgeoning and continuation of the achievement gap (Cohen, 1973; Jeynes, 2007a; Ravitch, 1974). And if this was the case, then supporting the family and inviting parental engagement were major keys to its elimination (Jeynes, 2003a, 2003b, 2005b, 2007b). Many educators and sociologists believe that the achievement gap both reflects racial inequality and causes it to continue (Cross & Slater, 2000; Green, 2001; Hedges & Nowell, 1999; Slavin & Madden, 2006). The nation's concern with the achievement gap helped to inspire research on parental involvement.

This concern has not only been expressed at the research level, but at the public policy level as well (Green, Blasik, Hartshorn, & Shatten-Jones, 2000; Jeynes, 2000a; Jones, 1984; Rumberger & Willms, 1992; Slavin & Madden, 2006). The gap exists across virtually every subject (Conciatore, 1990; Green et al., 2000; So & Chan, 1984).

The extent of concern about the achievement gap can hardly be overstated. Ronald Roach (2001) asserted, "In the academic and think tank world, pondering achievement gap remedies takes center stage" (p. 377). As a result of the Coleman report, a common solution that educators posited was that there needed to be more parental involvement (Green, Walker & Hoover-Dempsey, 2007; Domina, 2005; Englund, Luckner, Whaley & Egeland, 2004; Hara, 1998). The argument that these advocates proposed was that schools needed to become more parent-friendly and to "go the extra mile" in order to ensure full parental participation (Henderson & Mapp, 2002; Hoover-Dempsey et al., 2002; Mapp, Johnson, Strickland & Meza, 2010; Jeynes, 2003b). That is, the responsibility for parental involvement not only rested with the parents, but with educators as well (Garbers, Tunstill & Allnock, 2006; Jeynes, 2003b; Rimm-Kaufman & Pianta, 2005).

Educational Research, The Achievement Gap, and Parental Involvement

For about five or six decades, social scientists have dedicated a great deal of time examining poor minority children, particularly those who attend poor schools (Paik, 2007). Over the last four decades, one of the most persistent debates in education has been on how to close the achievement gap between white students on the one hand and black and Hispanic students on the other (Green, 2001; Simpson, 1981). This achievement gap exists in virtually every measure of educational progress, including standardized tests, GPA, the dropout rate, and the extent to which students are left back a grade (Conciatore, 1990; Green, 2001). The United States was founded on the principle of equality. As a result, Americans tend to feel uncomfortable when unequal results emerge, and American educators have frequently tried to reduce those inequalities (Green, 2001; Haycock, 2001; Osborne, 1999).

The intractable nature of the difference in academic outcomes that exists between students of certain races of color and white students, as well as those of low versus high socioeconomic status, has been of considerable concern to educators and the American public (Roscigno, 1998). Kozol (1991) and other researchers assert that low-SES youth and children of color are the most crucial for the U.S. educational system to reach. Given the persistence of this gap, the government has launched a plethora of initiatives designed to eradicate it, including Head Start, father and mother involvement, community partnerships and other programs (Orfield et al., 2000; Slavin & Madden, 2006). In recent years, there have emerged studies that indicate that the presence of high levels of parental involvement, especially in the context of two-biological-parent family homes, reduces the achievement gap (Jeynes, 2008b, 2008c).

In spite of the research that social scientists have conducted with the goal of reducing the achievement gap, these educational differences remain adamantly placed in the American educational landscape (Jeynes, 2008b, 2008c). Partially because of the relatively late development of family research on family structure and parental engagement, it has been a relatively recent development that academics have focused on family involvement as a means to reducing the achievement gap (Brown, Bakken, Nguyen & Von Bank, 2007; Jeynes, 1999a, 2003b, 2008b, 2008c).

One of the reasons for the slow response by scholars to family and academic realities is because the academic environment, unlike the world of community, religious, and political leaders is intensely specialized and focused and often lacks a broad perspective (McLanahan & Sandefur, 1994). What this means is that educators tend to propose educational solutions, psychologists tend to prefer psychological remedies, and family scientists focus on family factors (Jeynes,

2005b, 2008b, 2008c). There are very few solutions presented that transcend the disciplinary barriers that are inherent to the world of scholarship. For example, Sara Lawrence Lightfoot (1978), an educator, generally advocated school-based solutions and Andrew Cherlin (1978), a sociologist, advocated societal solutions to these issues. Although these works made important contributions to the field, their recommendations were primarily restricted to those promoted in their discipline.

Another major reason why academic recommendations were limited in their ameliorative impact is because unlike most Americans, scholars were hesitant to assert that certain family structures and parental practices were better for children than others (McLanahan & Sandefur, 1994; Wallerstein & Lewis, 1998). Their reluctance was in the name of being sensitive. However, McLanahan and Sandefur and other researchers averred that in the name of scholarly sensitivity, social scientists were being remarkably insensitive. McLanahan and Sandefur declared unapologetically, based on the examination of several nationwide data sets, that parental intact families were much better for families' children than non-intact family structures. In the mid-1980s, Joyce Epstein also made it clear that parental involvement was better than non-involvement. Although these statements made it clear how belated social scientists had been in recognizing what had been obvious for most for decades and even centuries, it was significant because it placed academics in a position in which they could offer advice to the broader community (Epstein, 2001).

Social scientists are now discovering just how vital parental involvement is not only to academic success, but also to positive social behavior among adolescents. As family and educational research has become broader, more informative, and increasingly sophisticated, social scientists have been able to provide guidance that transcends disciplinary divides. One consistent finding that researchers have uncovered is that in order to encourage parental engagement, there must be a relationship between the school leaders and each parent (Brown et al., 2007). This is not the easiest relationship to establish. Reaching out to single parent parents is particularly important because the African American youth who are struggling the most in school are frequently from single-parent families (Reglin, 1993). And reaching out in this way is particularly important because as Reglin (1993, p. 3) notes, "The survival of all our children depends on how well parents educate and support one another."

Federal Policy, Parental Involvement, and the Achievement Gap

For most of American history, the federal government did not engage in aggressive educational policies (Logsdon & Launius, 2000). The primary reason for this approach was the fact that throughout the history of the nation, the United States possessed a decentralized system of education (Cubberley, 1920: Spring, 1997). Almost by definition, the distinct settlements of the 1600s and 1700s did not combine into a comprehensive unit to establish a coordinated organization to address scholastic issues. In the late 1700s and early 1800s, the Democratic Republicans gradually triumphed over the Federalists in political power and in the educational debates of the era (Jeynes, 2007a; Johnson, 1997). The primary educational contribution of the Democratic Republicans is that they called for a decentralized system of education, in which it was the states and not the central government that was the locus of power (Jeynes, 2007a). This may or may not have been a perspicacious move, but what is incontrovertible is that America's decentralized system of education is largely explained by the fact that historically less than ten percent of the public school education dollar has come from the federal government and over ninety percent generally comes from state and local sources (Jeynes, 2007a, 2008b; U.S. Department of Education, 2008).

Largely because of the nation's affinity for a decentralized education paradigm, the federal government did not make a concerted effort to consistently influence educational policy until Dwight Eisenhower and the U.S. Congress responded to the Russian launch of the Sputnik in 1957 (Logsdon & Launius, 2000). There were isolated instances of the federal government influencing schooling, as in the case of its calling for algebra to be a required fourth grade class in the 1840s (Jeynes, 2007a). This was done out of a sense of national necessity, because many students dropped out of school by the eighth grade (Troen, 1988). Similarly in 1958 the U.S. Congress passed the National Defense Education Act in order to produce a coordinated educational response to what was considered a national crisis (Johnson, 1997).

The precedent established during the Eisenhower administration facilitated Lyndon Johnson attempt to relieve the achievement gap during the 1960s. The federal government's Head Start program inaugurated in 1965 (Carleton, 2002) was consistent with Lyndon Johnson's Great Society program in that it hoped to elevate all Americans to the level of enjoying the nation's prosperity (Johnson, 1997). Although the Head Start program in its original form called for some level of parental involvement, the primary focus of the Head Start program was designed to give poor children and some children of color an early introduction to schooling to help close the scholastic gap that existed between some children and color and white children (Carleton, 2002).

As originally conceptualized, Head Start's emphasis on parental involvement was wholly inadequate (Carleton, 2002). Nevertheless, two studies were released that would eventually be foundational in changing that fact. First James Coleman and his colleagues released the Coleman Report asserting that family factors were far more prominent in determining scholastic outcomes than school variables (U.S. Center for Education Statistics, 1966). During the 1960s Daniel Patrick Moynihan (1965) released a study, which also highlighted family factors, particularly family structure, as playing a major role in explaining both the racial and socio-economic achievement gap.

Many community, religious, and political leaders embraced the results of the Coleman and Moynihan studies as enlightening and called for the nation to emphasize the salience of the family (Jeynes, 2002a). Unfortunately, most academics and educators resisted these calls and instead focused on the role that the schools could play in bridging the gap (Jeynes, 2003b, 2008b).

Two trends, however, would eventually cause more people in the academic and education communities to acknowledge the relationship between family factors and achievement. The first trend is that divorce rates in the United States suddenly began to soar in 1963, ending a slow downtrend that lasted from 1948 until 1963 (Cherlin, 1978; Jeynes, 2002a). The surge lasted exactly seventeen years topping out in exactly 1980 (Jeynes, 2002a; McLanahan & Sandefur, 1994). The second trend is that SAT scores started a persistent seventeen-year drop in 1963, bottoming out in precisely 1980 (Jeynes, 2007a). The fact that the two trends occurred simultaneously over exactly the same seventeen-year period caused the growth of research that examined family and achievement, shortly before the period reached its conclusion. In 1977 the College Board, the makers of the SAT, declared that they believed that the deterioration of the family was a major cause behind the SAT score decline (Wirtz, 1977). Although the simultaneous nature of these trends could have been purely correlational rather than causal, an increasing number of academics began to concur with the community, religious, and political leaders who thought otherwise (McLanahan & Sandefur, 1994; Wallerstein & Lewis, 1998).

As the discipline examining family structure and school outcomes grew in the late 1970s and 1980s, it became ostensible that a causal relationship existed (McLanahan & Sandefur, 1994; Wallerstein & Lewis, 1998). Although several hypotheses emerged regarding the reasons behind this relationship, one of the most prominent was that divorce and other non-traditional family structures generally caused a lower level of involvement by the parents, particularly the father (Cherlin, 1978; McLanahan & Sandefur, 1994). This realization contributed to the rise of parental involvement research (Epstein, 2001; Jeynes, 2010).

The growth of research on the family gradually changed the nature of the Head Start program so that its parental involvement component became more prominent (Epstein, 2001; Jeynes, 2010). There are some who believe that the increased emphasis on parental involvement caused the Head Start program to become more effective (Epstein, 2001; Jeynes, 2010). To whatever extent the Head Start program has become more effective, it is difficult to determine whether an increased emphasis on parental involvement was the cause.

Politicians throughout the 1980s and 1990s continued to be one step ahead of academics in recognizing the inextricable connection between family factors and scholastic outcomes. Ronald Reagan lauded the advantages of the two-parent intact family and called on parents to become more involved in their children's education (Epstein, 2001; Jeynes, 2010). The federal report, *A Nation at Risk*, supported Reagan's assertions (National Commission on Excellence in Education, 1983). Bill Clinton advocated the growth of parental participation through charter schools, which he viewed as more father friendly than public schools (Epstein, 2001; Jeynes, 2010). George W. Bush's No Child Left Behind initiative eventually became controversial in many circles. Nevertheless, family science researchers such as Joyce Epstein have praised the initiative for its emphasis on both father and mother involvement (Epstein, 2001; Thompson, 2007). Many family scientists anticipate that now that academics have more fully comprehended the public's desire for more research-based guidance on parental involvement and have responded with more highly developed research since 2000, government involvement programs will become more research based.

The Relationship between Student–School Outcomes and Other Factors

In the early 1980s and continuing into the 1990s and 2000s social scientists hypothesized that parental involvement probably extended well beyond the educational sphere (Ratelle, Larose, & Guay, 2005; Wentzel, 2002; Yewchuk & Schlosser, 1995). This assertion was largely based on the observation that student achievement was highly related with other factors such as alcohol consumption, illegal drug intake, sexual promiscuity, and psychological adjustment (Jeynes, 2001a, 2001b, 2001c, 2002c). In addition, there was increasing evidence that parental family structure was associated with a number of these other factors (Jeynes, 2001a, 2001b, 2001c, 2002c; 2003b). And indeed if this was the case, it seemed quite possible that other family variables such as parental engagement would also influence these behavioral outcomes (Henderson & Mapp, 2002). Naturally, there were issues of causality that social scientists needed to disentangle. That is, although it is quite possible for parental involvement to affect both academic and behavioral outcomes, it is also reasonable and even undeniable that some of these behavioral outcomes influence school outcomes (Jeynes, 2001a, 2001b, 2001c, 2002d). It is important for academics and the general public to acknowledge this mutual causality when attempting to decipher the precise relationship between parental engagement and behavioral outcomes. It is also conceivable, although less patent, that some of these behavioral outcomes could influence the exercise of parental involvement in either one direction or the other. In fact, one could certainly make an argument that these behavioral factors could impact family engagement in one direction or the other. For example, if a youth had a social or drinking problem, one could make an argume t that this might cause parents, out of necessity, to become more engaged in their child's upbringing or it could potentially cause them to withdraw.

The Decline in Achievement Test Scores

Two concurrent trends also caused academics and most Americans generally to become more convinced that research on parental involvement needed to become more prominent in the United States. Divorce rates surged beginning in 1963, and continued to increase for an unprecedented seventeen consecutive years, topping out and then essentially stabilizing in 1980 (Jeynes, 2007a; U.S.

Department of Education, 2005; Wirtz, 1977). This unyielding upward trend caused concern enough among family scientists. A concurrent trend, however, only added to the concerns of the American public at large and particularly among politicians, ministers, and social workers. That is, achievement test scores after about eighty years of stability plummeted during precisely the same 1963–1980 period. It would not be overstating the typical American response at all to say that millions of its citizenry and leaders were alarmed (Wirtz, 1977). Suddenly, Americans were concerned that the dissolution of a plethora of American families was about to have monumental implications for its future economic prosperity (National Commission on Excellence in Education, 1983; Jeynes, 2007a; Stevenson & Stigler, 1992; Wirtz, 1977). The reason is because it is understood by virtually all the political and economic leaders of the world that that the health of a country's school system ultimately has an impact on the Gross Domestic Product (GDP) (National Commission on Excellence in Education, 1983; Jeynes, 2007a; Stevenson & Stigler, 1992; Wirtz, 1977). As one might expect, there is a certain degree of delay in the relationship between the two becoming clear, but the there is a copious degree of quantifiable data that indicate that the association is much more than mere coincidental juxtaposition (National Commission on Excellence in Education, 1983; Jeynes, 2007a; Stevenson & Stigler, 1992; Wirtz, 1977).

Generally speaking, there is about a ten-year delay between significant changes in the high school achievement of a nation and any changes in its economic output or standard of living (National Commission on Excellence in Education, 1983; Jeynes, 2007a). This ten-year delay is logical because the high school achievement data covers the age span of approximately fifteen to eighteen years of age. Ten years after this point, at ages twenty-five to twenty-eight, these same individuals are usually active in the workforce and exert a considerable influence on GDP. Therefore, it only makes sense that about a ten-year delay in education's effect on GDP would be plausible. This puissant relationship between educational outcomes and GDP is evident in the educational histories of several major nations and territories including Japan, Korea, Hong Kong, Taiwan, China, and innumerable countries in South America, Africa, and Europe. It therefore should come as no surprise that when American achievement test scores, as measured by a host of both national and state assessments, seemingly fell off the precipice in 1963 that economic growth stalled, beginning in 1973 (Jeynes, 2007a; Johnson, 1997; Wirtz, 1977). Most major economists are agreed that the U.S. economy has really never been the same as in 1973 (Jeynes, 2007a). They assert that the nation's standard of living really has not changed since then (Jeynes, 2007a). That is, when one adjusts for inflation, any real increase in American GDP per capita since then has only been a result of the tremendous influx of women into the workforce and the citizenry's obsession with incurring massive amounts of debt in order to procure an unsustainable loan-backed lifestyle (Goldberg, 2008; Leary, 2008).

As with myriad other developments in life, the American public became more focused on the family-structure-and-involvement quandary, as it became more evident that these family dynamics were having a dramatic impact on the economic conditions of the country (Jeynes, 2002c). In the aftermath of the divorce surge of the 1960s and 1970s, welfare rolls swelled, inundated especially with women and children who were there due either to divorce or as a result of pre-marital sex resulting in births during the mother's teens (Jeynes, 2006b). Beginning in the 1970s, in particular, an endless litany of research statistics became available providing a large storehouse of information adding credence to the claim that the teeming number of family transitions taking place in the United States was having devastating effects on the state of the economy and creating a new underclass of people inveterately caught in poverty and relegated to living in increasingly numerous enclaves that were worse than most slums called the inner cities (Hamburg, 1992; Jencks, 1992). Some of the most notable of these statistics included data that most people who were persistently on welfare started there as a result of being an unwed teen with child and that half of all sexually active single males had their first sexual experience by the time they were eleven (U.S. Department of Health & Human Services, 1998; U.S. Department of Justice, 1999).

With this background in mind, new debates emerged in academic and policy-making circles regarding whether the US government was one of the forces inadvertently fostering this new sense of family and child crisis (Hamburg, 1992; Jencks, 1992). In other words, was the attempt under President Lyndon B. Johnson's Great Society and related initiatives to ease economic pressures for those in single-parent households, actually acting as a major catalyst to encourage marital breakups and intercourse out of wedlock (Hamburg, 1992; Jencks, 1992)? That is: did the ostensible removal of many of the economic consequences for engaging in irresponsible relational behavior (including actions that might have provided short-term personal stimulation but yielded patent deleterious consequences for the offspring in the long term) actually encourage the incidence of divorce and pre-marital intercourse (Hamburg, 1992; Jencks, 1992). At the very minimum, it would be hard to argue that the social welfare proposals of the 1960s buttressed the strength of the family and discouraged behavior harmful to children. There is virtually no one who would argue that the government initiatives helped caregivers or potential caregivers to act responsibly in the best interests of intact families and children. Rather, the debate concentrates on the extent of the damage, some averring that the consequences were minimal to nearly nil and others presenting research evidence indicating that the effects were prodigious (Hamburg, 1992; Jencks, 1992).

However one dissects the above debate, it was almost axiomatic that a number of forces work at work in America, causing some immense family changes and requiring that children make adjustments to a host of parental transitions, ushered in an era of academics considering the effects of family much more seriously and intently than had previously been the case. Surely, one needed to forget for the moment that the knowledge of academics about family dynamics clearly lagged behind that of the American public who for centuries had experienced the realities of family living on a personal level. But in a very real sense, the fact that the common sense of the public was well ahead of the ivory tower knowledge of America's scholars was almost a moot point (Davis-Kean, 2005; Krivy, 1978; McDonald & Robinson, 2009; Smith, 2009). Clearly, no matter what conclusions the academic world arrived at, Americans were already personally cognizant of the multifarious baleful manifestations that non-intact family structures were creating and nothing that the scholarly world contributed to the debate would change that. Nevertheless, Americans were also keenly aware that the results of university-based research drove government policies that could ultimately affect families.

Many in the American public were poignantly aware that government policies usually implemented tended to be both tardy and insufficient. With this caveat in mind, however, many Americans were willing to live with these impediments as long as there was eventual government action taken. A salient, although somewhat disconcerting, example is the debate that extended for decades over whether children watching violence on television made it more likely for them to engage in acts of violence (Friedman & Schustock, 2001; Kirsh, 2006). One can certainly intelligently posit that because the debate over whether witnessing acts of violence increased the likelihood of further violence was resolved in classics of religious and philosophical thought such as in the Old Testament and in ancient Greek literature, what emerged as a debate never should have been a debate at all. That is, any person with even the most rudimentary knowledge of religion, philosophy, and history should have been able to resolve his question with the greatest of ease. Nevertheless, because Sigmund Freud in his theory of catharsis challenged the veracity of this belief, academics were not quickly convinced and in fact usually chose to support Freudian theory and hypotheses rather than the wisdom that had accrued through the ages. In fact, academics sided with Freud so willingly that the issue was not even subject to much debate until a Stanford Professor Albert Bandura (1977) declared that he believed that the common sense that had emerged over the ages was indeed correct. Naturally, he did not conceptualize his assertions quite this simply or else he probably would not have been published, but instead propounded a theory called Social Learning Theory, which simply restated the age-old truths that had represented apprehended common sense for most of recorded human history (Bandura, 1977; Salkind, 2006).

Once Bandura propounded his theory a debate ensured for three-and-a-half decades regarding the effect of children watching violence on television. Amazingly, it was not until 1997 that the American Psychological Association (APA) concluded that youth watching acts of violence did give them more of a propensity to commit acts of aggression (Kirsch, 2006; Salkind, 2006).

In spite of the public's general conclusion that academics were more often than not behind the curve of what the American public already acknowledged to be true, they also knew that such research was necessary in order to justify public policy that promoted parental involvement. Was such policy to encourage involvement belated? In the eyes of most Americans, it was. However, a delayed endorsement was better than none at all.

The Acceleration of Rates of Problematic Teenage Behavior

In addition to the scholastic slide that took place during the 1963–1980 period, there was also a dramatic increase in the frequency and degree of adolescent problematic behavior (U.S. Department of Health and Human Services, 1998; U.S. Department of Justice, 1999). The fact that it occurred during the identical seventeen years that divorce rates surged may be coincidental, but most social scientists do not believe so (Jeynes, 2007a). During this period, preadolescents and adolescents significantly increased their consumption of illegal drugs. The rate surged until exactly 1980, when the rate stabilized. In spite of this relative stabilization, the overall level of illegal drug consumption remains high, particularly compared to its pre-1963 levels (U.S. Department of Justice, 1999).

Second, youth are much more likely to engage in sexually promiscuous behavior than before prayer and moral education were removed from the public schools. Sexually promiscuous behavior was relatively stable during the 1940s and 1950s, but after prayer and moral education were removed from the schools, rates of adolescent and preadolescent rape surged by over three times during the 1963–1980 period and during the same time premarital pregnancy rates multiplied by seven times. Coincident to these changes surveys indicated that over half of single youth and adolescents had their first sexual experience at the age of eleven (Melody & Peterson, 1999; U.S. Department of Health & Human Services, 1998; U.S. Department of Justice, 1999).

There is no question that there were a variety of factors causing these changes in adolescent behavior (Jeynes, 2007a). For example, although there were changes in family dynamics beginning particularly in 1963, it is also true that there were other changes taking place simultaneously. For example, in a series of Supreme Court decisions in 1962 and 1963 prayer and Bible reading were removed from the public schools (Blanshard, 1963; Michaelsen, 1970; Ulich, 1968). Many social scientists note that at this time character education, as teachers shared it, was based on Judeo–Christian principles. Therefore, when prayer and Bible reading were removed from the public schools teachers also retreated from teaching moral instruction (Jeynes, 2007a). This was especially true because many people rightly or wrongly interpreted teaching about forgiveness, loving the helpless, respect for parents, and the golden rule as teachings from Christianity. A large number of researchers aver that the removal of these teachings had a deleterious influence on the sexual attitudes and behavior of adolescents as well as their patterns of substance abuse (Blanshard, 1963; Kliebard, 1969; Sikorski, 1993).

Whether one understood these trends as reflecting the increased rates of marital dissolution or the dearth of character education in the public schools, a large number of scholars saw the need for a renewed emphasis on character education to reverse these trends (Jeynes, 2009).

Conclusion

Although parental involvement has been a centerpiece of education in North America as early as the arrival of the pilgrims and the puritans, it really was not studied much until academics until the 1980s. Changes beginning around 1963 greatly contributed to the willingness of social scientists to examine this very important topic. Soaring rates of divorce, out-of-wedlock adolescent childbirth, and falling test scores among other factors all contributed to a call to rediscover the salience of parental engagement. There is little question that such an emphasis is overdue and is literally centuries behind the practices and comprehensions of the American people. As a result, there is little question that the academic community has a lot of catching up to do. Nevertheless, the general public generally welcomes the input of social sciences even though they are clearly behind the curve. They realize that more knowledge about parental engagement is definitely needed and that in the modern world such research must precede any real changes in policy and practice.

Chapter 3

Parental Involvement and Elementary School Achievement
A Meta-analysis

Over the last two decades, researchers have sought to quantify the influence of parental involvement on the academic outcomes of elementary school children (Marcon, 1999b; Peressini, 1998). Moreover, some educators have increasingly identified parental involvement as the primary vehicle by which to elevate academic achievement from current levels (e.g. Hara, 1998). Many social scientists have argued that in urban areas, in particular, parental involvement may be especially important due to high family dissolution rates, numerous two-parent working families, and unique sociological pressures on children (Hampton, Mumford, & Bond, 1998).

The question, therefore, emerges: can parental involvement really improve the educational outcomes children? More specifically, three issues are especially pertinent to parents and educators. First, to what degree is parental involvement associated with higher levels of school achievement among students? Second, what aspects of parental involvement help those students the most? Third, does the relationship between parental involvement and academic achievement hold across race and gender groups?

To answer these three key questions, it is important to know what the overall body of research indicates. A meta-analysis statistically combines all the relevant existing studies on a given subject in order to determine the aggregated results of said research. This study utilizes meta-analysis to examine the effects of parental involvement on elementary school children, addressing each of the three research questions listed.

The Importance of Parental Involvement and These Three Research Questions

Studies indicate that American teachers and educational psychologists place great importance on parental involvement to improve educational outcomes particularly among students who face other disadvantages (Eccles & Harold, 1993; Jeynes, 1999a, 2003b, 2005d). There is a dearth of knowledge about which aspects of parental involvement help student achievement and exactly what kind of parental involvement is most important (Christian, Morrison, & Bryant,

1998; Epstein, 2001; Henderson & Mapp, 2002). Both parents and teachers need specific information to maximize the efficacy of parental involvement.

With these facts in mind, the first research question addresses the degree of association between parental involvement and achievement outcomes among students. Some researchers have noted little is known about the effects of parental involvement on the educational attainment of students specifically (Jeynes, 2005d; Shaver & Walls, 1998). Instead, most research tends to focus on the influence of involvement on the general population rather than on students in particular. Further complicating the matter are the divergent results of two of the most comprehensive studies on the influence of parental involvement.

Mattingly and her colleagues (Prislin, McKenzie, Rodriguez, and Kayzar) (2002) recently published a research overview or synthesis focusing only on parental involvement programs. The Mattingly study makes no statistical or meta-analytical attempt to combine the results of the individual studies. Nonetheless, Mattingly et al. concluded that parental involvement programs demonstrated virtually no influence on student academic achievement. Conversely, Fan and Chen (2001) performed a meta-analysis examining the influence of parental involvement on the general student population and concluded parental involvement positively influenced educational outcomes. Adding to the debate is the fact that neither study included calculations for students, nor identified and tested components of parental involvement.

The second research question addresses specific aspects of parental involvement that help elementary school students the most. Ballantine (1999) identifies many components of parental involvement and asserts it would be helpful if researchers identified the aspects most beneficial to children. Grolnick, Benjet, Kurowski, and Apostoleris (1997) further assert that once the academic community knows the constructs inherent in parental involvement, it can better predict the family and social attributes most advantageous to producing parents who participate in the educational experience of their children. To fulfill this assertion, a meta-analysis needs to specify what aspects help the most (Hoover-Dempsey & Sandler, 1997).

The third research question addresses whether the relationship between parental involvement and educational outcomes holds across racial and gender groups. Clearly, if educators are to be able to espouse the practice of parental educational support, it would be crucial for parental involvement to have an influence that holds for virtually all groups (Jeynes, 2004; Muller, 1998).

The Need for a Meta-Analysis for Elementary School Students

Both the Mattingly and Fan and Chen studies contribute to initiating a broader debate about the influence of parental involvement. However, for the aforementioned reasons, a meta-analysis is needed to assess the effects of parental involvement on elementary school achievement, specific manifestations of parental involvement, and parental support programs specifically designed to help elementary school students. In addition to the three goals listed, this meta-analysis examines: what are the effects of parental involvement across different kinds of academic measures, especially standardized versus non-standardized?

Methods

Analytical Approach

This meta-analysis examined the relationship between parental involvement and elementary student achievement. The first analysis included determining effect sizes for the overall parental involvement variable (research question 1). The second analysis examined the association between specific components of parental involvement (e.g. parental expectations, participation in school events) with student achievement (research question 2). The third analysis examined the relationship between parental involvement and student achievement by race and gender (research question 3). The procedures employed to conduct the meta-analysis are outlined under this heading (Analytical Approach) and the following headings below: Data Collection Method, Study Quality Rating, Statistical Methods and Effect Size Statistics, and Defining of Variables.

Each study included in this meta-analysis met the following criteria:

1   It needed to examine parental involvement in a way that could be conceptually and statistically distinguished from other primary variables under consideration. For example, if a school implemented a program that involved nine key features, including parental involvement, and the influence of parental involvement could not be statistically isolated from the other features, the study was not included in the analysis.

2   It needed to include a sufficient amount of statistical information to determine effect sizes. That is, a study needed to contain enough information so that test statistics, such as those resulting from a t-test, analysis of variance, and so forth, were either provided in the study or could be determined from the means and measures of variance listed in the study.

3   If the study used a control group, it had to qualify as a true control group and therefore be a fair and accurate means of comparison. Moreover, if the research utilized a control group at some times but not others, only the former comparisons were included in the meta-analysis.

4   The study needed to be set in a school environment and could be a published or unpublished study.

Due to the nature of the criteria listed above, qualitative studies were not included in the analysis. Although qualitative studies are definitely valuable, they are difficult to code for quantitative purposes and any attempt to do so might bias the results of the meta-analysis.

Data Collection Method (Coding and Rater Reliability)

In order to obtain the studies used in the meta-analysis, a search was performed using every major social science research database (e.g. Psych Info, ERIC, Dissertation Abstracts International, Wilson Periodicals, Sociological Abstracts, and so forth) to find studies examining the relationship between parental involvement and the academic achievement of children from grades K-6. The search terms included parental involvement, parents, schools, family, education, parental support, partnership, programs, communication, expectations, reading, attendance, homework, household, rules, parental style, and several other terms. Reference sections from journal articles on parental involvement were also examined to find additional research articles. Although this search yielded over 5,000 articles and papers on parental involvement, nearly all of these articles were not quantitative in nature. This process yielded a total of fifty studies that quantitatively examined the relationship between parental involvement and elementary school student achievement. Of these, forty-one possessed a sufficient degree of quantitative data to include in this meta-analysis.

Study Quality Rating

Two researchers coded the studies independently for quality, the presence of randomization, and whether both the definitional criteria for parental involvement and specific aspects of parental involvement were met. Study quality and the use of random samples were graded on a 0 (lowest) to 3 (highest) scale. Quality was determined using the following:

1   Did it use randomization of assignment?
2   Did it avoid mono-method bias?
3   Did it avoid mono-operation bias?
4   Did it avoid selection bias?
5   Did it use a specific definition of parental involvement?

We calculated inter-rater reliability by computing percentage of agreement on: the definition of parental involvement, the specific components examined in each study, issues of randomization, and quality of the study. Inter-rater reliability was 100% on whether a study examined parental involvement, 97% for the specific components of parental involvement examined in a given study, and 94% for the quality of the study. For the specific components of quality, inter-rater agreement percentages were 98% for randomization, 94% for avoiding mono-method bias, 94% for avoiding mono-operation bias, 90% for avoiding selection bias, and 94% for using a specific definition of parental involvement.

Two supplementary analyses were done to include first, only those studies with quality ratings of 2 and 3 and second, only those studies with quality ratings of 1 to 3.

Statistical Methods and the Effect Size Statistic

Among the forty-one studies that possessed a sufficient degree of quantitative data to include in this meta-analysis, the total number of subjects exceeded 20,000. To ensure accurate statistical results, a number of steps were taken to make the meta-analysis more sophisticated. First, the Hedges' "g" measure of effect size was used (Hedges, 1981). Since it employs the pooled standard deviation in the denominator, it customarily provides a more conservative estimate of effect size. Hedges also provides a correction factor that helps to adjust for the impact of small samples. Effect sizes from data in such forms as t tests, F tests, p levels, frequencies, and r values were computed via conversion formulas provided by Glass and his colleagues (1981). When results were not significant, studies sometimes reported only a significance level. In the unusual case that the direction of these not significant results was not available, the effect size was calculated to be zero.

The analysis herein determines the overall relationship between parental involvement and achievement obtained for each study, as well as specific components of parental involvement mentioned earlier in the Methods section. Four different measures of academic achievement were used to assess the effects of parental involvement on achievement. First, there was an overall measure of all components of academic achievement combined. The other measures included grades, academic achievement as determined by standardized tests, and other measures that generally consisted of teacher rating scales and indices of academic behaviors and attitudes. The results presented in this study reflect the association between parental involvement and achievement found for each facet of parental involvement, using each of these academic categories.

Two sets of statistical procedures were also used to distinguish between those analyses that included sophisticated controls (socioeconomic status, race, gender, or previous achievement) and those studies that did not. The effect sizes were determined using weights based on the inverse of the variance, in order to give greater weight to studies with larger sample sizes (Hedges and Cooper, 1994). The results of these procedures are listed in different columns in the Results section, with the degree of statistical significance and 95% confidence intervals listed for each. An overall effect size was then determined, combining the studies that did and did not use sophisticated controls. No analyses of statistical significance were completed on the combined effect sizes given the different structure of the studies involved.

Supplementary analyses also examined what effect sizes emerged when adjusting for the quality of the study. In one set of analyses, only studies with an average quality rating of 2 or 3 (on a 0 to 3 scale) were included. In the second set of analyses only studies with an average quality rating of 1 to 3 (on a 0 to 3 scale) were included. Tests of homogeneity were completed on the specific components of parental involvement to gain a sense of the consistency of specific parental involvement measures across studies.

For all the analyses, when only one study was included using a specific academic outcome for a specific parental involvement variable, the regression coefficient for this study is listed with a notation indicating the table cell only included one study, in order to serve as a means of comparison with the various other effect sizes.

Defining Variables

For the purposes of this study, parental involvement was defined as parental participation in the educational processes and experiences of their children. The specific parental involvement variables, defined below, were those identified by educators as most frequently practiced by parents, examined by researchers (Deslandes, Royer, Turcott & Bertrand, 1997; Epstein, 2001), and hypothesized by theorists as the most fundamental aspects of parental involvement. The categorization of these specific parental involvement variables was based on the precise terms used in the original studies included in the meta-analysis. Given that these social scientists used widely accepted and recognized terms, the proper categorization of effect sizes was nearly always self-evident, e.g. those studies included in the meta-analysis for "parental expectations" generally used precisely the same term:

- *General Parental Involvement*: includes the overall measure of parental involvement, as defined by the researchers of a particular study. If a study did not have an overall measure of parental involvement, the effect size of this variable was determined by combining all its discrete measures.
- *Specific Parental Involvement*: includes a specific measure of parental involvement, as distinguished from other measures of parental involvement used in the study.
- *Communication*: the extent to which parents and their children communicated about school activities and reported a high level of communication overall.
- *Homework*: the extent to which parents checked their children's homework before the child handed it in to his or her teacher.
- *Parental Expectations*: the degree to which a student's parents held high expectations of the student's promise of achieving at high levels.
- *Reading*: the extent to which parents either have in the past or now in the present read regularly with their children.
- *Attendance/Participation*: whether and how frequently parents attend and participate in school functions.
- *Parental Style*: the extent to which a parent demonstrated a supportive and helpful parenting approach. In the studies included in the meta-analysis, most frequently this referred to a simultaneous ability to be loving and supportive and yet maintain an adequate level of discipline in the household. It

also included styles in which the parent demonstrated such qualities as trust and being approachable.

Results

Homogeneity tests

For most of the parental involvement variables herein the homogeneity tests were not statistically significant, indicating the researchers tested about the same aspect of parental involvement. The specific aspects of parental involvement that did indicate homogeneity included reading to children ($X^2 = 3.52$, n.s.), parental style ($X^2 = 0.02$, n.s.), communication ($X^2 = 1.89$, n.s.), parental attendance and participation ($X^2 = 4.68$, n.s.), and specific parental involvement ($X^2 = 0.16$, n.s.).

Effect Sizes for Overall Parental Involvement

Overall, the results of the meta-analysis indicate that the relationship between parental involvement and elementary school student achievement holds for overall measures of parental involvement and for most specific components of parental involvement. In addition, parental involvement is also associated with higher achievement for racial minority students and for both boys and girls. Statistically significant results emerged consistently across the various kinds of academic measures, although there was some degree of variation in the effect sizes.

The results of this study indicate the general parental involvement variable usually yielded statistically significant outcomes of approximately seven-tenths to three-fourths of a standard deviation. Table 3.1 lists the effects sizes of the forty-one studies in descending order. All but one of the effect sizes was in the positive direction and ranged from 0.00 to 1.78. The studies with the smallest samples produced the most extreme effect sizes on either end, consistent with the "funnel" pattern ideal in effect sizes (Greenhouse & Iyengar, 1994).

Table 3.2 lists the mean values, determined by the raters, for the quality of the studies, the quality of the definition of parental involvement researchers used in their studies, and the extent to which each study used a random sample. Table 3.2 also lists the study's mean year and the average sample size. The average quality of the study and the average quality of the definition of parental involvement were 2.15 and 2.05 respectively. The average rating for randomization was 1.44, which was slightly greater than the median of a 0 to 3 scale. The mean year a study was undertaken was 1992.1 and the average sample size was 558.9. The correlations between these variables are listed in Table 3.3. Among the most important correlations, there were no statistically significant relationships between effect size and study quality, year of the study, or randomization. Researchers were

Table 3.1 List of Studies used in the Meta-Analysis for Parental Involvement, the Year of the Study, and the Effect Sizes for the Various Studies

Study	Year	Student Sample Size	Effect Size[a] Without Sophisticated Controls	Effect Size[a] With Sophisticated Controls	Study Distinctions
Bal & Goc	1999	34	+1.78	—	Program
Hess, Holloway, Dickson & Price	1984	47	+1.62	—	A white children
Griffith	1997	98	+1.54	—	Information from parents alone
Griffith	1996	11,317	+1.11	+0.88	Very diverse group of students
Mantzicopoulos	1997	93	+1.04	—	Mostly Minority Children
Fantuzzo, Davis, & Ginsburg	1995	38	+0.97	—	Program
Woods, Barnard, & TeSelle	1974	80	+0.94	—	Program
Miliotis, Sesma & Maston	1999	59	—	+0.88	Disadvantaged children
Gilmore	1985	18	+0.85	—	Program
Villas-Boas	1998	77	+0.84	—	2 experimental groups
Grolnick & Slowiaczek	1994	301	+0.67	—	Large majority of white children
McKinney	1975	100	+0.60	—	Program
Marcon	1999b	708	+0.59	—	Many measures of parental involvement
Long	1991	77	+0.59	—	Different types of parental attendance
Koskinen, Blum, Bisson, Phillips & Creamer	2000	162	+0.57	—	Program
Collazo-Levy & Villegas	1984	98	+0.52	—	Program
Shaver & Walls	1998	257	+0.44	—	Program
Zellman & Waterman	1998	111	—	+0.43	Mostly minority children
Miedel & Reynolds	1999	704	+0.42	—	Program
Reynolds	1992	676	—	+0.39	All minority children

Author	Year	N			Notes
Taylor, Hinton & Wilson	1995	566	+0.37	—	Examined time spent with child and activities
Bermudez & Padron	1990	162	+0.37	—	Program
Uguroglu & Walberg	1986	970	+0.37	+0.17	Very diverse group of students
Marcon	1999a	434	—	+0.32	Program
Clarke	1993	23	+0.32	—	Program
Offenberg, Rodriguez-Acosta, & Epstein	1979	264	+0.31	—	Program
Williams	1999	467	+0.30	—	Mostly minority children
Hampton, Mumford & Bond	1998	676	+0.29	—	All African American students
Yap & Enoki	1995	328	+0.28	—	Many measures of parental involvement
Marcon	1993	168	+0.26	—	Almost all African American students
Brutsaert	1998	1,795	+0.25	—	Public and private schools
Georgiou	1999	413	+0.24	—	All minority students
Luchuck	1998	80	+0.20	—	Study covered 2-year period
Fuligni	1995	662	+0.20	—	One quarter minority students
Allen	1991	701	+0.19	—	Used California Achievement Test
Schwartz	1996	1,464	+0.19	—	Program
Revicki	1981	321	—	+0.13	Program
Austin	1988	77	+0.06	—	Program
Lipman	1985	156	+0.01	—	Focused on math
Nesbitt	1993	136	+0.01	—	Program
Buchanan, Hansen & Quilling	1969	83	0.00	—	Program

Note
a Effects sizes are in standard deviation units.

Table 3.2 Means for Measures Assessing the Quality of Study, whether a Random Sample was used, Year of Study, and Sample Size for the 41 Studies Included in the Meta-Analysis

	Mean	Standard Deviation or Percentage Distribution	Range
Year of Study	1992.1	7.4	1969–2000
Sample Size	558.9	1,000+ = 3	
		500–999 = 8	
		100–499 = 15	
		1–99 = 15	18–11,317
Quality of Study	2.15	3 = 18	
		2 = 13	
		1 = 8	
		0 = 3	0–3
Quality of Study's Definition of Parental Involvement	2.05	3 = 17	
		2 = 13	
		1 = 7	
		0 = 5	0–3
Random Sample	1.44	3 = 15	
		2 = 5	
		1 = 4	
		0 = 17	0–3

more likely to use randomization of assignment if the study occurred in a later year rather than an earlier one.

Table 3.4 lists the effect sizes that emerged for parental involvement as a whole addressed under research question #1. Beginning with parental involvement in general, the effect sizes were quite similar for the studies that used sophisticated controls, like race, socio-economic status, and gender, and those that did not. The regression coefficients for these studies were .75 ($p < 0.01$) and .73 ($p < 0.01$) respectively. For those studies that did not use elaborate controls the effect size for GPA was .85 ($p < 0.001$), 0.40 ($p < 0.01$) for standardized tests, and 0.34 ($p = $ n.s.) for other measures. For those analyses that did use controls the results were 0.86 ($p < 0.0001$) for GPA and 0.21 ($p < 0.05$) for standardized tests. Possible reasons for the larger GPA effect size are included in the Discussion section.

Study Quality

In the secondary set of analyses that adjusted for the average quality rating of the study, the effect sizes were slightly greater than when no quality adjustments were made. When only those studies rated 2 and 3 (on a 0 to 3 scale) were included, the effect sizes were 0.72 ($p < 0.01$) for those studies that did use sophisticated controls and 0.78 ($p < 0.01$) for those that did not. When studies rated 1 to 3 were included, the respective effect sizes were nearly the same at 0.72 ($p < 0.01$) and 0.77 ($p < 0.01$). As noted in Table 3, the correlation between

Table 3.3 Correlations between Measures Assessing the Quality of Study, whether a Random Sample was used, Year of Study, and Sample Size for the 41 studies included in the meta-analysis

	Correlation with Year of the Study	Correlation with Effect Size of the Study	Correlation with Quality of the Study	Correlation with Quality of Study's Definition of Parental Involvement	Correlation with whether a Random sample was used
Year of Study	—	−0.05	0.19	0.19	0.24*
Effect Size from Study	−0.05	—	0.05	−0.12	0.16
Quality of Study	0.19	0.05	—	0.53***	0.51***
Quality of Study's Definition of Parental Involvement	0.19	−0.12	0.51***	—	0.21
Random Sample	0.24*	0.16	0.51***	0.21	—

Note

* $p < 0.05$; ** $p < 0.01$; *** $p < 0.001$; **** $p < 0.0001$

the study's quality and its effect size was 0.05. As a result, across all the parental variables examined in this study no statistically significant differences in effect sizes emerged from adjusting for study quality.

Table 3.4 Effect Sizes for General Parental Involvement with 95% Confidence Intervals in Parentheses

Type of Parental Involvement and Academic Variables	Effect Size Without Sophisticated Controls	Effect Size With Sophisticated Controls	Overall Effect Size
General Parental Involvement			
Overall	0.75** (0.25, 1.25)	0.73** (0.23, 1.23)	0.74[a]
Grades	0.85**** (0.44, 1.29)	0.86**** (0.66, 1.06)	0.85[a]
Standardized Tests	0.40* (0.06, 0.74)	0.21* (0.02, 0.40)	0.37[a]
Other	0.34	NA	0.34[a]

Notes
* $p < 0.05$; ** $p < 0.01$; *** $p < 0.001$; **** $p < 0.0001$; NA = Not available
a Confidence intervals tabulation not undertaken for combined effect size because of difference in sample

Effect Sizes for Specific Components of Parental Involvement

Parental Expectations

Table 3.5 lists the effect sizes for various components of parental involvement, addressed in research question #3. Parental expectations yielded the largest effect sizes of the specific aspects of parental involvement. For all the analyses combined, the effect size for overall achievement was 0.58 ($p < 0.05$). The specific aspects of academic achievement yielded similar results. Technically, only the results listed for "other measures" involved a meta-analysis. This academic variable yielded an effect size of 0.58. However, the one study that examined the influence of parental expectations of standardized test scores yielded a result of 0.57 standard deviation units. This result is noted for the sake of comparison.

Parental Reading

Whether the mother and/or the father read with the child was also an important predictor of academic outcomes. The measures were not as substantial as for family expectations. Nevertheless, for all studies combined the results were 0.42 ($p < 0.0001$) of a standard deviation. In fact, for each one of the specific academic measures under consideration the effects size was 0.42 ($p < 0.0001$).

Communication

between the father and/or mother and children also had an effect size of about one quarter of a standard deviation. The effect for "other measures" was the highest of the achievement variables at 0.28 ($p < 0.01$). Standardized test scores yielded the lowest effect size at 0.21 ($p < 0.0001$). Overall, the effect size for communication was 0.24 ($p < 0.0001$). For both the reading and communication variables, as well as in several other sets of results, the "other measures" variable had the largest standard deviation of the academic variables examined. The possible reasons for this finding are addressed in the Discussion section.

Checking Homework

The effect sizes for checking homework manifested an entirely different pattern of results than the other facets of parental involvement. The effect sizes for checking homework were −0.08 for both overall academic outcomes and standardized tests. Neither of these results was statistically significant.

Parental Style

The numerical outcomes for parental style (see Table 3.5) were generally around three-tenths of a standard deviation, when one considered all the studies together. For all achievement measures combined the effect size was 0.31. The

Table 3.5 Effect Sizes for Specific Aspects of Parental Involvement with 95% Confidence Intervals in Parentheses

Type of Parental Involvement and Academic Variables	Effect Size Without Sophisticated Controls	Effect Size With Sophisticated Controls	Overall Effect Size
Expectations			
Overall	0.58* (0.12, 1.04)	NA	0.58[a]
Standardized Tests	0.57 {based on 1 study only}	NA	0.57 {based on 1 study only}
Other	0.58*(0.12, 1.04)	NA	0.58[a]
Reading			
Overall	0.42**** (30, 0.54)	NA	0.42[a]
Standardized Tests	0.42**** (33, 0.51)	NA	0.42[a]
Other	0.42**** (26, 0.58)	NA	0.42[a]
Communication			
Overall	0.24**** (0.22, 0.26)	NA	0.24[a]
Standardized Tests	0.21**** (0.19, 0.23)	NA	0.21[a]
Other	0.28** (0.12, 0.44)	NA	0.28[a]
Homework			
Overall	−0.08	NA	−0.08
Standardized Tests	−0.08	NA	−0.08
Parental Style			
Overall	0.35** (10, 0.60)	0.17**** (0.14, 0.20)	0.31[a]
Grades	0.33* (0.05, 0.61)	NA	0.33[a]
Standardized Tests	0.29* (04, 0.54)	0.17**** (0.14, 0.20)	0.28[a]
Other	0.31	NA	0.31[a]
Specific Parental Involvement			
Overall	0.35** (0.13, 0.57)	0.14*** (0.08, 0.20)	0.29[a]
Grades	0.37** (0.10, 0.64)	NA	0.37[a]
Standardized Tests	0.34*** (0.15, 0.53)	0.12** (0.04, 0.20)	0.21[a]
Other	0.27	0.15*** (0.13, 0.17)	0.23[a]
Attendance/ Participation			
Overall	0.21*(0.01, 0.41)	NA	0.21[a]
Grades	0.39 {based on 1 study only}	NA	0.39 {based on 1 study only}
Standardized Tests	0.22* (0.02, 0.42)	NA	0.22[a]
Other	0.08 {based on 1 study only}	NA	0.08 {based on 1 study only}

Notes

* $p < 0.05$; ** $p < 0.01$; *** $p < 0.001$; **** $p < 0.0001$; NA = Not available

a Confidence intervals tabulation not undertaken for combined effect size because of difference in sample distributions for the two sets of studies.

results were slightly higher than this for GPA (0.33) and other measures (0.31) and slightly lower for standardized tests (0.28). However, these differences were small, and it should be noted that only the overall achievement measure and the standardized test measure include both studies with sophisticated and those with unsophisticated controls.

One should also note the effect sizes that emerged for parental style were much higher in cases in which sophisticated controls were not used versus when they were. The effect size was for overall achievement was about half the size in studies using sophisticated controls (0.17, $p < 0.0001$) than in research results in which these controls were not used. Moreover, the standard deviations and confidence intervals were smaller when sophisticated controls were used. This pattern also emerged in a number of other results and is further elaborated on in the Discussion section.

Specific parental involvement

Although all studies included in this meta-analysis examined the influence of parental involvement on a broad general level, a number of studies also included a specific variable they called "parental involvement" as one of a number of different kinds of parental involvement variables. That is, a specific parental involvement variable was often included with other involvement variables, such as parental participation in school events, the expectations of the mother and father, family communication about school, and so forth.

As expected, the numerical outcomes were smaller than those measuring the overall impact of parental involvement. The effect size for specific measures of parental involvement was 0.29 for overall measures of achievement. When no elaborate controls were in place the effect size was 0.35 ($p < 0.01$) for over-all achievement. The results for specific measures of achievement were 0.37 ($p < 0.01$) for GPA, 0.34 for standardized tests ($p < 0.001$), and 0.27 ($p =$ n.s.) for other measures. The effect size for specific parental involvement was lower when sophisticated controls were used. However, as was the case with a number of the other measures, the confidence intervals were tighter when sophisticated controls were used. For overall achievement the result was 0.14 ($p < 0.001$). The effect sizes for standardized tests and other measures were very similar in size to the overall measure when sophisticated controls were used.

Parental participation or attendance

which is one of the most ostensible measures of parental involvement, had an overall effect size of 0.21 ($p < 0.05$) in studies that did not use sophisticated controls. This was also the outcome for all the research examined for this variable due to the lack of a study using sophisticated controls. Standardized test scores produced a result of 0.22 ($p < 0.05$).

Table 3.6 Effect Sizes for General Parental Involvement for Studies with Mostly Minority and All Minority Students, with 95% Confidence Intervals in Parentheses

Parental Involvement and Academic Variables	Effect Size without Sophisticated Controls	Effect Size with Sophisticated Controls	Overall Effect Size
General Parental Involvement			
Mostly Minority			
Overall	1.06****(0.68, 1.44)	0.84****(0.57, 1.11)	1.01[a]
Grades	1.11{based on 1 large study only}	0.85****(0.63, 1.07)	0.89[a]
Standardized Tests	0.48*(0.02, 0.94)	0.34****(0.32, 0.36)	0.43[a]
Other	0.52	NA	0.52[a]
All Minority			
Overall	0.29* (0.05, 0.53)	0.46** (0.11, 0.81)	0.41[a]
Grades	0.34** (0.07, 0.61)	0.26**** (0.16, 0.36)	0.32[a]
Standardized Tests	0.27* (0.02, 0.52)	0.26**** (0.24, 0.28)	0.26[a]
Other	NA	0.40** (0.11, 0.69)	0.40[a]
Overall	0.92** (0.27, 1.57)	0.69** (0.18, 1.20)	0.78[a]
Grades	1.03****(0.54, 1.52)	0.69** (0.20, 1.18)	0.86[a]
Standardized Tests	0.29* (0.01, 0.57)	0.28**** (0.21, 0.35)	0.29[a]
Other	0.52	0.40** (0.11, 0.69)	0.41[a]

Notes
* $p < 0.05$; ** $p < 0.01$; *** $p < 0.001$; **** $p < 0.0001$; NA = Not available
a Confidence intervals tabulation not undertaken for combined effect size because of difference in sample distributions for the two sets of studies.

Effect Sizes for Parental Involvement by Child's Race and Gender

One of the key questions (#4) on this issue is whether the relationship between parental involvement and educational outcomes holds by race and by gender. Tables 5.6 and 5.7 list the regression coefficients for parental involvement for racial minority students and for males and females of all those subjects examined, respectively. Regarding the results by race, the studies are divided into two different types. The first includes only those studies in which 100% of the subjects were racial minorities. The second includes those studies in which a majority (on average about 85%) of the students were racial minorities.

For those studies in the latter category, the effect sizes for overall achievement were 1.06 ($p < 0.0001$) when no controls were used and 0.84 ($p < 0.0001$) when sophisticated controls were in place. The 1.06 effect size was larger than the effect size for students primarily from white families ($p < 0.001$). However, no statistically significant difference emerged when comparing mostly minority and mostly white students when sophisticated controls were used. For those studies in which all subjects were of minority racial status the results were 0.29 ($p < 0.05$)

Table 3.7 Effect Sizes for General Parental Involvement for Studies for Boys and Girls, with 95% Confidence Intervals in Parentheses

Parental Involvement and Academic Variables	Effect Size without Sophisticated Controls	Effect Size with Sophisticated Controls	Overall Effect Size
General Parental Involvement			
Girls	0.52** (0.17, 0.87)	NA	0.52[a]
Boys	0.62** (0.27, 0.97)	NA	0.62[a]
Parental Attendance			
Girls	{based on 1 large study only}, 0.94	NA	{based on 1 large study only}, 0.94
Boys	{based on 1 large study only}, 0.94	NA	{based on 1 large study only}, 0.94
Parental Expectations			
Girls	0.34* (0.04, 0.64)	NA	0.34[a]
Boys	0.38**** (0.22, 0.54)	NA	0.38[a]
Parental Style			
Girls	{based on 1 study only}, 0.16	NA	{based on 1 study only}, 0.16
Boys	{based on 1 study only}, 0.42	NA	{based on 1 study only}, 0.42

Notes
* $p < 0.05$; ** $p < 0.01$; *** $p < 0.001$; **** $p < 0.0001$; NA = Not available
a Confidence intervals tabulation not undertaken for combined effect size because of difference in sample distributions for the two sets of studies.

with no sophisticated controls in place and 0.46 ($p < 0.01$) for those in which such controls were used. All the effect sizes were at least one-fourth of a standard deviation. No comparisons were made with studies of all white students, since so few filled this description.

If one combines the effect sizes for all studies that either examined mostly minority students or all minority students, the effect sizes were 0.92 ($p < 0.01$) when no controls were used and 0.69 ($p < 0.01$) when they were. As in the meta-analysis of all the students in all the studies combined, the effect sizes for grades and other measures were larger than for the standardized tests. The effect sizes for grades were 0.69 ($p < 0.01$) and 1.03 ($p < 0.0001$), when sophisticated controls were and were not used, respectively. The results for standardized tests were slightly less than three-tenths of a standard deviation using each of these models.

The results also indicate the relationship between parental involvement and achievement exists for both boys and girls. The overall effect size for parental involvement was somewhat larger for boys (0.62, $p < 0.01$) than for girls (0.52, $p < 0.01$). However, the effect sizes for parental expectations for boys and girls both exceeded three-tenths of a standard deviation and were nearly identical.

Overall, meta-analytic results indicate that almost every major facet of parental involvement examined herein yielded statistically significant results.

Discussion

This study's results indicate a considerable and consistent relationship between parental involvement and academic achievement among elementary school students. This also holds when disaggregated by gender and racial minority status.

Research Question #1: Overall Parental Involvement

Overall, parental involvement's relationship to elementary school student academic outcomes was about seven-tenths to three-quarters of a standard deviation. This is close to what Rosnow and Rosenthal (1996) describe as a large effect size (about 0.8). The regression coefficients were somewhat larger for those studies that did not use sophisticated controls versus those that did. This may indicate parental involvement enjoys an influence that largely transcends differences in socioeconomic status, (SES), race, and other factors. This is supported in the parental involvement data for racial minorities and by gender, which is encouraging in that any group can experience the advantages of parental involvement.

These results appear to support the findings of Fan and Chen (2001), which indicate that there is a strong relationship between parental involvement and academic outcomes. Furthermore, it is apparent from this study that this relationship holds for elementary school students. The fact that these results are different than those obtained by Mattingly et al. (2002) is less significant, because the Mattingly study focused only on parental involvement programs. These programs are school-initiated rather than parent-initiated and their involuntary nature is therefore likely to result in smaller effect sizes. Nevertheless, one should know the effects of these programs.

Research Question #2: Specific Components of Parental Involvement

In addition, nearly all of the individual components of parental involvement were positively and significantly related to educational outcomes. Naturally, the specific components of parental involvement were not correlated with school results as strongly as parental involvement as a whole. Nevertheless, the fact that the various aspects of parental involvement yielded statistically significant results highlights the extent to which parental involvement influences elementary school student achievement.

Much of this meta-analysis examines the specific aspects of parental involvement. These findings are particularly helpful in that they indicate which kinds of parental involvement influence academic success. One definite pattern that emerged is that some of the most potent facets of parental involvement are some of the more subtle aspects of family support. Most notably parental expectations and style each demonstrated a strong relationship with scholastic outcomes. Thus, it was not particular actions like attending school functions, establishing household rules, and checking student homework that yielded the statistically significant effect sizes. Rather, variables that reflected a general atmosphere of involvement produced the strongest results. Parental expectations and style may create an educationally oriented ambience, which establishes an understanding of a certain level of support and standards in the child's mind.

In two ways this finding is encouraging. First, some parents likely influence their child's educational achievements to a greater degree than they realize. Through their expectations for success and style of parenting, they establish an atmosphere conducive to strong achievement. Second, to those parents who inquire about how to become more involved, the answer may be easier than teachers commonly believe.

In contrast, it should be noted that parents checking on student homework did not yield statistically significant results. This does not necessarily suggest the practice's ineffectiveness. Rather, it may be that the meta-analysis measured an underlying dynamic across the studies. Namely, the students whose homework was most likely checked by their parents were those who most needed it, i.e. challenged students. However, this may also suggest that checking on children's homework may not be as effective an expression of parental involvement as many educators currently believe.

It should also be noted that parental attendance and participation did not yield large effect sizes as one might expect. Indeed, they were generally slightly greater than two-tenths of a standard deviation—substantively smaller than other parental involvement variables. This meta-analysis, therefore, questions current beliefs about parental support mechanisms considered exemplary (e.g. checking homework, attending school functions). The most important aspects of parental involvement appear to be more subtle.

Research Question #3: Parental Involvement by Race and Gender

One of the most remarkable patterns that emerged from this meta-analysis is the broad association between parental involvement and school achievement. The correlation generally held across race and gender. That the relationship between parental support and educational outcomes held across race is particularly important for both educators and parents in an increasingly diverse country. In fact, this meta-analysis included so many different types of samples one can conclude this relationship holds across different cultures, backgrounds, and situations.

The results of this study are particularly encouraging, because these findings suggest that parental involvement may be one means of reducing the achievement gap that exists between white students and some racial minority groups (Bronstein, Stoll, Clauson, Abrams & Briones, 1994; Hampton et al., 1998). A number of educators and sociologists have advocated this position and the results of this study support their theories (Bronstein et al., 1994; Hampton et al., 1998; Offenberg, Rodriguez-Acosta & Epstein, 1979). One should also note that many of the parental involvement programs included in this study focused on minority students. Therefore, this meta-analysis not only suggests that parental involvement overall may reduce the achievement gap, but also that programs of this nature may help as well.

This study's broad range of statistically significant effect sizes for parental involvement supports prior claims about the relationship between parental support and educational outcomes when applied to race (Mau, 1997; Sanders, 1998; Shaver & Walls, 1998; Villas-Boas, 1998), gender (Muller, 1998), and background (Griffith, 1996; Hampton et al., 1998). Nevertheless, encouraging parental involvement is not easy. Unquestionably, some family situations more easily lend themselves to greater parental involvement than others—for example, research indicates strong relationships between parental involvement, socioeconomic status, and whether a child is from an intact family (Jeynes, 2002a, 2002b; McLanahan & Sandefur, 1994).

Parental Involvement across Different Achievement Measures

Statistically significant effects emerged not only for overall academic achievement, but also for GPA, standardized tests, and other academic measures. One noticeable trend concerns a greater relationship between parental involvement and grades and other measures, such as teacher ratings, rather than standardized tests. This pattern is not surprising for at least two reasons. First, parental involvement tends to focus on classroom-based assignments rather than preparing for standardized tests.

Second, teachers themselves are influenced by parental involvement. A teacher plays a major role in the grades and ratings a student receives in class, and a high degree of parental involvement likely influences how the teacher perceives and even grades the child. Thus, unlike standardized tests, grades reflect: (a) a positive relationship between the parent and the teacher; (b) a sense of teamwork between the parent and the teacher, due to increased communication between the two; and (c) an acknowledgement by the teacher of parental efforts.

Another trend of note is tighter confidence intervals and smaller standard deviations for the standardized test scores. This reflects the high levels of reliability inherent in standardized tests as compared to less objective measures, like teacher ratings and grades, which can be more easily influenced by the unique perspective and biases of the assessor.

Finally, including only higher quality studies in the meta-analyses also did not markedly influence effect sizes, particularly for those studies with sophisticated controls. Not surprisingly, those studies with sophisticated controls were generally among the studies highest in quality. Of course, neither of the findings is surprising given the 0.02 correlation between study quality and effect size.

Limitations of Study

The primary limitation of this meta-analysis, or any meta-analysis, is that it is restricted to analyzing the existing body of literature. Therefore, even if the researcher conducting the quantitative integrations sees ways the studies included could have been improved, there is no way to implement those changes. A second limitation of a meta-analysis is that the social scientist is limited to addressing the same research questions addressed in the aggregated studies. For example, it would be advisable to have measures of parental expectations from all the studies included, but one can only aggregate the existing results.

Recommendations for Further Research

The results of this study are particularly important given the achievement gap between students of color and their white counterparts (Bronstein et al., 1994; Hampton et al., 1998). Indeed, this study's findings suggest parental involvement may effectively contribute to reducing that gap. Nevertheless, further research is needed to examine why certain aspects of parental involvement, particularly those that involve creating an educationally oriented atmosphere, are more noteworthy than others. Additional research can also help determine why parental involvement strongly influences the achievement of minority children in particular. Future research should also incorporate sophisticated statistical techniques, such as randomization and the use of hierarchical linear modeling. Qualitative research can also supplement the findings of this study by ascertaining the ways in which teachers, parents, and students perceive that parental involvement benefits students the most.

Chapter 4

Parental Involvement and Secondary School Achievement

A Meta-analysis

Parental involvement has become one of the most debated facets of education today. The discussion over parental support for children's studies has not been limited to educators, but has become an important topic among parents, social scientists, and politicians. Although a myriad of educators has focused on the importance of parental involvement to children excelling in school, a meta-analysis is of utmost utility because it gives insight into what the overall body of research indicates. This fact largely contributes to a limited body of knowledge that exists regarding which aspects of parental involvement help student education and just what components of this involvement are most important (Christian et al., 1998).

A large number of studies have been done that examine the impact of parental involvement on the general population. However, most of these studies have one of the following limitations that hurt the benefit of each of these individual studies (McBride & Lin, 1996, Muller, 1998, Peressini, 1998). First, most studies focus on only on parental involvement generally or on certain aspects of parental involvement. Consequently, most individual studies can offer little guidance to parents and educators regarding which aspects of parental involvement are most important (Christian et al., 1998). Second, a large number of these studies have small samples that make it difficult to estimate the influence of parental involvement on the general student population (Bauch & Goldring, 1995; Bronstein et al., 1994; Crouter et al., 1999). Third, a large number of the studies focus on only particular groups of students in certain situations (McBride & Lin, 1996; Muller, 1998; Peressini, 1998). Consequently, by examining the results of a single study, it may not be possible to come to develop principles about what aspects of parental involvement may be helpful to the broad spectrum of students.

Mattingly and her colleagues recently published a research synthesis, which is the closest any one has come to publishing a meta-analysis on this very important topic (Mattingly, Prislin, McKenzie, Rodriguez, & Kayzar, 2002). Nevertheless, this study possesses two major weaknesses. First, quite a number of prominent studies are not included in the research synthesis. Instead, about one half of the studies are unpublished studies. Unpublished studies are more likely to have statistically insignificant results. Therefore, the omission of a number of published studies likely biased the results in favor of the author's conclusion that parental support programs may have no impact. Second, Mattingly and her colleagues only examined parental involvement programs, rather than the general presence of parental involvement. In all fairness to their study, Mattingly and her associates only desired to address parental involvement programs. Third, Mattingly concludes that some of the studies that do show a statistically significant effect for parental involvement actually show no impact. However, since the Mattingly research synthesis did not examine the influence of parental involvement generally, the need to have an actual meta-analysis, rather than merely a research synthesis, is especially important.

Beyond undertaking a meta-analysis that assesses the overall impact of parental involvement, just as in the case with the elementary school meta-analysis in Chapter 3, it is also essential to address which aspects of parental support are most important using this approach. Over the last few years, researchers have attempted to become more specific in their studies, regarding just what they mean by parental involvement. Hoge, Smit, and Crist (1997) attempted to define parental involvement as consisting of four components: parental expectations, parental interest, parental involvement in school, and family community. They determined that of the four components, parental expectations were the most important. Other social scientists either qualify or dispute these findings. Mau's (1997) findings suggested that while parental expectations were important, parental supervision of homework was crucial. Mau also observed some racial differences in the types of parental involvement that parents engaged in. She found that while white parents were more likely to attend school functions than their Asian and Asian American counterparts, the latter parents had higher expectations and their children did more homework than the white students. Given that Asian and Asian American students generally academically outperformed white students, Mau doubted the significance of parents attending school functions. Some research suggests that parental expectations may backfire if they are not established in the context of an affirming parental style (Zellman & Waterman, 1998). Otherwise, potentially high expectations may place an unreasonable degree of pressure on the child. A meta-analysis could help resolve these debates as well as others.

The existing status of the body research knowledge is as follows. There have been a fair number of studies done on the influence of parental involvement. Nevertheless, the various limitations of many of these studies, referred to earlier, makes it challenging to come to any firm conclusions about which components of parental involvement have the greatest impact. Both these facts taken together lend themselves to undertaking a meta-analysis on parental involvement on. Two facts would make a meta-analysis on parental involvement especially helpful. First, although the individual studies themselves may be too narrowly focused to yield the necessary generalizations, the statistical combination of these studies in a meta-analysis would make this possible.

Second, the number of studies on this issue is large enough to warrant this approach.

Given that: 1) that many individual studies have certain limitations and 2) there has been a reasonably large amount of research on parental involvement, this suggests that this area of research has developed to a point at which a meta-analysis of secondary school students would be very beneficial. Enough studies have been done at the secondary school level to warrant a meta-analysis and this technique would also yield some answers to questions that the individual studies by themselves are too narrowly focused to address.

It is important to know not only the overall impact of parental involvement, but to know the specific components of this support that can help the most. After all, parental involvement can be a nebulous term, which can mean considerably different things to different people. In recent years some social scientists have attempted to more lucidly define what is meant by parental involvement (Crouter, Helms-Erickson, Updegraff, & McHale, 1999). Ballantine (1999) asserts that there are many aspects of parental involvement and that it would be beneficial if social scientists would identify which aspects of parental involvement have the greatest benefit on children. Grolnick, Benjet, Kurowski, and Apostoleris (1997) claim that once the academic community knows what parental involvement consists of, it can predict what parental attributes will contribute most to producing a family that participates in the educational journey of their children. Beyond this, parental involvement may reduce some of the downward impact on educational outcomes that broken homes (Bronstein et al., 1994) and deficient schools (Hampton et al., 1998; Hara, 1998) generally have on children. However, the question remains, what aspects of parental involvement help the most?

Methods

The methods used in this meta-analysis are similar to those used in the meta-analysis used for elementary schools. Nevertheless, because: 1) it facilitates the reading of the chapter and 2) there are some differences especially numerically, the methodology will be listed here.

Analytical Approach

This meta-analysis examined the relationship between parental involvement and urban secondary student achievement. The first analysis consisted of computing effect sizes for the overall parental involvement variable (research question 1). The second analysis assessed the association between specific types of parental involvement (e.g. checking homework and parental expectations) with student achievement (research question 2). The third analysis examined the relationship between parental involvement and student achievement by race and gender (research question 3). The procedures used to conduct the meta-analysis are outlined under this heading (Analytical Approach) and the following headings below: Data Collection Method, Study Quality Rating, Statistical Methods and Effect Size Statistics, and Defining of Variables.

Each study incorporated in this meta-analysis met the following criteria:

1   It needed to examine parental involvement in a way that could be conceptually and statistically distinguished from other primary variables under consideration. For example, if a study involved nine key variables, including parental involvement, and the impact of parental involvement could not be statistically isolated from the other features, the study was not included in the analysis.

2   It must include a sufficient amount of statistical information to ascertain effect sizes. That is, a study needed to possess enough information so that test statistics, such as those resulting from a t-test, analysis of variance, and so forth, were either provided in the study or could be determined from the means and measures of variance provided in the study.

3   If the study included a control group, it had to qualify as a true control group and therefore be a fair and accurate means of comparison. Furthermore, if the research utilized a control group at some times but not others, only the former comparisons were included in the meta-analysis.

4   The study needed to be set in an urban environment and could be a published or unpublished study.

Given the nature of the criteria listed above, qualitative studies were not included in the study. Qualitative studies are definitely valuable, but they are difficult to code for quantitative purposes and any attempt to do so might bias the results of the meta-analysis.

Data Collection Method (Coding and Rater Reliability)

In order to obtain the studies used in the meta-analysis, a search was performed using every major social science research database (e.g. Psych Info, ERIC, Dissertation Abstracts International, Wilson Periodicals, Sociological Abstracts, and so forth) to locate studies examining the relationship between parental involvement and the educational outcomes of students from grades 6–12. The search terms included parental involvement, parents, schools, family, partnership, education, expectations, parental support, communication, expectations, reading, attendance, homework, household, rules, parental style, and several other terms. Reference sections from journal articles on parental involvement were also examined to locate additional research articles. Although this search yielded over 5,000 articles and papers on parental involvement, nearly all of these articles were not quantitative in nature. This process yielded a total of sixty-seven studies that quantitatively assessed the relationship between parental involvement and urban secondary school student achievement. Of these, fifty-two had a sufficient degree of quantitative data to include in this meta-analysis.

Study Quality Rating

Two researchers coded the studies independently for quality, the presence of randomization, and whether both the definitional criteria for parental involvement and specific aspects of parental involvement were met. Study quality and the use of random samples were graded on a 0 (lowest) to 3 (highest) scale. Quality was determined using the following:

1   Did it use randomization of assignment?
2   Did it avoid mono-method bias?
3   Did it avoid mono-operation bias?
4   Did it avoid selection bias?
5   Did it use a specific definition of parental involvement?

We computed inter-rater reliability by calculating the percentage of agreement on: the definition of parental involvement, issues of randomization, the specific components examined in each study, and quality of the study. Inter-rater reliability was 100% on whether a study examined parental involvement, 96% for the specific components of parental involvement examined in a given study, and 92% for the quality of the study. For the specific components of quality, inter-rater agreement percentages were 98% for randomization, 94% for avoiding mono-method bias, 94% for avoiding mono-operation bias, 92% for avoiding selection bias, and 96% for using a specific definition of parental involvement.

Two supplementary analyses were done to include first, only those studies with quality ratings of 2 and 3 and second, only those studies with quality ratings of 1 to 3.

Statistical Methods and the Effect Size Statistic

Among the fifty-two studies that had a sufficient degree of quantitative data to include in this meta-analysis, the total number of subjects was well over 300,000. To ensure accurate statistical results, a number of steps were taken to make the meta-analysis more sophisticated. First, the Hedges' "g" measure of effect size was used (Hedges, 1981). Since it employs the pooled standard deviation in the denominator, it customarily provides a more conservative estimate of effect size. Hedges also provides a correction factor that helps to adjust for the impact of small samples. Effect sizes from data in such forms as t tests, F tests, p levels, frequencies, and r values were calculated via conversion formulas provided by Glass and his colleagues (1981). When results were not statistically significant, studies sometimes reported only a significance level. In the unusual case that the direction of these not significant results was not available, the effect size was calculated to be zero.

The analysis in this study determines the overall relationship between parental involvement and achievement obtained for each study, as well as specific types of parental involvement mentioned earlier in the Methods section. Four different measures of academic achievement were used to assess the effects of parental involvement on educational outcomes. First, there was an overall measure of all components of academic achievement combined. The other measures included grades, standardized tests, and other measures that generally included teacher rating scales and indices of academic attitudes and behaviors. The results that emerged in this study reflect the association between parental involvement and achievement found for each component of parental involvement, using each of these educational outcomes.

Two sets of statistical procedures were also used to distinguish between those analyses that included sophisticated controls (socioeconomic status, race, gender, or previous achievement) and those studies that did not. The effect sizes were determined using weights based on the inverse of the variance, in order to give greater weight to studies with larger sample sizes. The results of these procedures are listed in different columns in the Results section, with the degree of statistical significance and 95% confidence intervals listed for each. An overall effect size was then determined, combining the studies that did and did not use sophisticated controls. No analyses of statistical significance were completed on the combined effect sizes given the different structure of the studies involved.

Supplementary analyses also addressed what effect sizes arose when adjusting for the quality of the study. In one set of analyses, only studies with an average quality rating of 2 or 3 (on a 0 to 3 scale) were included. In the second set of analyses only studies with an average quality rating of 1 to 3 (on a 0 to 3 scale) were included. Tests of homogeneity were completed on the specific components of parental involvement to gain a sense of the consistency of specific parental involvement measures across studies.

For all the analyses, when only one study was included using a specific academic outcome for a specific parental involvement variable, the regression coefficient for this study is listed with a notation indicating the table cell only included one study, in order to serve as a means of comparison with the various other effect sizes.

Defining of Variables

For the purposes of this study, parental involvement was defined as parental participation in the educational processes and experiences of their children. The specific parental involvement variables, defined below, were the types of parental involvement identified by educators as most frequently practiced by parents, examined by researchers, and hypothesized by theorists as the most fundamental aspects of parental involvement (Deslandes et al., 1997; Epstein, 2001). The categorization of these specific parental involvement variables was based on the precise terms used in the original studies included in the meta-analysis. Fortunately, these researchers used widely accepted and recognized terms. Therefore, the proper categorization of effect sizes was nearly always self-evident, e.g. those studies included in the meta-analysis for "parental expectations" typically used precisely the same term.

General Parental Involvement

Includes the overall measure of parental involvement, as defined by the researchers of a particular study. If a study did not possess an overall measure of parental involvement, the effect size of this variable was determined by combining all its discrete measures.

Specific Parental Involvement

Includes a specific measure of parental involvement, as distinguished from other measures of parental involvement used in the study.

Parental Expectations

The degree to which a student's parents maintained high expectations of the student's ability to achieve at high levels.

Reading

The extent to which parents either have in the past or are in the present reading regularly with their children.

Attendance/Participation

Whether and how frequently parents attend and participate in school functions and activities.

Communication

The extent to which parents and their children communicated about school activities and reported a high level of communication overall.

Homework

The extent to which parents checked their children's homework before the child handed it in to his or her teacher.

Parental Style

The extent to which a parent demonstrated a supportive and helpful parenting approach. In the studies included in the meta-analysis, most frequently this referred to a simultaneous ability to be loving and supportive and yet maintain an adequate level of discipline in the household. It also included styles in which the parent demonstrated such qualities as trust and being approachable.

Results

The results of the meta-analysis indicate that parental involvement is associated with higher student achievement outcomes. This trend holds not only for parental involvement overall, but for most different components of parental involvement that were examined in the meta-analysis.

Table 4.1 lists the effects that emerged for the individual studies examined in this meta-analysis. The effects varied from 0.01 to 0.83. Generally speaking, the effects that were the largest and smallest in size were from studies that had small sample sizes. This fact contributed to a "funnel pattern" in the effects that is desirable when one is doing a meta-analysis. This is because the influence of a normal distribution tends to draw results toward the population mean, in the case of the studies with the larger sample sizes.

Table 4.1 List of Studies used in the Meta-Analysis for Parental Involvement, the Year of the Study, and the Effect Sizes for the Various Studies

Study	Year	Effect Size Without Sophisticated Controls	Effect Size With Sophisticated Controls
Wise	1972	+0.83	—
Ma	1999	+0.82	—
Singh, Bickley, Trivette, Keith, Patricia, & Anderson	1995	—	+0.81
Keith, Keith, Quirk, Cohen-Rosenthal, & Franzese	1996	+0.80	—
Simich-Dudgeon	1993	+0.76	—
Mau	1997	+0.74	—
Unger, McLeod, Brown, & Tressell	2000	+0.70	+0.65
Grolnick & Slowiaczek	1994	+0.67	—
Keith, Keith, Troutman, Bickley, Trivette, & Singh	1993	+0.67	—
Paulson	1994a	+0.67	—
Zdzinski	1992	+0.67	—
Keith & Lichtman	1994	+0.65	—
Steinberg, Elmen, & Mounts	1989	+0.63	+0.41
Russell & Elder	1997	—	+0.63
Keith, Reimers, Fehrmann, Pottebaum, & Aubey	1986	+0.63	—

Eagle	1989	—	+0.62
Paulson	1994b	+0.62	—
Keith, Keith, Bickley, & Singh	1992	—	+0.61
Brown & Madhere	1996	—	+0.60
Jeynes	2000	+0.60	+0.27
Shanham & Walberg	1985	+0.56	—
Steinberg, Lamborn, Dornbusch, & Darling	1992	—	+0.56
Melby & Conger	1996	+0.51	+0.35
Jeynes	2002e	+0.50	+0.29
Yan	1999	+0.49	+0.34
Taylor	1996	—	+0.49
Hoge, Smit, & Crist	1997	+0.47	—
O'Reilly	1992	+0.45	—
Deslandes, Royer, & Turcotte	1997	—	+0.43
Aeby, Thyer, & Carpenter-Aeby	1999	+0.42	—
Fehrmann, Keith, & Reimers	1987	+0.42	+0.33
Stevenson & Baker	1987	+0.38	—
Taylor, Hinton, & Wilson	1995	+0.37	—
Bermudez & Padron	1990	+0.37	—
Uguroglu & Walberg	1986	+0.37	+0.17
Sui-Chu & Willms	1996	—	+0.35
Williams	1999	+0.30	—
Hampton, Mumford, & Bond	1998	+0.29	—
Yap, & Enoki	1995	+0.28	—
Peng & Wright	1994	—	+0.27
Heiss	1996	—	+0.26
Desimone	1996	+0.28	+0.04
Sanders	1996	+0.26	—
Keith & Lichtman	1992	+0.25	—
Epstein, Herick, & Coates	1996	+0.25	—
Keith, Keith, Sperduto, Santillo, & Killings	1998	—	+0.23
Cardenas-Rivera	1994	+0.22	—
Fletcher	1994	+0.22	—
Brownell	1995	+0.20	—
McNeal	1999	+0.18	—
Cooper, Lindsay, & Nye	2000	+0.04	—
Veneziano	1996	+0.01	—

In table 4.2 are listed the effect sizes for parental involvement, in general, using the four academic achievement variables. For all the achievement variables combined the effect sizes were somewhat higher for studies that did not use sophisticated controls than those that did.

For the studies that did not use sophisticated controls, the overall effect size was 0.53 (p < 0.0001) of a standard deviation versus 0.38 (p < 0.05) for those studies hat did use sophisticated controls. For those studies that did not use sophisticated controls, the effect sizes were quite consistent across the academic measures, varying from 0.55 (p < 0.0001) for standardized test scores to 0.34 (p < 0.001) for other measures. For those studies with sophisticated controls, the

Table 4.2 Effect Sizes for General Parental Involvement with 95% Confidence
Intervals in Parentheses

Parental Involvement and Academic Variables	Effect Size Without Sophisticated Controls	Effect Size With Sophisticated Controls	Overall Effect Size
General Parental Involvement			
Overall	0.53**** (0.26, 0.80)	0.38* (0.07, 0.69)	0.46[a]
Grades	0.49*** (0.18, 0.86)	0.27* (0.05, 0.49)	0.40[a]
Standardized Tests	0.55**** (0.27, 0.83)	0.37* (0.07, 0.67)	0.47[a]
Other	0.34** (0.09, 0.51)	0.53**** (0.33, 0.73)	0.43[a]

Notes
* $p < 0.05$; ** $p < 0.01$; *** $p < 0.001$; **** $p < 0.0001$
a Confidence intervals tabulation not undertaken for combined effect size because of difference in sample distributions for the two sets of studies.

outcomes ranged from 0.53 ($p < 0.0001$) for other measures to 0.27 ($p < 0.05$) for grades. Further analysis, not listed here, indicated that there were no differences in the influence of parental involvement among the different subjects included in the standardized tests.

Table 4.3 lists the results for the various specific components of parental involvement. The largest effect sizes emerged for parental expectations. For overall academic achievement, the effect size for parental expectations was 0.88 ($p < 0.0001$) of a standard deviation. The results were similar for standardized tests and other measures.

The results for parental expectations were quite consistent among the various studies examined. Therefore, the confidence intervals were generally narrow, especially for standardized tests. For parental style the effect sizes were quite consistent across the different academic measures. In the case of overall achievement, the effect size was .40 ($p < 0.05$) of a standard deviation. The grades and standardized test variables yielded results of 0.45 ($p < 0.0001$) and 0.39 ($p < 0.05$) respectively.

The results for family communication about school were stronger when no sophisticated controls were used than when they were. For all the educational measures combined, the result was 0.32 ($p < 0.05$) standard deviation units. The effect sizes for standardized tests and grades were also statistically significant, but they were not statistically significant for other measures. When sophisticated controls were used, the effect sizes for overall achievement and standardized were in the positive direction, but were not statistically significant.

The impact of parents checking homework was somewhat similar to that of family communication regarding school. When no sophisticated controls were used, the effect size for overall academic achievement was 0.38 ($p < 0.05$) of a standard deviation. In terms of the specific measures of academic achievement the impact of grades was statistically significant, but the beta for standardized

Table 4.3 Effect Sizes for Specific Aspects of Parental Involvement with 95% Confidence Intervals in Parentheses

Parental Involvement and Academic Variables	Effect Size Without Sophisticated Controls	Effect Size With Sophisticated Controls	Overall Effect Size
Expectations			
Overall	0.88**** (0.72,1.04)	NA	0.88
Standardized Tests	NA	NA	NA
Grades	0.85**** (0.80, 0.90)	NA	0.85
Other	1.09**** (0.84, 1.34)	NA	1.09
Parental Style			
Overall	0.40* (05, 0.75)	NA	0.40
Grades	0.45**** (22, 0.68)	NA	0.45
Standardized Tests	0.39* (04, 0.74)	NA	0.39
Other	0.65 {based on 1 study}	NA	0.65 {based on 1 study}
Communication			
Overall	0.32* (0.01, 0.63)	0.15	0.24[a]
Grades	0.29* (0.03, 0.55)	0.04 {based on 1 study}	0.29[a]
Standardized Tests	0.30** (0.07, 0.53)	0.14	0.23[a]
Other	0.24	0.22 {based on 1 study}	0.24[a]
Homework			
Overall	0.38* (02, 0.74)	0.13 (0.14, 0.20)	0.32[a]
Grades	0.39* (0.03, 0.75)	−0.10{based on 1 study}	0.35[a]
Standardized Tests	0.24	0.14	0.20[a]

Notes
* p< 0.05; ** p < 0.01; *** p < 0.001; **** p < 0.0001
a Confidence intervals tabulation not undertaken for combined effect size because of difference in sample distributions for the two sets of studies.

tests was not. When sophisticated controls were used, the regression coefficients for overall achievement and standardized tests were in the positive direction, but they were not statistically significant.

Table 4.4 lists the effect sizes for specific variables for parental involvement, parents attending and participating in school events, and having household rules regarding schoolwork. Overall, the effect sizes for overall achievement for the specific parental involvement variable was 0.40 of a standard deviation variable, 0.29 when no sophisticated controls were used and .61 when these controls were used. Contrary to the general patterns evident for the other specific variables, the effect sizes for specific aspects of parental involvement were larger when sophisticated controls were utilized. The effect size for other measures when sophisticated controls were in place were 0.33 (p < 0.05) for grades, 0.59 (p < .0001) for standardized tests, and 0.99 for other measures.

Table 4.4 Effect Sizes for Additional Specific Aspects of Parental Involvement with 95% Confidence Intervals in Parentheses

	Effect Size Without Sophisticated Controls	*Effect Size With Sophisticated Controls*	*Overall Effect Size*
Specific Parental Involvement			
Overall	0.29** (0.09, 0.49)	0.61** (0.21, 1.01)	0.39[a]
Grades	0.32** (0.11, 0.53)	0.33* (0.07, 0.59)	0.32[a]
Standardized Tests	0.28* (0.04, 0.52)	0.59**** (0.41, 0.77)	0.34[a]
Other	0.25* (0.04, 0.46)	0.99*** (0.37, 1.61)	0.94[a]
Rules			
Overall	−0.00 (02, 0.74)	0.02 (0.14, 0.20)	0.02[a]
Grades	0.07 (0.03, 0.75)	0.07 {based on 1 study}	0.07[a]
Standardized Tests	0.00	0.02	0.02[a]
Other	0.12* (0.02, 0.22)	0.13 {based on 1 study}	0.12[a]
Attendance/Participation			
Overall	0.14	0.03	0.11[a]
Grades	0.21** (0.06, 0.36)	0.07 {based on 1 study}	0.18[a]
Standardized Tests	0.09	0.05	0.07[a]
Other	0.50** (0.13, 0.87)	0.21 {based on 1 study}	0.38[a]

Notes
* $p < 0.05$; ** $p < 0.01$; *** $p < 0.001$; **** $p < 0.0001$
a Confidence intervals tabulation not undertaken for combined effect size because of difference in sample distributions for the two sets of studies.

The pattern that emerged for parental participation and attendance is that, for studies not using sophisticated controls, statistically significant results emerged for grades, 0.21 ($p < 0.01$) and other measures, 0.50 ($p < 0.01$), but not for overall achievement and standardized tests. When sophisticated controls were used, no statistically significant results emerged.

Of all the parental involvement variables examined, the outcomes for rules yielded the smallest effect sizes. Overall, the effect size for overall achievement was 0.00 (n.s.), when no sophisticated controls were used. Of the individual academic variables examined, only the effect sizes for other measures were statistically significant, 0.12 ($p < 0.05$). It was in the positive direction. When sophisticated controls were used, the effect sizes for overall achievement and standardized tests were not statistically significant. For grades and other measures, only one study was done that included sophisticated controls. Although, no meta-analysis could therefore be done for these specific variables, the results were roughly the same for these individual studies as for the meta-analysis undertaken for the set of studies with no sophisticated controls.

Homogeneity tests were performed to assess the extent to which the specific aspects of parental involvement across the various studies included were comparable. Generally speaking, for the same educational outcome measure, the results usually indicated that the tests for homogeneity were not statistically significant. These results indicate that within each specific component of parental involvement, the various measures of parental involvement were relatively homogeneous across studies.

Among the specific parental variables that did not test statistically significant for heterogeneity were parental expectations ($X^2 = 4.33$, n.s.), specific parental involvement ($X^2 = 4.44$, n.s.), and parental style ($X^2 = 8.66$, n.s.). Nevertheless, some of the other specific variables tested as heterogeneous, e.g. parental participation/attendance ($X^2 = 13.80$, p < 0.001) and household rules ($X^2 = 5.59$, p < 0.05).

The effect sizes for parental involvement for minority children (see Table 4.5) showed consistent statistically significant positive results. For those studies that examined students that were 100% minority the effect sizes were, 0.46 (p < 0.001) for overall achievement, 0.42 (p < 0.0001), for grades, and 0.49 (p < 0.0001) for standardized tests, when sophisticated controls were not used. The effect sizes were generally lower when sophisticated controls were used versus when they were not.

The effect size for overall achievement was 0.33 (p < 0.01). For the specific educational variables, the outcomes varied from 0.26 (p < 0.0001) for grades to 0.48 (p < 0.0001) for other measures.

Table 4.5 Effect Sizes for General Parental Involvement for Studies with Mostly Minority and All Minority Students with 95% Confidence Intervals in Parentheses

Parental Involvement and Academic Variables	Effect Size without Sophisticated Controls	Effect Size with Sophisticated Controls	Overall Effect Size
General Parental Involvement			
Mostly Minority			
Overall	0.53* (0.02, 1.04)	0.36**** (0.24, 0.48)	0.53[a]
Grades	NA	0.32 {based on 1 study only}	NA
Standardized Tests	1.08 {based on 1 study only}	0.36**** (0.24, 0.48)	0.43[a]
Other	0.52* (01, 1.04)	NA	0.52[a]
All Minority			
Overall	0.46*** (0.17, 0.75)	0.33** (0.10, 0.56)	0.42[a]
Grades	0.42**** (0.33, 0.51)	0.26**** (0.18, 0.34)	0.33[a]
Standardized Tests	0.49*** (0.10, 0.88)	0.27**** (0.21, 0.33)	0.26[a]
Other	0.49 {based on 1 study only}	0.48**** (0.26, 0.76)	0.40[a]

Notes
* p < 0.05; ** p < 0.01; *** p < 0.001; **** p < 0.0001
a Confidence intervals tabulation not undertaken for combined effect size because of difference in sample distributions for the two sets of studies

For those studies that examined samples of mostly minority students (on average about 85% minority students), the effect sizes were very close to those found for student samples made up of 100% minority students. The effect size for overall academic achievement was 0.53 ($p < 0.05$), when sophisticated controls were not used, and 0.36 ($p < 0.0001$) when these controls were utilized.

Discussion

The results of this study indicate that parental involvement has a positive impact on secondary school student's academic achievement. This overall results holds for all measures of academic achievement that were examined. This pattern holds not only for the overall student population, but for minority students as well. For the overall population of students, the effect sizes were in the general range of about one half of a standard deviation for overall educational outcomes, grades and academic achievement when no sophisticated controls were used. The results for studies examining 100% minority students and mostly minority students were also close to about half a standard deviation unit. For overall achievement, the effect size was 0.46 for studies that examined all minority children and 0.53 for those studies that included mostly minority children. These results highlight the consistency of the impact of parental involvement.

The results on the influence of overall parental involvement should cheer those who desire to know whether parental involvement holds across populations and cultures. Although the United States is a diverse country, the impact of parental involvement apparently holds across different types of populations of children. Even when sophisticated controls were used, the overall impact of parental involvement was 0.38 for the overall population of students and nearly that high for racial minority children.

One of the most vital aspects of this study was its examination of specific components of parental involvement to see which aspects influenced student achievement. One of the patterns that emerged from the findings is that subtle aspects of parental involvement such as parental style and expectations had a greater impact on student educational outcomes than some of the more demonstrative aspects of parental involvement such as having household rules and parental attendance and participation at school functions.

The effect sizes for parental style were generally around .40 of a standard deviation. The effect sizes for parental expectations were over 0.80. These regressions coefficients were the largest of all the specific components of parental involvement that were examined. The beta for other measures, under the parental expectations variable, was 1.09. Not only were the results for parental expectations quite large in standard deviation units, but they had 95% confidence intervals that were pretty narrow. This fact yielded effect sizes that were statistically significant at the 0.0001 level of probability.

The effect sizes for family communication about school were smaller than for either parental style or expectations. Nevertheless, when sophisticated controls were not used the effect sizes were generally around three-tenths of a standard deviation unit. However, when sophisticated controls were used although the regression coefficients were in the positive direction, they were no longer statistically significant.

Among some of the more ostensible facets of parental involvement, the effect sizes were generally smaller than those found for the more subtle aspects of parental involvement. The effect sizes for the influence of household rules on overall academic achievement were not statistically significant either for studies that used sophisticated controls or those that did not. The effect size for other measures was statistically significant. Nevertheless, for the remaining measures the size was not statistically significant. Parental participation and attendance had a mixed impact on academic achievement. Parental participation and attendance had no statistically significant impact on overall academic achievement, whether on not sophisticated controls were used. However, parental participation did have an impact on grades and other measures. Some possible explanations for this phenomenon include: 1) parental attendance is more likely to help students assimilate material covered in school than it is to help students excel in understanding the broad range of knowledge that is usually covered in standardized tests and 2) parental participation enhances the relationship between parents and teachers, which positively impacts grades.

In fact, other measures and grades were somewhat more likely in the various elements of the meta-analysis to produce statistically significant results than standardized test scores. This result likely emerged for many of the same reasons that parental participation influenced other measures and grades more than it did standardized test scores. That is, first, parents generally focus their involvement on school outcomes more than the results of standardized tests. Second, parental involvement generally improves the relationship between parents and teachers, which likely positively impacts school outcomes.

While it is true that the influence of parental involvement largely transcended socioeconomic factors, the inclusion of the SES and other variables somewhat reduced the effects for parental involvement versus those that emerged when no sophisticated controls were used. The fact that the inclusion of these addition variables, especially SES, did have a little impact is not a surprise, given the fact that past research indicates that there is a high correlation between SES and parental involvement. Highly educated parents are often more likely acknowledge the importance of parental support in education (Legutko, 1998; Mulroy, Goldman, & Wales, 1998; Portes & MacLeod, 1996). Parents with a high SES level are also likely to appreciate the importance of a good education in terms of living a successful adult life (Grayson, 1999; Mulroy et al., 1998; Portes & MacLeod, 1996). Ascertaining the causal relationship between parental involvement and SES is a challenging one.

Clearly, some of the same attributes that help make a parent supportive are also likely to produce high SES parents. For example, a parent who believes diligence in school is important is more likely than most to be highly educated and is also more likely than most to support his or her children in scholastic endeavors. Moreover, a person with a supportive personality is more likely to excel as a boss and is also more likely to excel as an involved parent. One can make the argument that the addition of the SES variables dilutes the effects for parental involvement not because the causal nature of SES so much, as the fact that there are other causal components beyond SES and parental involvement that influence both variables. In terms of SES specifically, a growing number of studies indicate that the level of SES can be a result of various other factors, rather than a primary cause (Gortmaker, Must, Perrin, Sobol, et al., 1993; Jeynes, 1998; Zakrisson & Ekehammer, 1998). Crane (1996) demonstrated that the influence of SES, as a causal variable, can be overestimated if mediating family factors are not taken into account. More research is needed to effectively understand the relationship between parental family structure and SES.

Taken together, the results of this study are very enlightening. First, these findings that support the notion that parental involvement has salient effects that hold across various populations are fairly substantial. Second, this meta-analysis suggests that among the most important aspects of parental involvement are some of the more subtle facets of this practice. Among these more subtle aspects of parental involvement are parental style and parental expectations. Third, although the influence of parental involvement generally holds across academic variables, it appeared to produce statistically significant effects slightly more often for grades and other measures than for standardized tests.

The findings of this study give an overall sense of the extent of the influence of parental involvement, based on the present body of research. This study also gives teachers and parents guidance about which aspects of parental involvement are most helpful. Further research can examine whether utilizing the most influential aspects of parental involvement, as uncovered by this study, will yield more effective parental involvement and parental support programs.

Chapter 5

Parental Involvement and Minority Student Achievement
A Meta-analysis

Parental involvement has become one of the centerpieces of educational dialogue among educators, parents, and political leaders. The presence of more parents in the work force, the fast pace of modern society as a whole, and the declining role of the family have all been reasons that some social scientists have pointed to, in order to explain an apparent decline in parental involvement in education. Although many educators have highlighted the importance of parental involvement, if children are to do well in school, the research that has been done on this issue has frequently been unable to give guidance regarding the extent to which parental involvement helps student achievement and just what kind of parental involvement is most important, which may be particularly helpful for parents and students of color.

Parental involvement research has been on the increase during the last two decades. Social Scientists are giving parental involvement a special place of importance in influencing the academic outcomes of the youth. Hara (1998) goes so far as to claim that increased parental involvement is the key to improving the academic achievement of children. Various studies indicate that parental involvement is salient in determining how well children do in school at both the elementary and secondary school levels (Christian et al., 1998; Mau, 1997; McBride & Lin, 1996; Muller, 1998; Singh et al. 1995). Research by Singh et al. (1995) suggests that the effects of parental involvement may be greater at the elementary school level. Deslandes, Royer, Turcott, and Bertrand (1997) reported results that suggest the parenting style might determine how great an effect the involvement of parents has at the secondary level. The impact of parental involvement emerges in mathematics achievement (Muller, 1998; Peressini, 1998; Shaver & Walls; 1998), reading achievement (Jeynes, 2003b, 2005e, 2007b; Shaver & Walls, 1998), and in other subjects as well (Jeynes, 1998, 2003a, 2005b, 2006a, 2007b; Zdzinski, 1996).

The research that has been done thus far also indicates that the effects of parental involvement are quite broad. That is, they hold across a variety of different types of populations and situations. For example, the place of parental involvement on academic achievement holds no matter what level of parental education one examines (Bogenschneider, 1997) and at all levels of economic background (Shaver & Walls, 1998). Most relevant to this study, the research evidence also indicates that parental involvement positively impacts the academic achievement of children no matter the racial heritage of the children being studied (Mau, 1997; Sanders, 1998; Villas-Boas, 1998). However, those studies that have made this assertion have generally examined only one ethnic group and have defined parental involvement as only having a one-to-three components. Muller's (1998) research indicates that parental involvement may help reduce the mathematics achievement gap between boys and girls. Studies undertaken overseas suggest that parental involvement has positive effects on international children as well (Deslandes et al., 1997, Mau, 1997, Villas-Boas, 1998). The willingness of parents to participate in the education of their children apparently also transcends the distinction between whether a school is from the inner city or the suburbs (Griffith, 1996, 1997, Hampton et al., 1998). To the extent that minority children are more likely than whites to reside in urban areas, these results may have some bearing on what one might predict for this study. That is, parental involvement may indeed have an impact.

Research by Bauch and Goldring (1995) suggests that high levels of parental involvement are more easily achieved when parents have chosen a particular school for their child. Other studies indicate that parental involvement is greatly facilitated if a child comes from an intact family (Onatsu-Arvibani & Nurmi, 1997), when the parents are enthusiastic generally (Zellman & Waterman, 1998), and if the family is religious (Riley, 1996, Sanders, 1998).

Parental involvement and the educational outcomes of children of color have emerged as two of the most discussed topics in educational circles today. Parental involvement has especially become a popular topic because the stability of the American family has declined over the last four decades (Hetherington & Jodl, 1994; Wallerstein & Lewis, 1998). Although social scientists have conducted a number of studies indicating that parental involvement has a beneficial impact, these studies have generally not focused on students of color specifically and generally have had either small sample sizes or have been specialized samples. Concurrently, over the last four decades perhaps the most persistent debate in education has been on how to close the achievement gap between white students on the one hand and black and Hispanic students on the other (Green, 2001; Simpson, 1981). This achievement gap exists in virtually every measure of educational progress, including standardized tests, GPA, the dropout rate, the extent to which students are left back a grade, and so forth. The United States was founded on the principle of equality. As a result, Americans tend to feel uncomfortable when unequal results emerge. When inequalities emerge, American educators have frequently tried to reduce those inequalities (Green, 2001).

The benefits of parental involvement are well documented and therefore there is reason to believe that a high level of parental involvement could benefit children of color. Research indicates that parental involvement makes it more likely for children to do their homework (Balli, 1998; Balli, Demo, & Wedman

1998; Villas-Boas, 1998), improve their language skills (Bermudez & Padron, 1990), have low school absentee rates (Nesbitt, 1993), and even have strong musical skills (Zdzinski, 1992).

Of all the inequalities that exist in the American education system, researchers have probably tried to address racial inequality more than any other (Orfield, Kahlenberg, Gordon, Genessee, Slocumb, & Payne, 2000). One indication that racial inequality still exists in the United States is the presence of a persistent academic achievement gap between African Americans, as well as Latinos, and white Americans. Many educators and sociologists note that this achievement gap both reflects racial inequality and causes it to continue (Cross & Slater, 1995, Green, 2001, Hedges & Nowell, 1999, Slavin & Madden, 2006). In spite of many attempts to reduce the achievement gap, a large difference in scores still exists (Green, 2001). By some measures, the achievement gap declined during the 1980s. Nevertheless, the achievement gap remains a thorny issue among American educators. Given that parental involvement has been demonstrated to help the general population of students, some researchers believe that parental participation in education as one possible way of bridging the achievement gap.

Numerous educators and social scientists have raised concerns about the achievement gap between many non-white and white students (Green, 2001; Green et al., 2000; Haycock, 2001; Jeynes, 2003b; Slavin & Madden, 2006), especially because there is a general consensus that if people took the appropriate actions the gap could be substantially reduced or eliminated (Jeynes, 2003b; Slavin & Madden, 2006). This concern has not only been expressed at the research level, but at the public policy level as well (Green et al., 2000; Jackson, 1978; Jones, 1984; Rumberger & Willms, 1992; Slavin & Madden, 2006). Prominent individuals like Jesse Jackson (1978) have brought this issue to the forefront of public awareness. Researchers have known for years that an achievement gap has existed between whites and certain racial minorities, including African Americans (Cross & Slater, 2000; Slater, 1999). The gap exists across virtually every subject (Conciatore, 1990; Gordon, 1976; Green et al., 2000; So & Chan, 1984).

Although researchers and educators acknowledge that an achievement gap exists, social scientists differ widely in terms of their suggestions about how to bridge the gap. Ronald Roach (2001) asserted, "In the academic and think tank world, pondering achievement gap remedies takes center stage" (p. 377). One of the most common solutions that educators propound is that there needs to be more parental involvement (Hara, 1998). Although some parents naturally become strong partners in their children's education, these educators assert that teachers, principals, and society's leaders need to become actively engaged in encouraging high levels of parental involvement (Jeynes, 2003b). These advocates claim that schools need to become more parent-friendly and "go the extra mile" in order to ensure full parental participation (Jeynes, 2003b). In other words, the responsibility for parental involvement not only rests with the parents, but with educators as well (Jeynes, 2003b). For example, Slavin and Madden (2001) argue that parental involvement is one of the most crucial factors necessary for raising the achievement of minority and disadvantaged children. Ross, Smith, and Casey's (1999) study supports this assertion. Green (2001) avers that parental and community partnerships are absolutely essential to improving educational outcomes for minority children.

There have been a fair number of studies done on the effects of parental involvement. However, this meta-analysis focuses on children of color specifically. The number of studies on this issue is large enough to warrant this approach. Second, although the individual studies themselves may be too narrowly focused to yield the necessary generalizations to know how much parental involvement can aid the achievement of children of color, the statistical combination of these studies in a meta-analysis would make this possible.

Methods

Chapters 3–4 describe generally the methodology that was employed in this study, as well as those used in these previous two chapters. The Methods section here only highlights whatever differences might exist between the analyses. In this project, I searched every major database (Psych Info, ERIC, Sociological Abstracts, Wilson Periodicals and so forth) to find studies examining the effects of parental involvement on the academic achievement of children from grades K-12. I also searched journal articles on parental involvement, especially with respect to minority students, to find additional research articles that addressed this issue. I obtained a total of twenty-seven studies that addressed the relationship under study and found twenty-one studies that had a sufficient degree of quantitative data to include in this meta-analysis. The total number of subjects included in these studies was nearly 12,000.

In this project, a statistical analysis was done to determine the overall effects of parental involvement obtained for each study, as well as specific components of parental involvement. These specific components include the extent to which parents communicated with their children about school, whether parents checked their children's homework, parental expectations for the academic success of their children, whether parents encouraged their children to do outside reading, whether the parents attended or participated in school functions, the extent to which there were household rules regarding school and/or leisure activities, parenting style and warmth, and other specific measures of parental involvement.

Four different measures of academic achievement were used to assess the effects of parental involvement on academic achievement. First, there was an overall measure of all components of academic achievement combined. The other measures included grades, academic achievement as determined by standardized tests, and other measures, which generally consisted of teacher rating scales and indices of academic behaviors and attitudes. The results presented in this study reflect the effects found for each facet of parental involvement, using each of these academic categories. The possible differing effects of parental involvement by gender and socioeconomic status were also considered. Two statistical measures were used to reduce sampling and publication bias.

Results

The results indicate that parental involvement does generally impact the academic achievement of the minority groups under study. Table 5.1 lists the studies used in this meta-analysis and the overall effect size for each.

Table 5.2 compares the effects of general parental involvement among the minority groups under study. In all cases where there were data, the effect sizes are above two-tenths of a standard deviation. Overall, the effect sizes varied from over two-tenths of a standard deviation to over four-tenths of a standard deviation. For the group consisting of mostly African Americans and 100% African Americans the effect sizes are 0.44 ($p < 0.01$) and 0.48 ($p < 0.01$) respectively, with the 95% confidence intervals in the latter case of 0.17–0.79. For the group consisting of mostly Latinos and Asians and 100% Latinos and Asians, the effect sizes are 0.43 ($p < 0.05$) for the former group and 0.48 ($p < 0.05$) for the latter. For the Asian subjects alone, the effects sizes are smaller, but the confidence intervals are quite narrow.

Table 5.1 List of Studies used in the Meta-Analysis for Parental Involvement, the Year of the Study, and the Effect Sizes for the Various Studies

Study	Year	Effect Size
Keith & Lichtman	1994	+0.74
Yan	1999	+0.67
Brown & Madhere	1996	+0.60
Taylor	1996	+0.49
Zellman & Waterman	1998	+0.43
Reynolds	1992	+0.39
Taylor, Hinton, & Wilson	1995	+0.37
Williams	1999	+0.34
Marcon	1999a	+0.32
Hampton	1998	+0.29
Sanders	1996	+0.28
Fletcher	1994	+0.28
Strage & Brandt	1999	+0.28
Marcon	1993	+0.26
Keith & Lichtman	1992	+0.25
Cardenas-Rivera	1994	+0.22
Mau	1997	+0.21
Austin	1988	+0.06
Georgiou	1999	+0.05
Nesbitt	1993	+0.01

Table 5.2 Effect Sizes for General Parental Involvement with Confidence Intervals in Parentheses

Parental Involvement and Academic Variables	Overall Academic Achievement	GPA	Academic Achievement Tests	Other Measures
General Parental Involvement				
African Americans— Studies with Mostly or All of this Group as Subjects	0.44** (0.14, 0.74)	0.32**** (0.22, 0.42)	0.31**** (0.17, 0.45)	0.62**** (0.53, 0.71)
African Americans— Studies with All of this Group as Subjects	0.48** (0.17, 0.79)	0.33**** (0.21, 0.45)	No data	0.62**** (0.53, 0.71)
Latinos and Asian Americans—Studies with Mostly or All of this Group as Subjects	0.43* (0.01, 0.85)	0.25**** (0.23, 0.27)	0.44*	No data 0.02, 0.86)
Latinos and Asian Americans—Studies with All of this Group as Subjects	0.48* (0.03, 0.93)	No data	0.48*	No data (0.03, 0.93)
Asian Americans— Studies with Mostly or All of this Group as Subjects	0.22**** (0.20, 0.24)	No data	0.22****	No data (0.20, 0.24)
Asian Americans— Studies with All of this Group as Subjects	0.22**** (0.20, 0.24)	0.No data	0.22****	No data (0.20, 0.24)

Note: *$p < 0.05$; **$p < 0.01$; ***$p < 0.001$; ****$p < 0.0001$

For the GPA measure the effect sizes were generally somewhat smaller than for the overall measures of academic achievement. In terms of standard deviation units, the effect sizes varied from 0.25 ($p < 0.0001$) for groups consisting of mostly Latinos and Asian Americans to 0.33 ($p < 0.0001$) for studies in which all of the subjects were African American students. The numerical outcomes that emerged for standardized tests were larger, on average, than for GPA, although they covered a wide range. Studies in which all the subjects were Latino and Asian Americans produced an effect size of 0.48 ($p < 0.05$). This was greater than for students that included mostly Latino and Asian American students (0.44, $p < 0.05$). The effect size was 0.31 ($p < 0.0001$) for studies with mostly African

American students and 0.22 (p < .0001) for both the mostly and 100% Asian American groups.

Of all the academic measures under examination, it was the conglomeration of all the other measures that yielded the largest regression coefficients. For this academic measure effect sizes were available only for studies for mostly or all African American subjects. In each case the effect size was 0.62 (p < 0.0001).

In Table 5.3 the various aspects of parental involvement are broken down in order to assess their overall influence on overall academic achievement. The influence of each of the parental involvement variables differs in effect by race in some cases. Overall, the various specific measures of parental involvement had, on average, overall achievement test (p < 0.05) and 0.25 for GPA (p < 0.0001). For the studies made up of 100% Latinos, the effect size was 0.48 for both overall was 0.48 for both overall achievement and achievement tests. Among the studies examining mostly or 100% Asians, the effect sizes were smaller but were very consistent across all the studies included in the meta-analysis. Therefore, the effect sizes were all statistically significant to the 0.0001 level of probability. The effect sizes were all between 0.20 and 0.25 in size.

For the studies examining mostly African Americans and 100% African Americans the effect sizes for the general measures of parental involvement ranged from over three-tenths of a standard deviation to over sixth-tenths of a standard deviation. The effect sizes for overall academic achievement were 0.44 (p < 0.01) examining studies that had primarily African American subjects to 0.48 (p <0.01) for those studies that had all African American subjects. For GPA and Achievement tests all the effect sizes were slightly larger than three tenths of a standard deviation (p < 0.0001). The effect size for other academic measures was the largest of the academic variables measured at 0.62 (p < 0.0001) of a standard deviation. The 95% confidence interval had a range of 0.53 to 0.71. Some possible reasons for the differences in the size of these regression coefficients are examined in the Discussion section.

For studies in which the subjects were Latinos and Asians combined the overall effects of parental involvement were 0.25 (p < 0.0001) for GPA and 0.44 (p < 0.05) for standardized tests for studies with most subjects from this racial group. The effect size was slightly higher (0.48, p < 0.05) when all the subjects were either Latino or Asian American. When subjects were mostly or all Asian Americans the effect size for standardized tests was 0.22 (p < 0.0001). The effect sizes for the studies that included Asian subjects, tended to be quite consistent across studies.

Table 5.3 lists the effect sizes for parental involvement for overall academic achievement by different aspects of parental involvement. In the case of African Americans all of the aspects of parental involvement in which a meta-analysis could be done (i.e. that included more than one study) had a statistically significant positive influence. The magnitude of this impact varied by the

Table 5.3 Effect Sizes for Overall Academic Achievement by Different Aspects of Parental Involvement

Parental Involvement and Academic Variables	African Americans—Studies with Mostly or All of this Group as Subjects	African Americans—Studies with All of this Group as Subjects	Latinos and Asian Americans—Studies with Mostly or All of this Group as Subjects	Latinos and Asian Americans—Studies with All of this Group as Subjects	Asian Americans—Studies with Mostly or All of this Group as Subjects	Asian Americans—Studies with All of this Group as Subjects
Specific Parental Involvement	0.30**** (0.16, 0.44)	0.31**** (0.25, 0.37)	No Data	No Data	No Data	No Data
Parental Style	0.44** (0.18, 0.70)	0.44** (0.18, 0.70)	−0.01	−0.01	−0.00	−0.00
Parental Attendance	0.51** (0.22, 0.80)	0.62 (1 study)	−0.29	−0.29	−0.29	−0.29
Expectations	0.57** (0.23, 0.91)	0.57**	No Data	No Data	No Data	No Data
Reading	0.39 (1 study)	0.39 (1 study)	0.21* (0.03, 0.39)	0.21* (0.03, 0.39)	0.21* (0.03, 0.39)	0.21* (0.03, 0.39)
Communication	0.53** (0.18, 0.88)	0.53** (0.18, 0.88)	No Data	No Data	No Data	No Data
Rules	0.35 (1 study)	0.35 (1 study)	−0.25 (−0.03, −0.47)	−0.25 (−0.03, −0.47)	−0.25 (−0.03, −0.47)	−0.25 (−0.03, −0.47)
Homework	0.72**** (0.46, 0.98)	0.72**** (0.46, 0.98)	No Data	No Data	No Data	No Data

Note
* $p < 0.05$; ** $p < 0.01$; *** $p < 0.001$; **** $p < 0.0001$

parental involvement variable. The effect size for those studies that included a specific variable (not merely a general all-encompassing variable) for parental involvement was 0.30 (p < 0.0001) for those studies that included mostly African American subjects and 0.31 (p < 0.0001) for the studies that included all African American subjects. The effect sizes for parents helping and checking their children's homework yielded the largest effect size of over seven-tenths of a standard deviation. The effect sizes for parents communicating with their children about school and parental expectations were both over half of a standard deviation.

Parental attendance yielded an effect size of 0.51 (p < 0.01) in the case of studies including mostly African American subjects, but only one study included subjects that were all African American. Therefore, a meta-analysis could not be done for the category of all African American subjects. Nevertheless, the one study that was done yielded a result of 0.62 of a standard deviation, which is similar to the effect size for studies including mostly African American subjects. Parental Style produced an effect size of 0.44 (p < 0.01) for studies including mostly African American students as well as those including all African American students.

The results for the other racial groups were quite different than those that emerged for African Americans. Although, this study has already determined that parental involvement impacts the academic achievement of all the groups incorporated into this study, the pattern for the specific components of parental involvement was quite different for the combinations of Asian and Latino groups studied than it was for African Americans. The extent to which a parent read with a child both in the past and the present positively influenced academic achievement. The effect size for Reading was 0.21 (p < 0.05). Only one study examined the impact of this aspect of parental involvement on African American achievement and therefore a meta-analysis could not be done. However, the effect for this study was 0.39 of a standard deviation. The effect sizes for parental style and parental attendance, which were positive for African Americans, were not statistically significant for the other groups under study. Also, the effect size for Rules regarding school work had a negative influence, yielding an effect size of –0.25 (p < 0.05). Although only one study examined this issue for African Americans and therefore no meta-analysis was undertaken in this case, the results of this study were in the positive direction. The significance of these results is examined in the Discussion Section.

Table 5.4 lists the effect sizes for specific measures of academic achievement by different aspects of parental involvement. These results once again indicate very consistent effects for parental involvement, no matter what variable is examined, for African American students. In the case of parental style, the effects for this variable are considerably larger for "Other" (0.57, p < 0.0001) measures of academic achievement than for grades (0.34, p < 0.01). The confidence intervals were generally pretty narrow for most of the variables producing statistically significant results.

Table 5.4 Effect Sizes for Specific Measures of Academic Achievement by Different Aspects of Parental Involvement

Parental Involvement and Academic Variables	African Americans—Studies with Mostly or All of this Group as Subjects	African Americans—Studies with All of this Group as Subjects	Latinos and Asian Americans—Studies with Mostly or All of this Group as Subjects	Latinos and Asian Americans—Studies with All of this Group as Subjects	Asian Americans—Studies with Mostly or All of this Group as Subjects	Asian Americans—Studies with All of this Group as Subjects
Specific Parental Involvement						
Grades	0.31**** (0.27, 0.35)	0.31**** (0.27, 0.35)	No Data	No Data	No Data	No Data
Parental Style						
Grades	0.34** (0.19, 0.49)	0.34** (0.19, 0.49)	No Data	No Data	No Data	No Data
Standardized Tests	No Data	No Data	−0.03	−0.03	−0.03	−0.03
Other	0.57**** (0.49, 0.65)	0.57**** (0.49, 0.65)	No Data	No Data	No Data	No Data
Parental Attendance	0.51** (0.22, 0.80)	0.62 (1 study)	−0.29	−0.29	−0.29	−0.29
Reading Standardized Tests	0.39 (1 study)	0.39 (1 study)	0.21* (0.03, 0.39)	0.21* (0.03, 0.39)	0.21* (0.03, 0.39)	0.21* (0.03, 0.39)
Homework Standardized Tests	0.72**** (0.46, 0.98)	0.72**** (0.46, 0.98)	No Data	No Data	No Data	No Data

Note
* $p < 0.05$; ** $p < 0.01$; *** $p < 0.001$; **** $p < 0.0001$

Discussion

The results indicate that parental involvement impacts the academic achievement of minority students. Several notable patterns emerged in the results.

First, the effects of parental involvement held across all the races under study. The effect sizes for parental involvement were over four-tenths of a standard deviation for studies that had either most or all African American subjects. Similar results were found for those studies that had either most or all Latinos and Asian Americans as their subjects. Those studies that used most or all Asian American students as subjects yielded smaller effect sizes. Nevertheless, a meta-analysis examining these studies found that the effect size was still over two-tenths of a standard deviation.

When specific academic measures were examined separately, the same overall pattern emerged. All of the academic measures yielded statistically significant quantitative outcomes. What this indicates is that parental involvement appears to impact all levels of academic achievement: GPA, standardized tests, and other measures as well. Overall, one can conclude that parental involvement has a significant positive impact on children across race and across academic outcomes. This is an important finding for urban educators and parents.

Second, the effect sizes that emerged for GPA were typically smaller than those of the other academic variables. If one takes the average effect size for each academic variable and averages them across the racial groups included in this study, "Other" measures yield the largest average effect size and GPA produces the least. The fact that "Other" measures were associated with the largest effect sizes would seem to be a reasonable and logical outcome. As mentioned in the Methods Section, "Other" measures consisted largely of teacher ratings. Teachers are among the first to recognize and appreciate parental involvement. Therefore, one might expect that teacher ratings might be among the primary measures to reflect parental involvement. It is likely that teacher ratings may be affected by teacher perceptions of the level of cooperation exhibited by the child and the family as a whole. To the extent that parental involvement may be the major component of that perceived cooperation, teachers may view children and their families more positively as a result of that perceived cooperation. In addition, "Other" measures are more likely to be influenced by the perceived motives of the child and family. Pure motives do not always translate into educational success. Standardized test scores and grade point average may or may not partially reflect pure motives. Teachers, however, may feel inclined to reward good motives by the child and the family. Teacher ratings are more likely than other academic measures to reflect: (a) a positive relationship between the parent and the teacher, (b) a sense of teamwork between the parent and the teacher, due to increased communication between the two, (c) an acknowledgement by the teacher of parental efforts. The combination of these factors probably explains a substantial part of the reason why other measures of achievement yielded larger effect sizes than the other measures.

It is more challenging to explain why parental involvement appeared to influence standardized test scores more than GPA. One possible explanation is that when parents get involved in their children's education, they offer not only information specific to the classroom, but likely help in giving children a broader level of academic information. To the extent that this is true, parental involvement may give minority children a larger advantage in standardized tests than in classroom tests. Standardized tests usually measure a broader area of study than is covered within the classroom. Classroom material may be easily garnered by students from the teachers or other classmates. However, this broader information is likely harder to obtain and when parents provide it, this gives those who have involved parents a decided advantage on standardized tests.

Third, although the effects of parental involvement were apparent for all the racial groups under study, it is also clear that the effects of parental involvement were greater for some groups more than others. Parental involvement apparently benefited African Americans and Latinos more than they did Asian Americans. African American children benefited from all kinds of parental involvement. Latino and Asian Americans combined benefited from overall parental involvement more than Asian Americans alone, indicating that Latino students apparently benefit from parental involvement more than Asian American students.

The question emerges as to why African Americans likely benefit the most and Asian Americans benefit the least from parental involvement. This question is especially interesting, given that the parental involvement of parents of Asian descent is well documented and well publicized. In attempting to answer this question it must be remembered that the effect sizes for parental involvement do not measure the likelihood of parental involvement, but the effect of parental involvement when it takes place. In other words, what the results indicate is that when there is parental involvement, African American students, on the average, benefit more than the average Asian American student. Harold Stevenson, James Stigler, and other researchers have noted that there is a great deal of educational emphasis in the Asian and Asian American culture (Stevenson & Stigler, 1992). It may be that there are enough educational incentives present in other aspects of Asian American culture, so that even without a large degree of parental involvement students still do relatively well. It may well be that parental involvement has the greatest impact where there are no other cultural factors that are working to raise academic achievement.

A second reason for Asian Americans being affected less than Latinos and African American students, probably relates to the likelihood that children come from single-parent families. Of the three racial groups included in this study, African American children are most likely to come from a single-parent family, Latino children are the second most likely to come from this family structure, and Asian Americans are least likely to come from this family structure. Research supports the notion that family structure is the most important facet of parental involvement (Jeynes, 2005e).

To the extent that the average child from a certain group is not likely to have a certain parent present or involved, the impact of parents actually being involved is likely to be that much greater. These two possibilities likely explain much of the reason why parental involvement makes more of an impact on African American students and Latino Students than it does on Asian American students.

Further research is needed to examine why it is that particular kinds of parental involvement are especially beneficial for certain racial groups. Although the results of this study provide many insights into the effects of parental involvement on the academic achievement of minority children, it also raises some interesting questions about parental involvement, which can help guide research in years to come.

Parental Involvement and the Academic Achievement of African American Youth

Parental involvement and African American educational outcomes have emerged as two of the most discussed topics in educational circles today. Parental involvement has especially become a popular topic because the stability of the American family has declined over the last four decades (Hetherington & Jodl, 1994, Wallerstein & Lewis, 1998). Although social scientists have conducted a number of studies indicating that parental involvement has a beneficial impact, these studies have generally not focused on African American students specifically and generally have had either small sample sizes or have been specialized samples. Concurrently, over the last four decades perhaps the most persistent debate in education has been on how to close the achievement gap between white students on the one hand and black and Hispanic students on the other (Green, 2001, Simpson, 1981). This study uses the National Educational Longitudinal Study (NELS) to assess the relationship between parental involvement and African American student achievement.

One of the major reasons why researchers have increased their investigation of the impact of parental involvement is because society at large has become so focused on this concept. The presence of more parents in the work force, the fast pace of modern society as a whole, and the declining role of the family have all been reasons that both social scientists and the general public have pointed to, in order to explain an apparent decline in parental involvement in education (Coleman & Hoffer, 1987, Jeynes, 2002b). The African American community is no less influenced by these trends than any other group in the United States. There is a need for researchers to more fully grasp the impact of parental involvement among Americans generally and African Americans specifically.

Parental involvement research has been on the increase during the last two decades. Social scientists are giving parental involvement a special place of importance in influencing the academic outcomes of the youth. Nevertheless, there is dearth of knowledge about the effect of parental involvement overall on African American children, little is known about whether parents are more likely to be involved in the education of boys or girls. Ogbu (1992, 1993) expresses concern about the low percentage of African American males who attend college. He points to statistics that indicate that about 65% of African Americans who attend college are women. Ogbu argues that part of the reason for this gender gap among African Americans is that different elements of society, such as the media, schools, and athletic organizations, communicate to children that educational achievement is a white and female orientation. Ogbu points to a number of aspects of society contributing to this stereotype, including the lack of African American male elementary school teachers. Although Ogbu deals most specifically with the schools declaring this hidden message, he suggests that it applies to other aspects of society as well. Given that the gender gap among African American college attendees is substantial, Ogbu's point is worth considering in relation to parental involvement. The question that emerges based on Ogbu's assertions is whether parents reinforce the message that educational achievement is more of a female orientation than a male orientation, or a white male orientation but not an African American male orientation, by being more involved in the education of females?

Methods

Sample

The population that National Education Longitudinal Survey (NELS) study draws from includes students who participated in the NELS for the years 1990 and 1992. This consisted of a total of 18,726, of which 2,260 were African American. The U.S. Department of Education's National Center for Statistics sponsored the NELS project. The National Opinion Research Center (NORC) and NORC subcontractors designed the study. The Educational Testing Service (ETS) created the achievement tests used in this study. Among the African Americans, the median family income level was between $35,000 and $40,000. Among the parents, 19% had at least a four-year college degree and 82% had earned a high school diploma.

The NELS database that this study used has a nationally representative sample of African Americans. In order to address the issue of causality, parental involvement measures were taken from the 1990 (tenth grade) data set and the academic measures were taken from the 1992 (twelfth grade) data set. From the NELS questionnaires parental involvement questions were combined to create a parental involvement variable to be used in General Linear Model (GLM) regression analysis. Parents were considered involved in their children's education if they communicated with their children about their school work requirements and what events took place during the school day, were almost always available to help their children with school work, were aware of class assignments and activities, and communicated their academic expectations to their children.

Procedure

General Linear Model (GLM) regression and Logistic regression analysis was undertaken to compare the achievement test scores of African American children with "highly involved parents" versus African American children with "less involved parents." The regression coefficients that measured differences between the two groups were converted into standard deviation units to facilitate the comparison across different measures of academic achievement, gender and SES variables, and the different models used in the analysis.

In order to address issues of causality, parental involvement variables were taken from the tenth grade data set and achievement measures were taken from the twelfth grade data set. By doing this, one could not argue that twelfth grade achievement influenced a parent's willingness to get involved in a student's education.

Variables

Parental Involvement

These variables were ratings based on the response of parents in self-report surveys administered by the NELS representatives. If parents asserted that they were involved in their children's education in each of the following areas they were coded as highly involved in their children's education. These areas were attending school functions, communicating with their children about school, maintaining high expectations of their children's success, and checking their children's homework. If parents showed educational involvement in all these areas they were coded as "highly involved parents." If parents were *not* involved in all or some of these areas, they were coded as "less involved parents."

Academic Achievement

Standardized Tests

Standardized test scores were obtained using tests developed by ETS. IRT scores (Item Response Theory scores) were obtained for the Reading Comprehension Test, the Mathematics Comprehension Test, the Social Studies (History/Citizenship/Geography) Comprehension Test, the Science Comprehension Test, and the Test Composite (Reading and Math test results combined).

Left Back (a Grade)

A child who had been left back a grade at some point in his or her schooling was coded with the value 1. If a child had not been left back at any point, the child was coded with the value 0.

Gender

A child was coded with the value 1 for female. A child was coded with the value 0 for male.

Socioeconomic Status

The socioeconomic status of a child's family was determined "using parent questionnaire data, when available." The socioeconomic status variables consisted of five components: a) father's level of education, b) mother's level of education, c) father's occupation, d) mother's occupation, and e) family income. The occupational data were recoded using the Duncan SEI (Socioeconomic Index) scale, which was also used in the High School and Beyond Survey. If any of the components were missing from the parent questionnaire, equivalent or related questions were used from the student questionnaire to determine socioeconomic status (SES). Three coded SES variables were used to measure the effect of the SES quartile to which an African American student belonged.

Each student was coded with the value 1 for the SES quartile to which the student belonged and the value 0 for the other three quartiles. The first (lowest) SES quartile was considered the base. The effects of a child being from the second (second lowest), third (second highest), and fourth (highest) SES quartiles were assessed. The influence of being from each SES quartile on achievement was compared versus those who were in the first SES quartile. The differences were converted into standard deviation units. For example, if students from the second SES quartile, on average, scored 0.25 of a standard deviation higher than students from the first SES quartile on the Science test, then the effect of being from the second SES quartile would read 0.25.

Models

Two sets of models totaling four models were used in analyzing the effects of parental involvement. The Basic (1 and 2) Models constituted the first set and the SES (1 and 2) Models was the second set. The Basic 1 Model included only the parental involvement variable and the Basic 2 Model included the parental involvement variable plus the gender variable. The Basic 1 Model was designed to measure the overall effect of "highly involved parents" without considering the impact of the other variables. Each of the SES models included the addition of SES variables, specifically the SES quartile variables. The SES 1 Model included the parental involvement variable and the variables for the second, third, and fourth SES quartiles. Three SES 2 Models included the parental involvement variable, the gender variable, and the variables for the second, third, and fourth SES quartiles.

Results

The results indicate that having "highly involved parents" is associated with higher academic outcomes for African American senior students. The effects are statistically significant even if one controls for gender. However, parental involvement is correlated with socioeconomic status.

Therefore, once one adds variables for SES, although the regression coefficients are in the positive direction, they are no longer statistically significant. Overall, the results were consistently statistically significant using the Basic 1 and 2 Models and only generally approached statistical significance using the SES 1 and 2 Models.

Table 5.5 lists the test scores for the African American seniors whose parents were quite involved in their education versus those parents who were not. The standard deviations for each test score variable are also listed. The results indicate that for all the test scores available African American students whose parents were involved in their education had an advantage over those whose parents were not involved. The average difference in the scores was 4.08 points, with the smallest difference being for the Reading test and the largest difference for Social Studies. Nevertheless, the test score differences were quite consistent across the test measures.

Table 5.6 lists the betas in standard deviation units for each of the academic variables using both the Basic 1 and Basic 2 Models. Using the Basic 1 Model, the regression coefficients varied from 0.38 for the Reading, $F(1, 1394) = 7.08$, $p < 0.01$, and Math, $F(1, 1394) = 8.15$, $p < 0.01$ tests to 0.56, $F(1, 1659) = 10.35$, $p < 0.01$, for the Left Back variable. All the regression coefficients were statistically significant at a 0.01 level of probability.

Table 5.5 Mean Test Scores with Standard Deviations in Parentheses for African American Students with Highly Involved Parents versus Those with Less Involved Parents (N = 2,260)

Academic Measure	African American Students With Highly Involved Parents	African American Students With Less Involved Parents
	Mean (Standard Deviation)	Mean (Standard Deviation)
Reading Test	48.68 (9.89)	44.88 (9.99)
Math Test	47.98 (9.96)	44.10 (10.04)
Science Test	47.09 (9.87)	43.07 (9.97)
Social Studies Test	49.78 (9.82)	45.15 (10.00)
Test Composite	48.14 (9.90)	44.09 (10.03)

Table 5.6 Effects in Standard Deviation Units of Students having Highly Involved African American parents for various 12th grade academic measures using the Basic 1 and Basic 2 Models (N = 2,260)

Academic Measure	Basic 1 Model	Basic 2 Model
Reading Test	0.38**	0.30*
Math Test	0.38**	0.35*
Science Test	0.40**	0.40**
Social Studies Test	0.46***	0.42**
Test Composite	0.40**	0.34*
Left Back a Grade	0.56**	0.41*

Note
* $p < 0.05$; ** $p < 0.01$; *** $p < 0.001$; **** $p < 0.0001$

Using the Basic 2 Model, which adds a gender variable, all the betas remained statistically significant. The Left Back variable was the most impacted by the addition of the gender variable. Nevertheless, the regression coefficient for being left back a grade was still 0.41, $F (1, 1595) = 5.83$, $p < 0.05$. The beta for the Science test remained unchanged at 0.40, $F(1, 1209) = 9.48$, $p < 0.01$. The regression coefficients ranged from 0.30, $F (1, 1226) = 4.25$, $p < 0.05$, for the Reading test to 42, $F (1, 1201) = 8.81$, $p < 0.01$, for the Social Studies test. Overall, the average for the Basic 2 was 0.06 of a standard deviation lower than using the Basic 1 Model. However, for the standardized test measures the reduction was an average of only 0.04 lower.

In Tables 5.7–5.11 one sees the effects of adding the SES variables to the regression equation for each of the individualized standardized tests and the Left Back variable. All the regression coefficients for these tables are in standard deviation units. Table 5.7 lists the regression coefficients using the SES 1 and the SES 2

Table 5.7 Effects on Reading Achievement in Standard Deviation Units of Students having Highly Involved Parents and the Other Variables using the Basic 1 & 2 and the SES 1 & 2 Models for 12th Grade African American Students (N = 2,260)

Variable	Basic 1 Model for Reading Test	Basic 2 Model for Reading Test	SES 1 Model for Reading Test	SES 2 Model Reading Test
Parental Involvement	0.38**	0.30*	0.15[a]	0.07
Gender	—	0.20**	—	0.24****
SES Quartile 2	—	—	0.20**	0.19**
SES Quartile 3	—	—	0.39**	0.39**
SES Quartile 4	—	—	0.90****	0.94****

Notes
*$p < 0.05$; **$p < 0.01$; ***$p < 0.001$; ****$p < 0.0001$
a Approached, but did not reach statistical significance, $p < 0.100$.

models, in addition to the Basic 1 and 2 models, using the Reading Achievement Test variable. In both models the betas for "highly involved" parents: remain positive. However, in the cases of both models no statistically significant effects emerge for this high level of parental involvement. Using the SES 1 Model, the beta for parental involvement approached, but did not exceed, statistical significance.

Tables 5.8–5.11 show similar patterns for the other academic variables that emerged for the Reading test. Using the SES 1 model the regression coefficients ranged from 0.12, $F(1, 1240) = 0.88$, $p > 0.05$, for the Math test to 0.32, $F(1, 1471) = 3.51$, $p > 0.05$ for the Left Back variable. In the cases of the Left Back and Social Studies test variables the effects of "highly involved parents" especially approached, but did not exceed, statistical significance. Using the SES 2 Model,

Table 5.8 Effects on Math Achievement in Standard Deviation Units of Students having Highly Involved Parents and the Other Variables using the Basic 1 & 2 and the SES 1 & 2 Models for 12th Grade African American Students (N = 2,260)

Variable	Basic 1 Model for Reading Test	Basic 2 Model for Reading Test	SES 1 Model for Reading Test	SES 2 Model for Reading Test
Parental Involvement	0.38**	0.35*	0.12[a]	0.09
Gender	—	0.20**	—	0.03
SES Quartile 2	—	—	0.14**	0.16*
SES Quartile 3	—	—	0.41****	0.40****
SES Quartile 4	—	—	0.96****	0.99****

Notes
* $p < 0.05$; ** $p < 0.01$; *** $p < 0.001$; **** $p < 0.0001$
a Approached, but did not reach statistical significance, $p < 0.10$.

Table 5.9 Effects on Science Achievement (in Standard Deviation Units) of Students having Highly Involved Parents and the Other Variables using the Basic 1 & 2 and the SES 1 & 2 Models for 12th Grade African American Students (N = 2,260)

Variable	Basic 1 Model for Reading Test	Basic 2 Model for Reading Test	SES 1 Model for Reading Test	SES 2 Model for Reading Test
Parental Involvement	0.40**	0.40**	0.17[a]	0.18[a]
Gender	—	−0.19	—	−0.14**
SES Quartile 2	—	—	0.18**	0.19**
SES Quartile 3	—	—	0.34****	0.35**
SES Quartile 4	—	—	0.87****	0.92****

Notes
* $p < 0.05$; ** $p < 0.01$; *** $p < 0.001$; **** $p < 0.0001$
a Approached, but did not reach statistical significance, $p < 0.10$.

Table 5.10 Effects on Social Studies Achievement (in Standard Deviation Units) of Students having Highly Involved Parents and the Other Variables using the Basic 1 & 2 and the SES 1 & 2 Models for 12th Grade African American Students (N = 2,260)

Variable	Basic 1 Model for Reading Test	Basic 2 Model for Reading Test	SES 1 Model for Reading Test	SES 2 Model for Reading Test
Parental Involvement	0.38**	0.30*	0.23[a]	0.20[a]
Gender	—	0.20**	—	−0.00
SES Quartile 2	—	—	0.31****	0.34****
SES Quartile 3	—	—	0.43****	0.41****
SES Quartile 4	—	—	0.90****	0.95****

Notes
* $p < 0.05$; ** $p < 0.01$; *** $p < 0.001$; **** $p < 0.0001$
a   Approached, but did not reach statistical significance, $p < 0.10$.

all of the betas were in the positive direction. However, none of them yielded statistically significant results. In most cases, the regression coefficients for this high level of parental involvement were slightly lower than when the SES 1 Model was used. Once again, Tables 5.8–5.11 note the regression coefficients for "highly involved parents" that approached statistical significance. The regression coefficients tended to be largest for the Left Back and Social Studies variables.

Table 5.11 lists the results of testing Ogbu's hypothesis that American education is geared more toward African American females than African American males. Naturally, this analysis does not test the entirety of Ogbu's belief, only the parental involvement component of his theory.

Table 5.11 Effects on Math Achievement in Standard Deviation Units of Students having Highly Involved Parents and the Other Variables using the Basic 1 & 2 and the SES 1 & 2 Models for 12th Grade African American Students (N = 2,260)

Variable	Basic 1 Model for Reading Test	Basic 2 Model for Reading Test	SES 1 Model for Reading Test	SES 2 Model for Reading Test
Parental Involvement	0.56**	0.41*	0.32[a]	0.18[a]
Gender	—	0.24****	—	0.29****
SES Quartile 2	—	—	0.20**	0.18**
SES Quartile 3	—	—	0.39**	0.36****
SES Quartile 4	—	—	0.90****	0.59****

Notes
* $p < 0.05$; ** $p < 0.01$; *** $p < 0.001$; **** $p < 0.0001$
a   Approached, but did not reach statistical significance, $p < 0.10$.

Table 5.12 Differences in the Extent of Overall Parental Involvement by Child's Gender for African American Children and the Overall Sample (N = 2,260)

Academic measure	Basic 2 Model for Parental Involvement for African American Children	SES 2 Model for Parental Involvement for African American Children	Basic 2 Model for Parental Involvement for the Overall Sample of Children	SES 2 Model for Parental Involvement for the Overall Sample of Children
Parental Involvement	0.015[a]	0.02*	0.013****	0.02****
SES Quartile 2	—	0.02	—	0.02**
SES Quartile 3	—	0.05****	—	0.04****
SES Quartile 4	—	0.07****	—	0.08****

Notes
* $p < 0.05$; ** $p < 0.01$; *** $p < 0.001$; **** $p < 0.0001$
a Approached, but did not reach statistical significance, $p < 0.100$.

The results, listed in Table 5.12, indicate that when controlling for SES, parents are more likely to be involved in the education of African American girls than they are involved in the education of boys. However, although the difference was statistically significant, it was only 0.02 of a standard deviation, $F(1, 1515) = 4.03$, $p < 0.05$. Using the Basic 1 Model, the advantage for girls falls just shy of statistical significance at 0.015 standard deviation units, $F(1, 1900) = 3.73$, *n.s.*

The question then emerges whether parents are only more likely to be involved in the education of girls in the case of African Americans or whether it applies generally. Ogbu suggests that it especially applies to African Americans, although it may apply generally. Table 5.8 shows that the tendency for parents to be somewhat more involved in the education of girls holds true for the entire sample. When controlling for SES, the regression coefficient of 0.02 standard deviation units, is identical to the one that emerged for African Americans using this model. This result was statistically significant at the 0.0001 level of probability $F(1, 14783) = 38.90$, $p < 0.0001$. When the Base 1 Model was used the results were also statistically significant at the 0.0001 level of probability.

Discussion

The results suggest that parental involvement does have a positive influence on the academic outcomes of African American seniors. The difference in test scores between African American students from highly involved parents versus those parents who were less involved was generally about 0.4 of a standard deviation. However, the results also indicate that the extent of parental involvement is also highly related to SES. Once SES variables were added into the analysis, the betas for highly involved parents remained positive. However, these regression coefficients were no longer statistically significant, but only generally approached statistical significance. This indicates that parental involvement is strongly related to SES.

The relationship that this study found between parental involvement and SES confirms the findings of a number of other studies that have divulged the same pattern (Griffith, 1997; Hess, Holloway, Dickson & Price, 1984; Jeynes, 2010; Revicki, 1981). The presence of this pattern does not negate the influence of parental involvement, but rather raises the question why SES and parental involvement are closely connected? If the logic behind this relationship can be understood, then one can more easily understand parental involvement and encourage its activity.

Limitations

There arise a number of limitations common to examining large data sets, such as NELS, and virtually any study examining the effects of parental involvement. While none of these limitations is particularly serious, they should be noted. As in almost any study, there are certain relevant characteristics of the sample that one would like to know about, but are not accessible. In this study the most important of these characteristics of the sample involves those students who dropped out of the study. A fair number of students dropped out of the NELS sample at some point during the 1988–1992 period for various reasons that included moving to another school or moving to a different location. Past studies that have examined how such dropouts from a study differ from the remainder of a sample indicate that 1) this group of students generally performs less well academically than the remainder of a given sample and 2) that this group of students has a disproportionately high percentage of students coming from challenging family backgrounds. These facts combined will probably cause the effects for parental involvement to be lower in this study than they otherwise would be if we had access to the group of students that dropped out. This is probably the most important limitation of this study.

It would have also been nice to have reliable measures of parental involvement during earlier periods, when the students were younger. In that way, one could compare the influence of parental involvement for parents who had been involved during a long period of time versus those whose involvement had been more recent.

Parental Involvement and SES

There are several reasons why parental involvement and SES may be so closely related. Firstly, fathers and mothers who have high educational and occupational attainment are likely to have high personal drive and determination. It is only natural that these attributes carry over to their relationships with their children and their desire to see their children succeed (Crane, 1996, Jeynes 2002a, 2000b).

Secondly, to the extent that high-achieving SES parents have been the beneficiaries of an educational system that provided them with income and occupational status, they are more likely to be convinced that a good education is the most reliable means of partaking in the American dream. These parents are likely to make more sacrifices in order to establish their children's educational success. Highly educated parents, for example, are often more likely to acknowledge the importance of parental support in education (Legutko, 1998; Mulroy et al., 1998; Portes & MacLeod, 1996). As a result, they are more likely to place a high priority on becoming involved themselves. Consequently, the children of these parents benefit directly from the confidence that the parents have in the long-term rewards of parental support and the education system.

Thirdly, research indicates that parental involvement is highly related to family structure and availability. Single parents and poor families are more likely to be faced with under-employment in which they must work long hours or multiple jobs in order to make ends meet (Dixon, 1994; Jeynes, 2002a, 2002d; Juliusdottir, 1997). Dixon (1994) and Juliusdottir (1997) found that single parents, especially those who were poor, worked significantly more hours each week than their counterparts in two-biological-parent families. To the degree to which this is true, their presence at work will reduce their accessibility to their children. Furthermore, given that a single parent does not have a spouse at home to compensate for his or her absence from the home, this will tend to reduce the overall level of that household's parental participation in the child's education (Dixon, 1994).

Fourthly, to the extent that involved parents try to address the educational needs of their children, these parents may also try to purchase educational aids for their children (Stevenson & Stigler, 1992). These aids may include anything from supplementary textbooks, educational videotapes and audiotapes, tutors, desks, and additional supplies. To whatever extent the ability to buy these supplies increases when income rises, one would expect that this facet of parental involvement would rise along with SES.

Fifthly, sometimes increased SES can be, in and of itself, an expression of parental involvement (Grayson, 1999; Mulroy et al., 1998; Portes & MacLeod, 1996). There are times when parents seek a certain occupation, income level, or educational accomplishment for the benefit of their children. These parents believe that by having a high income or strong educational or occupational background, their children will experience a higher quality of life and be the beneficiaries of better education. Higher parental SES can sometimes be one expression of a higher level of parental involvement. To some parents, parental involvement as it is commonly conceived is just a one-dimensional variable— something that measures a parent's input of time. Accordingly to this fifth point, the father and mother seeking a higher SES level is partially another expression of their desire to be involved in their child's education. The parents seek a better income to send their children to better schools. They seek a better education in order to provide more opportunities for not only themselves, but also for their families. As a result, some parents view their willingness to spend time on their children's education and provide a better life for their children as two sides of the same coin. Many parents would view parental involvement as encompassing both an aspect that dictates that the parent spend time with the child, but also another that emphasizes giving the child a better life.

Although it might be tempting to try to encourage a higher level of parental involvement that is distinguished for SES, one is likely to meet with only limited success. To some extent, the same drives and motives that cause parents to become major participants in their child's education also causes them to pursue a higher SES level. Many researchers point out that SES is the ultimate "catchall" variable, reflecting various levels rather than being a pure, causal variable. (Gortmaker et al., 1993; Jeynes, 2002a, 2002c; Zakrisson, & Ekehammer, 1998). In this case, SES itself probably reflects certain aspects of parental involvement.

The results of this study also indicate that African American parents spend somewhat more time participating in the education of their girls than the education of their boys. This relationship not only holds with African American children, but in the overall student population. It should be noted, however, that the difference is quite small albeit statistically significant. Despite the small gender gap, for the overall sample this gap is statistically significant at the 0.0001 level of probability, indicating a strong level of consistency in the difference.

Given that Ogbu (1992, 1993) points to many societal dimensions that discourage achievement among African American males, a higher level of parental involvement for African American females may constitute one piece of a larger puzzle. The fact that the gender gap was also apparent in the general student population indicates that Ogbu's assertions, although focused on African Americans, may have a broader application to the student population as a whole. The fact that parents are more likely to be involved in the education of their girls more so than their boys is rather disconcerting, particularly because African American females are far more likely to go to college than African American males. The gender gap for the overall sample should also create some degree of concern. Although the gender gap for college entrance and graduation is substantially smaller for the general population than it is for African Americans, it nevertheless exists. The fact that parents are more involved in the education of girls than boys could be a small contributing factor to this gap.

The results of this study support the notion that parental involvement predicts the academic outcomes of African American students. Although the introduction of SES variables substantially reduces the impact of parental involvement, it is unwise to assume that the SES variables are primarily causal variables in this case. Rather, it is likely that there is a complex relationship between parental involvement and SES. In addition, this study lends some support to Ogbu's belief that various aspects of educational society, in this case, parents, subtly communicate to children that an educational emphasis is more appropriate for

African American females than it is for African American males. The fact that parents are apparently more involved in their girl's education than in that of their boys lends some support to Ogbu's theory that at least the parental involvement aspect of the societal message may apply to males and females in general. Ogbu's claim that American educational society depicts schooling as more of a female enterprise than a male one warrants a closer look. In future research, social scientists should test Ogbu's theory on other aspects of educational society.

This study likely raises as many questions as it does answers. Most notable among those questions include what is the complex relationship between parental involvement and SES? To what extent do other aspects of educational society discourage an academic orientation among African American males, specifically, and males, in general? Both of these questions are important and need to be addressed in order to more fully comprehend the role of parental involvement and other educational factors.

Chapter 6

Parental Involvement and Issues of Diversity

When examining the influence of parental involvement, it is important to consider the diversity of its implementation and efficacy across cultures and individual families (Brooks & Goldstein, 2001; Davalos et al., 2005; Delgado-Gaitan, 2004; Jeynes, 2003b). It is vital that social scientists not view the expressions of parental participation as a monolithic entity that must assume a particular form in every household. Rather, even the most all-encompassing data needs to be viewed with the understanding that the results are averages and designed to provide general principles to help educators and family guide the practice of parental involvement (Mapp et al., 2010).

It is vital for teachers and administrators to apprehend the themes just presented, so that they are able to recommend certain familial emphases in parental involvement and develop programs that reflect the friends that have emerged in the data, but are also sensitive to the individual situations apparent in families (Brooks & Goldstein, 2001; Domina, 2005; Epstein, 2001; Jeynes, 1999a). Many theorists argue that parental involvement is a more important practice than ever before in order to ensure successful student outcomes, because of the diverse nature of the nation's population. Due to cultural differences and sundry practices by different families, individual differences, and misunderstandings between teachers and families have the potential for increasing exponentially in modern society, parental involvement appears more vital than ever before (Borruel, 2002). It is therefore imperative that teachers and parents work concurrently to develop bonds as early as possible and as thoroughly as possible. To facilitate communication, it is also important for educators to develop an awareness of the parental involvement practices historically and in contemporary society in other countries. By educators reaching out to engage parents whose first language is not English, immigrant parents who otherwise might feel somehow ostracized by the American school system can conclude that they are an integral part of the scholastic success of their children (Davalos et al., 2005; Delgado-Gaitan, 2004; Domina, 2005). In addition, if educators reach out to parents, it can spawn higher levels parental involvement among family members of other groups that are often not sufficiently emphasized, including students with disabilities and those with learning and/or emotional issues.

Patterns in Parental Involvement Research and Diversity

There are some unequivocal patterns emerging in parental involvement research. Meta-analyses and the examination of nationwide data sets, in particular, have provided a boon of valuable information to provide insight into what components of parental participation are most salient. And indeed, educators need to expose one another, parents, and students (depending on their age) to the findings of these studies. Nationwide data sets are valuable because they provide a large nationally representative randomized sample that is generally undertaken by a large agency such as the federal government that is unattached to the social scientist conducting the study. There are a number of salient features of the nationwide data set that make the results of such analyses, on average, much more trustworthy than localized studies undertaken by the individual researchers conducting the study. The first advantage is the prodigious nature of this study, which generally includes thousands or tens of thousands of students from across the country. Second, the data collection is usually undertaken by an agency other than the researcher, usually the federal government, which significantly reduces the chances for bias in the data collection. Third, those undertaking such a large data collection effort with the agency usually abide by a strict data collection etiquette that helps ensure the reliability of the nationwide data set. Fourth, the fact that it is almost always a randomly selected nationwide data set makes it less subject to the vagaries of local culture or the (capricious nature of a biased or undereducated social scientist who does know how to procure on his or her own merits the most representative sample possible. For example, how does one know whether the findings that emerge in a study undertaken in San Francisco or Eugene are representative of the nation and able to be generalized to the entire American population? It is even conceivable the researcher chose certain locations because he or she was quite confident that the findings she or he longed for would be more likely to manifest themselves. When one utilizes a nationwide data set, such issues are far less likely to emerge. A meta-analysis is valuable because it, by definition, numerically summarizes the entire body of research. As a result, rather than base parental involvement practices on localized samples, anecdotal evidence, and personal experiences, it becomes based on the overall trends that one finds in dozens of studies that have been undertaken examining the issue. As one might examine, meta-analyses that include a fair number of studies utilizing nationwide data sets can be particularly valuable.

Teachers need to be sensitive to the fact that even meta-analyses that generally provide the broadest picture of the influence of parental involvement are simply presenting averages. This is particularly important to remember when advising family members regarding the various components of parental participation. Yes, it is undeniable that on average certain expressions of parental involvement are more effective than others (Jeynes, 2003b, 2005b, 2007b). Nevertheless, it is also true that different parents possess a vast array of distinct strengths and weaknesses (Domina, 2005; Epstein, 2001; Green et al., 2007; Kennedy, 2001). When educators advise family members on the most efficacious way of partnering with other children and teachers, one should keep this truism in mind.

Considering Parental Strengths

The advising educator should seek to play to the parents' strengths. If one knows that a parent is skilled at reading with their youth, teachers should encourage this exercise to a degree greater than they would otherwise. If the instructor notices that a mother or father has excellent communication skills, they should emphasize its application to the children in their home. Although this approach should certainly not eliminate training parents in areas in which they need help and growth if efficacious partnering potential already exists, it is vital to first build upon what is already strong. This approach will first maximize the positive influence of parental involvement and second, enhance the speed in which this participation is deployed (Brooks & Goldstein, 2001; Domina, 2005; Epstein, 2001).

If a teacher is working with two parents, he or she should be cognizant of the likelihood that these family members will have different strengths in terms of participation. For example, one parent might demonstrate strength in eliciting high expectations in the minds of children. The other parent might employ open-minded communication skills. Although the teacher should exhort these family members to excel at each of these skills, one should attempt to foster the expression of strengths that are already present (Domina, 2005; Epstein, 2001; Jeynes, 2006a).

Important Questions to Ask Regarding Diversity

There is no question that there is diversity that exists in the world and that this diversity takes on a variety of different forms. Nevertheless, it is important that one not stop at simply stating that diversity exists and therefore there must be different applications of parental involvement, any more than it would be sagacious to assert that parental participation generally has positive effects and leave it at that. Rather, there are particular questions that are especially important to ask in issues regarding diversity, even as there are key areas that should be addressed when communicating about parental involvement generally. First, to what extent does parental involvement benefit children of all hues? Second, do the most efficacious types of parental involvement vary depending on one's race or cultural background? Third, to what extent does diversity among individuals trump diversity among groups in terms of its importance to the application of parental involvement? Fourth, what are the most vital forms of diversity when applying various manifestations of parental involvement? In order to most appropriately utilize truths about parental involvement it is important to cogitate about these key questions. Let us now examine them (Davalos et al., 2005, Delgado-Gaitan, 2004, Kennedy, 2001).

First, to what extent does parental involvement benefit children of all hues? The meta-analyses that have been done on parental involvement and distinguish between children of different races, or at least between white and nonwhite children, indicate that parental engagement generally benefits children of all races and those of all the cultural backgrounds under study (Jeynes, 2003b, 2005b, 2007b). In these meta-analyses the overall impact of parental involvement appears to be fairly consistent across race (Jeynes, 2003b, 2005b, 2007b). This is especially encouraging because it means that parents and educators can focus on parental engagement, with the knowledge that they are working to benefit all kinds of children.

Second, do the most efficacious types of parental involvement vary depending on one's race or cultural background? The meta-analyses undertaken thus far and other studies on parental engagement indicate that there is some degree of difference between the aspects of parental involvement that are most effective for some racial groups versus others. The evidence suggests that although the various modes of family engagement are successful for all racial groups, there are some facets that are more successful for some groups than others (Jeynes, 2003b).

Third, to what extent does diversity among individuals trump diversity among groups in terms of its importance to the application of parental involvement? The evidence from research studies indicates that, in terms of the efficacy of parental involvement, the difference among children from different racial backgrounds is minimal. In addition, it is to some extent true that some differences emerge between different racial and ethic groups, as well as socioeconomically, in terms of the distinct facets of parental engagement. What is important to note, however, is that these distinct patterns vary only in the extent of their influence rather than whether they have any effect at all. Instead, what the body of research indicates is that there is considerably more variation among individual students and various seemingly similar groups of students in the various studies themselves than there was between any particular racial or cultural groups (Jeynes, 2003b, 2005b, 2007b; Mapp et al., 2010).

Fourth, what are the most vital forms of diversity when applying various manifestations of parental involvement? Based on the results of a plethora of studies on parental involvement it appears that several types of diversity among families and individuals are the most salient if one is to apprehend the differences in the varied experiences and practices of mother and father participation among youth. One of the most ostensible differences among individuals is the extent to which parents want to become involved. Some fathers and mothers have made it a real priority to participate in the day-to-day experiences and personal growth of their children (Green et al., 2007; Kennedy, 2001).

There may be a variety of reasons for their perceived exigency of this involvement. These adult family members may arrive at this conclusion because they themselves did or did not have fathers and mothers who were actively engaged in their education and by means of their example these adult family members were motivated to become more engaged in the schooling and development of their young (Green et al., 2007; Kennedy, 2001). Another reason may be because various parents differ in the degree of their conviction that parental involvement actually works. Fathers and mothers may arrive at different conclusions regarding this for a variety of reasons. For example, some may believe that educators are the only ones qualified to train youth and that parents are not properly equipped to have much of an influence in this regard (Egan, 2002). In other words, a copious number of parents regard teachers as the professionals and view them as specialists on whom parents can depend to inculcate their children with the appropriate information and principles that will enable youth to thrive (Green et al., 2007; Leary, 2008).

A third reason why there is a variation in a parental sense of exigency is because some parents, particularly some immigrants, do not have a high degree of trust in those who are employed by the government. Consequently, they are averse to partnering with educators. Such an attitude may seem relatively foreign to many Americans. It should be noted, however, that an abundant number of immigrants come from nations in which the government is extremely corrupt and even oppressive (Bennett, 1998; Morris & McGann, 2007; Phillips, 1994; Romero, 2008). It is easy for Americans for forget that myriad immigrants come to the United States, which they view as a land of opportunity, in order to escape from the oppression of dominating governments (Johnson, 1997). Recently, in the midst of massive government initiated bailouts and the prospect that government spending might go from 25% of Gross Domestic Product to over 50% in a very short period of time, Americans' cognizance of US government corruption has surged (Bracket, 2009; Malkin, 2009). Perhaps this heightened awareness will foster a new understanding and compassion for immigrant parents who possess a depressed level of trust for people in the government's employ.

Parental Involvement and Issues of Diversity Culture

In any parental involvement initiative, especially one undertaken by a school, it is important to consider the culture from which children and parents originate (Davalos et al., 2005; Delgado-Gaitan, 2004; Domina, 2005; Epstein, 2001; Saint Clair & Jackson, 2006). Different cultures do often have varying expectations about both the extent and type of family involvement that is expected (Davalos et al., 2005; Delgado-Gaitan, 2004; Mau, 1997; Schonpflug, 2008; Stevenson & Stigler, 1992). Part of this variation stems from the fact that citizens from different countries possess certain levels of expectations about the degree to which parents, schools, and young people are responsible for determining educational outcomes (Green et al., 2007; Kennedy, 2001; Mau, 1997). That is, some societies believe that in spite of the existence of schools, it is the parents who are ultimately the primary teachers of children (Jeynes, 2006a, 2007b). Other societies lean somewhat in this direction, but as the students mature they put an increasing degree of responsibility on the youth to learn the material that they are taught (Mau, 1997; Schonpflug, 2008). Still other nations view teachers as the instructional specialists that should take both the credit and the blame for student achievement (Egan, 2002; Leary, 2008).

Parents from different cultures may vary in their willingness to participate in scholastic exercises largely because their culture maintains a particular perspective about the relative responsibilities of parents, students, and teachers in the schooling process (Brooks & Goldstein, 2001; Davalos et al., 2005; Delgado-Gaitan, 2004). One must be careful not to prematurely judge a particular culture's orientation on this particular question (Davalos et al., 2005; Delgado-Gaitan, 2004). The United States tends to emphasize the role of the teacher more than in most societies, because this nation assumes that increased levels of specialization is generally advantageous for society (Egan, 2002; Johnson, 1997; Leary, 2008). Nevertheless, this should not cause Americans to in any way disparage those cultures who believe differently (Davalos et al., 2005; Delgado-Gaitan, 2004; Mapp et al., 2010; Vasquez, 2004). There are a number of truths that should discourage Americans from arriving at premature conclusions regarding the viewpoints that are frequently maintained by people from other cultures.

First, although many Americans opine that teachers are at the forefront of determining scholastic outcomes and are the nation's education specialists, this topic remains highly debatable even to this day (Brooks & Goldstein, 2001; Jeynes, 2007a; Wentzel, 2002). Second, at earlier periods in America's history, people believed that parents were the ones primarily responsible for ensuring academic success. The belief that the role of parents was secondary to teachers is a relatively recent phenomenon and was adhered to by a small minority until the heyday of John Dewey in the 1920s and may not have been maintained by a majority of the American people until the early-to-mid-1960s (Jeynes, 2007a; Leary, 2008). Third, there is no clear indication that Americans are correct in their views. Although there may be some evidence that the American perspective is correct, there is also evidence that suggests that the alternative perspectives may have merit. For example, most people in East Asian countries view parents as the primary educators and youth in their countries generally score about two years ahead of American children on international comparison tests (Benjamin, 1997; Jeynes, 2008d; White, 1987). Many scholars who study international education assert that it is the East Asian emphasis on the primacy of the parent that is one of the main reasons why students from this area of the world consistently outperform American students is because their cultures emphasize the place of parents in education (Benjamin, 1997; Mau, 1997; White, 1987).

If the Asian academic edge was exclusively limited to the Asian continent, a person could easily conclude that the Asian advantage was simply a result of better schools, teachers, and educational techniques. The Asian advantage, however, extends to the United States. Of all the primary racial groups in the United

States, Asian Americans consistently perform the best on major standardized tests (Nishida, 1999). Even if one breaks down the various racial groups by ethnicity, Asian Americans generally rank with Jewish and Northern European groups as those attaining the highest scores on standardized tests (Nakanishi & Nishida, 1999). Asian Americans are also very well represented at many of America's top universities like Harvard, Yale, Princeton, Stanford, and the University of Chicago (Nakanishi & Nishida, 1999).

The success of Asian American youth in the nation, indicates that variables outside the schools also play a role in explaining this degree of Asian ascendancy (Nakanishi & Nishida, 1999). When researchers list the factors outside the school that they believe contribute to East Asians' educational strength, parental involvement almost always heads the list (White, 1987). The fact that parental involvement in East Asia plays such a key role has fostered the interest of many social scientists. It is also true that the nature of parental involvement in Japan and other East Asian nations is different than what one commonly finds in the United States. In East Asia these nations encourage parents to emphasize effort over ability.

In a report entitled, *Japanese Education Today*, U.S. Department of Education (1987, p.3) reported that in Japan, "The amount of time and effort spent in study is believed to be more important than intelligence in determining educational outcomes." In that report, however, the salience of the parental role along these lines is emphasized. The report states, "The cultural emphasis on student effort and diligence is balanced by a recognition of the important responsibility borne by teachers, parents, parents and schools to awaken the desire to try" (p.4).

Various social scientists, however, have pointed out that one must be careful not to draw too great a distinction between the American and East Asian, especially the Japanese educational philosophy on the role of parents. As Stevenson and Stigler (1992) point out, several of these nations imitated the American schooling system in the second half of the nineteenth century and therefore it would be either naïve or disingenuous to exaggerate the differences. In 1868, Emperor Meiji assumed the throne and asserted that unless Japan adopted certain Western modern ways, Japanese society could not succeed (Hood, 2003; Shimizu, 1992). Emperor Meiji therefore asked several Western educators to come to Japan and construct a Japanese education system that would be based on the Western model (Amano, 1990; Hood, 2001). These educators were led by David Murray from Rutgers College, who became the Superintendent of Schools and served in that capacity from 1873–1878 (Amano, 1990; Keenleyside & Thomas, 1937). Shortly after these changes in Japan, American and European missionaries also started Western style schools in Korea and China (Reynolds, 2001). Consequently, it is important to draw a balance between appreciating the differences between cultures, but also being able to identify similarities due to imitation and other factors.

Socioeconomic Status

Socioeconomic status (SES) is another facet of diversity that is worthy of consideration in considering the implementation of parental engagement programs. The primary reason why it is key to understand the role of SES is because studies indicate that parental involvement and SES are highly correlated (Crane & Heaton, 2008; Mapp et al., 2010). That is, fathers and mothers who are highly engaged in their children's academic training and development also tend to be highly educated, have high status jobs, and make healthy levels of income (Crane & Heaton, 2008; Mapp et al., 2010; Wartman & Savage, 2008). There are a number of reasons why that this linkage likely exists. First, people who are successful as parents tend to have that success spill over to other areas of their lives (Epstein, 2001). Second, those parents who have benefited by the system are more likely to be involved in their children's lives, so that their progeny can also reap rewards from the system (Green et al., 2007; Kennedy, 2001). Stated in an inverse sense, some parents do not become involved in their children's education because they are not convinced the system has really worked for them. That is, they believe that participating in their child's life and training may not yield the effects that some would assume it does (Crane & Heaton, 2008, Green et al., 2007). Third, the component of socioeconomic status that generally has the highest level of predictive value, that is mother and father's education level, may also enable parents to have greater access to knowledge about the advantages of parental engagement that less educated family members may not have (Crane & Heaton, 2008; Domina, 2005; Epstein, 2001; Wartman & Savage, 2008).

Although there is currently a strong relationship between parental engagement and socioeconomic status, some theorists note that the vibrant relationship between these two variables may not be as patent in the future (Jeynes, 2007b). This possible prediction does not aver prognosticate that this relationship will disappear, but rather that it is conceivable that it might diminish. The possible reason for this fading in the relationship is due to an increased decoupling between family income and family education. Historically, throughout much of America's development there has been a vibrant relationship between one's highest level of schooling and one's income (Jeynes, 2007b). For example, in the 1930s teachers generally made three or four times what construction workers did (Jeynes, 2007a; Ravitch, 1974). This was largely justified on the basis of how important schooling was to the future of the nation and the college training that teachers required to fulfill that role of preparing America's future workers and leaders (Byrd & McIntyre, 1997; Ravitch, 1974). In that day, it was understood that the nation needed to reward the sacrifice and delayed gratification in terms of income that teachers engaged in order to become the nation's instructors and purveyors of truth for the future generations.

In the modern era the relationship between education and wages is much more precarious (Bousquet, 2008; Byrd & McIntyre, 1997). It does seem that there is still a relationship between procuring a high school diploma and obtaining a certain degree of income (Bousquet, 2008; Byrd & McIntyre, 1997). However, even this correlation is likely not as predictable as it might seem. There are generally two reasons for this. First, government statistics on the relationship between one's highest schooling level and family income usually exclude the government payments that one receives, e.g. welfare payments and food stamps. Government statistics generally examine the relationship between *earned* income and one's highest level of schooling. When these statistics are examined the gap in the income between those who have a high school diploma and those that do not appears quite formidable, but when *unearned government-based* income is included, the gap closes markedly. Second, part of the reason a gap exists between those that earn a high school diploma and those that do not possess a high school diploma are more likely to have gotten entangled in problems that substantially reduced their likelihood of procuring a high school diploma, e.g. getting involved in substance abuse, joining a gang, engaging in premarital intercourse that resulted in the birth of a child during his or her adolescence.

Overall, the propensity of those who have higher levels of schooling to have higher levels of income is far less certain than in was in previous generation (Bousquet, 2008; Byrd & McIntyre, 1997; Jeynes, 2007a). In today's society, the highest levels of annual incomes are associated with actors, athletes, and other celebrities whose incomes are not associated with level of schooling or intellectual prowess (Bousquet, 2008, Byrd & McIntyre, 1997). Beyond this, other than these examples, the people who make the highest levels of income on average are frequently those who own their own businesses. The degree of education attained by these individuals or required to excel at these positions varies considerably. Some of these individuals went to college and even attended graduate school, while others did not. Bill Gates, a frequent holder of the "title" the "richest man in the world" dropped out of Harvard and financially speaking, he has never looked back (Bousquet, 2008; Byrd & McIntyre, 1997).

Moreover, in addition to these trends, there are countless thousands of carpenters, plumbers, and truck drivers who may or may not possess a high school diploma who make more income than many teachers, professors, and especially ministers (Bousquet, 2008; Byrd & McIntyre, 1997). The days are evanescent when one can assume that there is an ostensible relationship between one's highest level of school attained and one's income. It is important not only that educators and society at large appreciate and understand the puissant relationship between SES and parental involvement, but also that they appreciate the fact that the relationship could be somewhat diluted in the future. That is, there is a possibility that educated parents who might normally become involved in their children's schooling, as a result of concluding that education yields higher levels of success, might conclude differently on today's society. As time progresses, increasingly parents may conclude that the economic payoff for education is not what it once was and choose to invest their time in other activities or in their children in other ways, because the long-term yield from education is less clear.

By Ethnicity and Race

Few would deny that issues of ethnicity and race are almost omnipresent in American society. It is also important to acknowledge that issues of ethnicity and race are inextricably connected with culture (Davalos et al., 2005; Delgado-Gaitan, 2004; Domina, 2005; Epstein, 2001). What research utilizing meta-analyses and nationwide data sets communicates is that it is important that educators and Americans at large develop a balance between appreciating the distinctions that exist by race and yet acknowledging the commonalities that people from all races share. It would also be sagacious to realize that in spite of the fact that human beings of different racial backgrounds are over 98% similar, people tend to focus on the differences (Jeynes, 2007a). Perhaps this reflects the superficial nature of people, that they emphasize qualities that are skin deep rather than the more profound realities of the heart.

The challenge of those educators who desire to foster parental involvement is to realize that the research suggests that the differences in the response and actual practice of parental involvement among the various races, appears to be minimal. Therefore, on the one hand, this fact can be very encouraging both to teachers and parents in the sense that people as a whole, no matter what their racial heritage generally respond favorably and convincingly to parental participation (Jeynes, 2003b, 2005f, 2007b). On the other hand, youth from racial backgrounds differ regarding parental involvement in one important way. That is, their parents may vary in their willingness or ability to be involved, but this is likely due more to their level of education and mastery of the English language rather than racial issues per se.

By Gender

The body of research suggests a number of truths regarding gender differences in parental involvement. First, there is little difference between how parental involvement benefits boys and girls (Jeynes, 2005b, 2005f, 2007b). Second, parents tend to be somewhat more actively engaged in the education of their girls rather than that of their boys (Farrell, Svoboda & Sterba, 2008, Jeynes, 2005f, Sommers, 2000). Third, there is some evidence, albeit inconsistent, that boys benefit a bit more than girls from the presence of their fathers and girls benefit a bit more than boys from the presence of their mothers (Hetherington & Jodl, 1994; Wallerstein & Blakeslee, 1989). It is important that teachers be aware of these trends. Once again it is almost becoming an axiomatic truth that parental engagement appears to benefit virtually all types of students, i.e. both genders and students of all races and socioeconomic backgrounds (Jeynes, 2003b, 2005b, 2007b). Moreover, it may be especially salient that educators realize that parents tend to be more actively engaged in helping their daughters in school than helping their sons. This is crucial to understand because a plethora of those in the public assume that parents are more faithful to support their sons in attaining their educational aspirations than their daughters in seeking these goals (Farrell et al., 2008; Sommers, 2000). National statistics, however, indicate that precisely the reverse is the case. There is a considerably higher percentage of females who attend college in the United States than there are males (Chronicle of Higher Education, 2003; U.S. Department of Education, 2002). The percentage is close to 60/40%, which is a substantial difference. For some racial groups, such as African Americans, the ratio of females to males going to college is nearly two to one (Chronicle of Higher Education, 2003; U.S. Department of Education, 2002).

Although there are elements of American society that are more sensitive to males than they are females, parental involvement clearly is not one of them. Research indicates that parents generally spend more time working with their daughters on school than they do with their sons (Jeynes, 2005f). It is conceivable that part of the difference between the amount of time that parents spend in helping their sons and daughters can be attributed to the sober realties of modern day family structure. That is, to the extent that fathers are more likely than mothers to be the non-custodial parent, it may be that the custodial mothers that remain in the home tend to spend more time helping their daughters in school than they do their sons who are in school. Although it is not certain that this is in fact is what is taking place and more research needs to be undertaken, it is clearly logical. It may well be that mothers feel on average inherently more comfortable supplying succor to other females than they do that same help to males (Jeynes, 2005f, Ogbu, 1992, 1993). It may be that as hard as mothers might try, they simply cannot relate to their sons as well as their daughters. It may be that fathers tend to have a more facile time than mothers relating to their sons. If this is the case, then part of the key to inspiring more ethereal levels of parental engagement may be realizing the influence of parental family structure (Jeynes, 2002a).

With this in mind, it then becomes important for the United States to decide whether it wants to generate policy that will encourage families to remain intact and adjust more appropriately to the families who have endured various transitions and dissolutions. Government policies and attitudes that support the two-parent family are not difficult to develop, if one allows a gush of compassion to well up with him or her and overcome his hesitancy about helping children that previously one did not know. Tax policies that in contemporary America discriminate against married couples, those typically referred to as the "marriage penalty," can easily be lifted to give families a financial incentive to remain together rather than split apart (Brown & Fellows, 1996; Lambro, 1980). In addition, the government can also reassess welfare support so that it does not help single-parent impoverished families disproportionately more than two-parent poor families. Because when such a policy exists, children from financially struggling two-parent families are discriminated against are the ones who are hurt at levels greater than their counterparts in single-parent families. In addition, it is important to note that many couples who get a divorce later regret not trying more diligently to keep their marriage together (Jeynes, 2002a; Wallerstein & Blakeslee, 1989). Myriad of these families later possess these attitudes because they realize now that at the time of the breakup they gave up on the relationship because they asserted that "the feeling is gone." As they have gotten older, however, they matured to the point at which they realized that love is not merely a feeling, but an act of the will (Jeynes, 2002a). It would not take a very aggressive family policy initiative at all to offer counseling and literature to couples considering divorce to carefully consider the possibility that if they have the will to work at their marriage, over time it might well succeed (Brown & Fellows, 1996; Lambro, 1980). The possibility that parental family structure could potentially explain a portion of the low levels of parental involvement for young males is a topic worthy of further study.

By Location

It is a salient sign of sensitivity if teachers acknowledge and adapt to the fact that different parts of the country possess different expectations and levels of parental engagement. This fact is a product of a multifarious number of factors that combined imbue the citizenry of that area with certain convictions about the way and degree parents should get involved. One of the factors that influences these perceptions is whether the school is in an urban, suburban, or rural area (Crane & Heaton, 2008). That is not to say that schools residing in these always differ in the same way and extent. What the research does indicate, however, is that on average these communities and the culture of these locations differ from one another. The distinctiveness of each of these types of environments is a result of factors such as the length of one's commute, the crime rate, the extent to which relationships or possessions is emphasized more. All of these variables affect the degree to which parental participation is feasible and the manifestations that are most likely. Long commutes, a loss of the sense of community, a high crime rate, a lascivious culture with few moral absolutes can all contribute to a sense of atrophy in family cohesiveness and mutual commitment in the household (Crane & Heaton, 2008). Although these developments do not by necessity have to take place when these location factors are at work, there is nevertheless a propensity for them to happen (Crane & Heaton, 2008).

Educators need to be sensitive to the challenges and obstacles that parents in their community typically face and seek to address these issues and allay parental and student fears about these issues (Crane & Heaton, 2008; Mapp et al., 2010). It is also vital for educators to apprehend the fact that the situations faced by parents may be different from those faced by the family. For example, teachers frequently live closer to the school than parents typically are from their work. And although it is true that considering their level of college education, teachers generally enjoy a higher standard of living than the families that they instruct (U.S. Department of Education, 2007). One indication of this fact is that surveys indicate that about 90% of teachers own their own home or condominium, which is a much higher percentage than the approximately 65% of the American public that can make the same claim (Byrd & McIntyre, 1997; Heim, 1992; U.S. Department of Education, 2007). Moreover, principals and vice principals make salaries that are exceeded only by the elite of a given township (U.S. Department of Education, 2007). Consequently, educators are usually not going to face the financial strain faced by those that they teach. To the extent that this is true it is imperative that educators maintain hearts of empathy toward the families of those that they teach.

Usually when modern day sociologists address the issue of diversity, they think in terms of race and ethnicity, but what is important to understand is that plenteous foreigners believe that Americans possess a very narrow definition of diversity. Europeans, for example, especially find it enigmatic that Americans teach ethnic tolerance, but show little acceptance toward people of faith. From the European perspective, Americans have little patience for people who do not espouse a secular humanistic point of view (Geisler, 1983; Hughes, 1983). But beyond this, it is evident that the American definition of diversity is very narrow. Diversity can refer to a full gamut of realities including political views, one's family situation, one's moral compass, location, lifestyle, personal philosophy, etc. Although American society often dismisses these facets of diversity as relatively unimportant or at least secondary to other aspects of diversity, it is nevertheless vital to examine these diversity issues. Although Americans rarely peruse research about these issues, it is key to possessing a truly well rounded perspective to maintain a broad view on diversity.

By Language

It should come as no surprise that research indicates that the number one predictor variable of whether an immigrant parent becomes involved in his or her child's education is the extent to which that parent knows English fluently (Turney & Kao, 2009). This is information that is key for teachers to know if they are to effectively reach students who live in homes in which English is not the primary language that is spoken in the household. Moreover, it is vital that teachers are cognizant of the fact that it is not simply a matter of the extent that the parent is conversant with English or not, but the sense of embarrassment that a parent might feel for not being strong in English (Turney & Kao, 2009). There are some teachers who criticize parents for not having as much working knowledge of English as they should. For example, the educators might find it unwise for an immigrant parent to have lived in the United States twenty-five years and still have a vocabulary of less than one hundred words. And indeed this concern may well be valid. Nevertheless, what is important for instructors to realize is that these family members are often cognizant of their rather feeble abilities in English, they are embarrassed by them, and these very facts reduce the likelihood that these parents will do well in school (Turney & Kao, 2009).

Because fluency in English is such a major predictor of parental involvement, it is important for teachers to do their best to reach out to these parents. It is wise to do what one can to bridge the language gap between the parent and the school educators (Jeynes, 2010). There are two salient actions that one can take to help facilitate and maximize parental participation in this situation. First, if there is a second dominant language in the area the teacher can do what is possible to learn that language (Jeynes, 2010). Although it is unlikely that fluency will be obtained, the parents will greatly appreciate the fact that one is making a sincere attempt to learn the language and will likely feel a sense of special affinity with the instructor. Clearly, if the neighborhood environment is such that that is a plethora of languages spoken, this recommendation will prove to be impractical. Nevertheless, if there is a second dominant language special bonds can be created. It would also ameliorate the situation if the school offers language classes in order to help the parents master English so that they likely will become more involved.

By Religion

Although American acceptance of people's ethnicities is frequently emphasized in the nation's schools, the United States has not been as open-minded when it comes to accepting people of faith (Geisler, 1983; Jeynes, 2007a). In contrast, European nations believe that religious faith is even more important than race and ethnicity when it comes to defining one's self-concept (Podell, 1987). Research indicates that religious faith may even more important than ethnicity in defining how a person views oneself (Podell, 1987). It is an act of both sensitivity and compassion to realize and appreciate the fact that families of faith generally have parental involvement as exceptionally high on their priority list. On the surface, this may appear to be a purely positive reality and no detracting features. Nevertheless, one should note that with this higher degree of engagement, family members typically possess high expectations of teachers and are more likely to participate in the classroom at levels that may prove irritating to teachers (Gatto, 2001). It is important that teachers respect how people of faith differ from people who are not as inclined in this direction and also sensitize themselves to differing roles of the parents in education among the variety of religious faiths (Podell, 1987).

Chapter 7

Parental Involvement Programs

Do They Work?

In the previous chapters, using meta-analysis, it has been established that there is a relationship between parental involvement and children's academic success. The results indicate that this pattern exists at both the elementary and secondary school levels and that it exists both for white children and children from the full gamut of racial backgrounds. Nevertheless, it should be noted that these findings emerge using studies that for the most part examine parental engagement that is previously extant and based on volunteerism (Jeynes, 2010).

The existence of these findings are vital, but an apposite question becomes manifest when one cogitates over these results. That is, is parental involvement still influential when a school-based program is the origin of that initiative? It is conceivable and potentially even logical to opine that although parental involvement has a positive impact on student educational outcomes, it only possesses such influence if is based on self-motivation and resides as a personal goal rather than one that is imposed by the school (Jeynes 1999a, 2003b, 2010). In fact, one could imagine a situation in which the imposition of family engagement might actually backfire and diminish parental participation in school activities.

The facts described above provide the impetus for conducting a meta-analysis to determine whether parental involvement programs are efficacious. Because the motivations behind such engagement are different in programs as opposed to acts of volunteerism and because self-generated involvement would appear almost by definition to yield more plentiful results, conducting such a distinct meta-analysis would seem to be of paramount importance. There are patently some examples of parental involvement programs that work, but a meta-analysis is designed to propound what the overall body of research indicates as opposed to relying on what could be the insular assumptions of an individual study or two (Aeby, Thyer & Carpenter-Abey, 1999; Hampton, Munford & Bond, 1998; Wise, 1972).

Parental involvement programs are school-sponsored initiatives that are designed to require or encourage parental participation in their children's education. It is important to determine if these programs have an impact, because even though voluntary acts of parental involvement may positively impact educational outcomes the same may or may not be true of programs in which schools require or encourage involvement. Fan and Chen (2001) did not distinguish those studies examining parental involvement programs from other studies that examined parental involvement without the use of programs. This proves problematic in that even if parental involvement effectively raises achievement, this does not necessarily mean that parental involvement programs work as well. They are, in essence, two different research questions.

Mattingly and her colleagues (2002) conducted a summary of the existing body of research on parental involvement programs which was not based on quantitative analysis, but was rather based on a vote counting method (Jeynes, 2005b, 2007b). This analysis also neglected to include various published analyses in their vote count, for reasons that the authors never explicitly stated. Consequently, it is unclear whether these studies were not included due to oversight or another reason. Mattingly did not include a number of prominent studies in the research synthesis (e.g. Koskinen, Blum, Bisson, Phillips, & Creamer, 2000; Miedel & Reynolds, 1999; Shaver & Walls, 1998). Instead, about one half of the studies were unpublished. Given that unpublished research more likely suffers from statistically insignificant results, their omission of published studies could bias the results in favor of the authors' conclusion; namely, parental involvement programs may have no impact. Moreover, for some studies Mattingly included only certain results that were subsets of the overall results rather than the overall results themselves. Once again, the authors do not explicate the reasoning for this rather counterintuitive procedure. Furthermore, Mattingly concludes that some of the studies indicating a statistically significant effect for parental involvement programs actually show no impact.

These facts being the case the need for a meta-analysis on this topic is obvious. The salience of such a study is undeniable. On the one hand, it is clearly important for teachers to know whether it is advantageous for school officials to encourage parental involvement and even to exhort family members to engage in its practice. This in and of itself is valuable information. It should be noted, however, that above and beyond this question is the issue of whether schools should actuate parents into practicing this engagement, utilizing school-based programs. This is an entirely different question. And indeed it is essential that parents, teachers, and students be cognizant of what the appropriate levels of action for schools to take regarding family involvement. First, should schools encourage parental involvement, and if so, is it sufficient that they stop at this point? Second, should schools actually exhort family members to become more active participants in the latter's educational development and if so, how can this be accomplished? Third, should schools actually provide programs by which even reluctant and recalcitrant parents are obligated to become involved? Different aspects of the analyses presented in these chapters address various and sundry parts of this progression of key questions. The research questions that focus on parental involvement in the general sense focus primarily on the first question. The research questions that divulge the specific facets of parental involvement that yield the strongest results direct attention primarily to the second question. It is the aspect of the meta-analysis that focuses on programs of parental engagement that addresses the third question. To the extent that Chapters 3–5 in particular address the first two questions propounded above, this chapter is concerned with whether schools should go beyond merely encouraging and directing parents to become more active participants in leading the fathers and mothers to become more engaged, and actually require them to do so.

Results of Examining the Relationship between Parental Involvement Programs and the Academic Achievement of Youth

Effect Sizes for Elementary School Level Parental Involvement Programs

Table 7.1 lists the effect sizes for the impact of parental involvement programs on the academic achievement of elementary school students. That is, these results do not assess the influence of parental involvement, which already exists, but attempts by schools to improve parental practices along these lines. For all the analyses combined, parental involvement programs yielded an effect size of 0.27. For those studies in which no sophisticated controls were used, the effect size was 0.31 ($p < 0.05$) and for studies with controls the result was 0.19 ($p < 0.05$). For all the academic measures examined with no controls used, standardized tests yielded the highest effect size at 0.40 ($p < 0.01$). In addition, for all the analyses combined, standardized tests yielded the largest effect size (0.40). Nevertheless, all the academic measures yielded very similar effect sizes for all the analyses combined. The effect sizes were generally about three-tenths of a standard deviation. Tests of homogeneity for parental involvement programs

Table 7.1 Effect Sizes for Programs of Parental Involvement at the Elementary School Level with 95% Confidence Intervals in Parentheses

Type of Parental Involvement and Academic Variables	Effect Size Without Sophisticated Controls	Effect Size With Sophisticated Controls	Overall Effect Size
Programs of Parental Involvement			
Overall	0.31* (0.06, 0.56)	0.19* (0.03, 0.35)	0.27[a]
Grades	NA	0.32 {based on 1 study only}	0.32 {based on 1 study only}
Standardized Tests	0.40** (0.10, 0.70)	NA	0.40[a]
Other	0.30* (0.04, 0.56)	NA	0.30[a]

Notes
* $p < 0.05$; ** $p < 0.01$; *** $p < 0.001$; **** $p < 0.0001$; NA = Not available
a Confidence intervals tabulation not undertaken for combined effect size because of difference in sample distributions for the two sets of studies.

indicated that the programs were relatively homogeneous when sophisticated controls were used ($X^2 = 2.87$, p = n.s.) but were heterogeneous when sophisticated controls were not included ($X^2 = 80.46$, $p < 0.0001$).

Effect Sizes for Secondary School Level Parental Involvement Programs

Table 7.2 lists the effect sizes for the relationship between parental involvement programs and the academic outcomes of secondary school students. In the case of secondary school students all the studies did not include sophisticated controls. Some of the studies examining the efficacy of the programs included statements to the effect that the schools ideally wanted to incorporate the programs as soon as possible, and this sense of urgency in some cases may have precluded the use of sophisticated controls in the analyses. For the analyses for secondary school, parental involvement programs yielded an effect size of 0.36 ($p < 0.05$). Standardized tests yielded the highest effect size at 0.42 ($p < 0.05$), whereas for grades and other non-standardized measures the effect sizes were both at 0.25 ($p < 0.001$) of a standard deviation. Secondary school parental programs were also homogeneous as indicated by this test ($X^2 = 1.81$, n.s.).

Discussion

The results of this study indicate that programs meant to ensure parental support in their child's schooling are positively related to achievement for youth. As expected, the effect sizes that emerge from these analyses are not as large as those that address the impact of parental involvement as a whole. This is because parents already enthusiastic about supporting the educational progress of their children will, on average, tend to help their children more than parents whose participation is fostered by the presence of a particular program. The

Table 7.2 Effect Sizes for Programs of Parental Involvement at the Secondary School Level with 95% Confidence Intervals in Parentheses

Type of Parental Involvement and Academic Variables	Effect Size Without Sophisticated Controls	Effect Size With Sophisticated Controls	Overall Effect Size
Programs of Parental Involvement			
Overall	0.36* (0.03, 0.69)	NA	0.36* (0.03, 0.69)
Grades	0.25*** (0.11, 0.39)	NA	0.25*** (0.11, 0.39)
Standardized Tests	0.42* (0.04, 0.80)	NA	0.42* (0.04, 0.80)
Other	0.25*** (0.10, 0.40)	NA	0.25*** (0.10, 0.40)

Note
* $p < 0.05$; ** $p < 0.01$; *** $p < 0.001$; **** $p < 0.0001$; NA = Not available

positive association between parental involvement programs and educational outcomes also suggests a direction of causality. That is, academic achievement would not influence the presence of parental involvement programs: rather, the inverse would be true.

Although fathers and mothers who initiate high levels of support are more likely to have an ameliorative effect than those parents responding to a particular parental support initiative, it is nevertheless important to discover whether parental involvement programs work. For years, teachers and others have held that many of the scholastically weakest students suffer from a lack of parental support and engagement. Therefore, inspiring parents to become involved, through various programmatic means, could spawn a considerable increase in achievement among these students.

These findings ostensibly contradict the claims by Mattingly and her colleagues (2002) indicating that parental involvement programs do not work. The effect sizes that emerge from the parental involvement programs are noteworthy for a number of reasons. First, they indicate that emboldening parental support of student academics appears to produce some positive impact for all students. This finding will indubitably comfort numerous teachers attempting to abet additional parental involvement. Second, they indicate parental involvement may represent an important means of raising the educational outcomes of struggling urban students specifically. The fact that most of the studies that initiated programs of parental support involved struggling school children suggests that parental involvement can be a means of reducing the achievement gap between these students and those more advanced scholastically (Green, 2001; Green et al., 2000; Griffith, 1997; Haycock, 2001; Slavin & Madden, 2006).

Third, it points to the benefits of teachers encouraging a higher level of parental participation in their child's education. Research indicates a myriad of teachers claim reaching out to parents will yield little fruit, as parents either cannot or will not become involved (Jeynes, 2010). However, the examination of urban parental involvement programs in this meta-analysis suggests otherwise. Finally, the finding that parental involvement programs were effective for urban students is particularly encouraging, since studies have indicated how low SES, urban parents are generally less educationally supportive than most other parents (Hampton et al., 1998).

Encouraging Findings

The results of this study are particularly encouraging, because these findings suggest that parental involvement programs may be one means of reducing the achievement gap that exists between white students and some racial minority groups (Bronstein et al., 1994; Hampton et al., 1998). A number of educators and sociologists have advocated this position and the results of this study support their theories (Bronstein et al., 1994; Hampton et al.,

1998). One should also note that many of the parental involvement programs included in this study focused on minority students. Therefore, this meta-analysis not only suggests that parental involvement overall may reduce the achievement gap, but also that programs of this nature may help as well.

This study's broad range of statistically significant effect sizes for parental involvement supports prior claims about the relationship between parental support and educational outcomes when applied to race (Mau, 1997; Sanders, 1998; Shaver & Walls, 1998; Villas-Boas, 1998), gender (Muller, 1998), and background (Griffith, 1996; Hampton et al., 1998). Nevertheless, encouraging parental involvement is not easy. Unquestionably, some family situations more easily lend themselves to greater parental involvement than others. For example, research indicates strong relationships between parental involvement, socioeconomic status, and whether a child is from an intact family (Jeynes, 2002a, 2006b; McLanahan & Sandefur, 1994). Nevertheless, results of this meta-analysis indicate the success of parental involvement programs and the worth inherent in efforts to increase parental participation in their children's education.

Even in the case of parental family structure, the results of the analyses on parental involvement programs could offer some solace. Although, it is almost axiomatic that two-parent families, on average, are going to find it more facile to offer high levels of access to their children than one is going to uncover in the case of single-parent families, it is clear that at least a portion of that disadvantage that usually accrues to the dissolution of a given family structure can be redeemed. This potential is particularly important, because even if a family unit that is broken is reunited, it is vital in the interim for some strategy to be in place to help youth overcome the handicaps that are often associated with coming from a single-biological-parent family (Pong et al., 2003; Rodgers & Rose, 2002).

Understanding the Influence of Parental Involvement Programs

Via the utilization especially of meta-analysis and the examination of nationwide data sets it is now clear that parental involvement has a positive impact on children's academic achievement. Now that this has been determined, the focus of the research has been on the extent to which schools and other valuable institutions can initiate programs of parental participation that can also enhance student outcome. If one examines this possibility in a cursory way, it appears only logical that such programs would have a positive impact (Miedel & Reynolds, 1999; Slavin & Madden, 2006). If one chooses, however, to cogitate about the issue more thoroughly, one apprehends a potentially poignant reality, i.e. it is quite possible that the success of the expression of family involvement is contingent upon a certain degree of volunteerism (Jeynes, 2010). In other words, one could cogently argue that parental involvement yields bountiful outcomes because it is done voluntarily out of heartfelt beliefs and emotions such as love, commitment, responsibility and so forth (Jeynes, 2010). Two centuries ago, in fact, Johann Pestalozzi, one of the founders of the public schools, posed a rhetorical question. He asked why it was that children learn best at home. He then asserted that it was because they were loved at home (Pestalozzi, 1801, 1916). Indeed, one could easily add the word "voluntarily" to that declaration, because love is, among other things, an act of the will (Jeynes, 2010). A person makes a decision whether he or she will release love (May, 1970; Pagitt & Jones, 2007). There is no question that parental involvement, as it is almost axiomatically a voluntary expression that is relatively free from coercion, is the vast majority of time an expression of maternal or paternal love (Gatto, 2001; Hoover-Dempsey et al., 2002).

To the extent that it is true that involvement is described is a voluntary action and generally also one of love, it is conceivable that school-based programs that exhort parents to become actively engaged in education and in many cases is going to require involuntary participation, are bound to fail. Even if one is not predisposed to arrive at this conclusion, at a logical level one cannot help but conclude that such an outcome is possible (Mattingly et al., 2002). With this in mind, it is vital that at least these questions regarding parental involvement be addressed and answered.

First, to what extent is parental involvement diluted by calling on parents to involuntarily become involved, as opposed to when guardians voluntarily engage in it. One would clearly expect some degree of dilution simply from observing human nature. One can discern that people apply more inertia to their actions when they act voluntarily. Second, to what degree is it possible to teach parents to apply dimensions of participation that have proved to be successful in the application of parental engagement. Even if has been demonstrated via relatively recent sophisticated analyses that certain components of parental participation yield laudable efforts, it is not clear whether these attributes and practices can be taught (Jeynes, 2010).

Third, it is essential to determine whether the aspects of family engagement that are most efficacious when done as a voluntary act are also the most effective when originating from a school or community-based program (Jeynes, 2010). For example, the meta-analyses used in this study indicate that parental expectations may be the manifestation of engagement that is the most salient for the educational success of one's children when it is voluntarily expressed. What is undetermined, however, whether a school-, church-, or community-based program, for example, that exhorted family leaders to maintain high expectations of their offspring yield anything close to the same results one would obtain from the voluntary expression of these expectations.

Fourth, and related to the previous question, is whether the order of effectiveness of various components of voluntary parental involvement is even the same as one finds in programs designed to foster this behavior.

On the one hand, it seems reasonable to think that certain aspects of parental involvement are beneficial whether they are expressed voluntarily or involuntarily. Nevertheless, it is also true that when an institution exhorts parents to take initiatives of one type or another, family members may resist for one reason or another. For example, first, parents could easily interpret any parental interpretation mandate as meddling into their affairs (Borruel, 2002; Gatto, 2001). Second, family members might not even resent the intrusion of school leaders, but they might take issue with the specifics of the actual advice given. Third, unless the family possesses an intimate relationship with the school the family may not have a proclivity to act on that advice.

There are other questions too that social scientists might seek to answer before it is sagacious to proceed full force into funding myriad parental engagement programs. This is of course not to say that Americans should be dilatory about inaugurating such programs across the country. Rather, the United States education system should proceed out of a copious degree of knowledge rather than out of ignorance. American public policy has sometimes had a tendency to plunge into inaugurating an ostensibly promising and provocative idea without thoroughly examining its ramifications (Borruel, 2002; Gatto, 2001; Jeynes, 1999a). There is a patent need for American society generally and public policy makers specifically to become more cognizant about what the results and broader implication of parental involvement program will be before its promotion and initiation.

One Unintended Consequence of Programs

Although school-based programs sound desirable and appear to have the potential to really be a boon to student educational outcomes, one should also be cognizant of one of the potential pitfalls of such initiatives. Probably the most prominent possible quandaries is that in the ideal world mothers and fathers should themselves initiate efforts at parental participation. One can certainly logically argue that by launching such projects, educators could be usurping the role of the parent. That is to say, parents are looking increasingly to the schools to undertake tasks that the parents themselves should practice. For example, educators often clean students, or feed students, when parents will not (Gatto, 2001).

Ideas for Further Research

Although the research presented in this chapter answers several questions about the meritorious nature of parental involvement programs, it also should inspire social scientists to address other important questions regarding these programs. Two lines of research could especially prove fruitful. Given that this meta-analysis provides evidence that parental involvement programs help struggling urban students, social scientists should undertake more studies to determine which programs work best and why. Second, future studies could consider the effects of parental involvement programs on a broader range of outcome variables, in much the same way family scholars examine the influence of parental involvement generally. Such undertakings will give the academic community and the general populace a broader knowledge of the dynamics of family involvement programs.

Chapter 8

Parental Involvement and Family Structure's Influence on Educational Outcomes

An Intact Biological Parental Family Structure Facilitates Involvement

Ever since the study of family structure has emerged, there has been an understanding overt or unstated, that family engagement is easiest when an intact two-biological-parent family structure is present (Jeynes, 2003a, 2005b, 2007b). In fact, for decades social scientists did not aggressively study parental involvement for two reasons because: 1) such a high percentage of parents in the first half of the twentieth century was actively engaged in their children's education and 2) there was an assumption that parental involvement was highly correlated with family structure (Jeynes, 2003a, 2005b, 2007b). This latter assumption was not meant in any sense to disparage the efforts of many American single parents across the country. Rather, it emerged out of an understanding that it takes time and commitment to reach a level of involvement with which parents are satisfied (Jeynes, 2003a, 2005b, 2007b). The reality is that with only one parent caring for a child there is no other parent available to provide a "relief" to custodial mothers or fathers that every caretaker, no matter how skilled or energetic, needs in order to continue to function at the fullest rested capacity (Bengston, 2005).

It is also a reality that in certain highly populated urban areas, in particular, where the cost of living is especially high, it is very difficult for a single-parent to provide both a sufficient level of income and be available a plenteous level of time (Bengston, 2005; Wallerstein & Blakeslee, 2003). In such instances the parent generally makes a decision in one direction or the other. That is, they either decide to sacrifice a middle-class standard of living in order to be available personally to the child or they decide to pursue a more typical American monetary lifestyle, but at the expense of being available to the child at a level that most of those knowledgeable about children's needs would recommend (Bengston, 2005; Frost, 2005; Mack, 1997; Wallerstein & Blakeslee, 2003).

Historical Trends in Family Structure and Parental Involvement

As various educational historians and parental involvement researchers have pointed out, high levels of mother and father participation is hardly new. Such engagement was vivid even going back to the era of the Pilgrims and the Puritans (McClellan & Reese, 1988). Moreover, caregivers in the settlements and the United States maintained a high level of parental involvement for at least three centuries (Jeynes, 2007a). There are several reasons for this elevated level of participation, but clearly one of them was because it was an integral part of American culture to believe that parents were of central importance in schooling children (Eavey, 1964; Mack, 1997). As much as people in the United States valued the teaching profession, they surmised that the year-round love, nurturing, encouraging and educational support that parents was indispensable for children to succeed (Jeynes, 2007a). To the vast majority of Americans, teachers, although important, were active for only a portion of a given year and then not until a youth's fifth year or afterward. In contrast, they surmised that it was the first five years of a child's life that were both the most important and foundational to a child's intellectual development. In their view the family involvement at this point was particularly intense and in their minds it is consequently particularly unwise to equate the importance of the role of the teacher and the parent (Eavey, 1964; Mack, 1997).

In spite of this parental orientation in terms of educational importance, John Dewey convinced the American people that the industrial evolution required a change in educational orientation (Dewey, 1915, 1920, Lawson & Lean, 1964). To Dewey, just as the industrial revolution produced an emphasis on individual specialization, so did it require a new orientation toward educational specialization. From Dewey's perspective, teachers in their professionalism were to be regarded as such by parents and entrusted with the academic development of children. Dewey's approach was no doubt well meaning, but the result was to relegate the position of parents as instructors to a patent secondary level (Mack, 1997; Ryan & Cooper, 1992). This development was not only significant in and of itself, but it established a pattern in which over the last number of decades parents have increasingly looked to the schools to perform functions that had in the past been associated with parents (Mack, 1997; Ryan & Cooper, 1992; Stotsky, 1999).

There were several ways in which Dewey's new industrial model of schools contributed to the parental abdication of some of the responsibilities that had generally been heirs in the past. First, Dewey's model caused many parents to view teachers as the professionals responsible for the academic development of their children, which parents often believed reduced the time commitments that were necessary of their part. Second, this new paradigm as convenient because it reduced some of the guilt that mothers and fathers felt for accruing a growing number of hours in the workplace and reducing the number of hours they spent at home (Egan, 2002). Third, increasingly, first fathers and eventually mothers began to view themselves as the material providers for children rather than having the overwhelming degree of influence on the emotional development of children. Such a conclusion was also in harmony with Dewey's general belief that: a) parents (and teachers) needed to allow youth to explore the world for themselves free from the predispositions and presuppositions that adults usually encumber upon children (Dewey, 1902, 1915, 1990) and b) schools needed to direct children away from the values of their parents, so that they could develop their own values (Jeynes, 2007a). It as healthier, in Dewey's view, for children to procure their values from their own experiences and those of their peers than it was for their values to be instilled in them from the convictions and beliefs of their parents (Egan, 2002; Jeynes, 2007a). These perspectives that Dewey inculcated into his college students, colleagues, and American society at large changed how many Americans viewed the process of child rearing. Previous to Dewey, most Americans had viewed raising children as primarily the duty of the parent with supplementation on the part of the community (Jeynes, 2003a, 2005b, 2007b). Now, an increasing number of the nation's citizenry viewed it as a mutual compact between the parents and the state (Mack, 1997; Ryan & Cooper, 1992; Stotsky, 1999). And indeed, as time passed a debate emerged as to how much of the responsibility rested with the maternal and paternal facets and how much should be the responsibility of the state.

Just how much of these developments could be attributed to some of the realities of capitalism or even in the worst case, the brutalities of industrial development and how much could be blamed an emerging socialism of which John Dewey was a part, is difficult to determine. In fact, it may be disturbingly difficult to separate these two trends. That is, historically, cries for socialism have generally followed the excesses of capitalism that emerge when the latter is not morally restrained by love, compassion, and moral responsibility (Cohen, 2000; Hahnel, 2005). Nevertheless, it is also true that the change in parental roles and significance, as perceived in the schools particularly by the 1960s (by which time nearly every teacher had been trained in Deweyism) likely was one of many contributing factors to parents viewing the intact two-biological-parent family as having a less decisive role in rearing well adjusted children (Egan, 2002; Mack, 1997).

Parental Involvement Becomes More Difficult in the 1960s

In precisely 1963, after fourteen years of edging downward, the American divorce rate surged (U.S. Census Bureau, 2001). This rend was significant not only in its own right, but because the changing trends in family structure ultimately made father and mother involvement more difficult. More frequently than not, marital dissolution particularly made paternal participation more challenging because 90% of the time that there was parental absence, it was the father who as not available (Lamb, 1997). Nevertheless, even though it was generally the father who was absent, marital dissolution on average also ultimately made an impact on the levels of mother participation that were possible as well (Lamb, 1997). This is because there were now new financial and time pressures on the mother to financially provide for the family and perform everyday tasks such as working on the house and running various errands that often the family's father had done previously. Clearly, as a result of the surge in divorce rates and out-of-wedlock births, youth generally had less access not only to the father but also to the mother.

As a consequence of the rising tide of marital dissolutions, it was inevitable that social scientists should not only manifest a new interest in studying family structure, but also examine the axiom that American people had known for centuries, that maternal and paternal involvement had a wide array of benefits for children (Jeynes, 2003a, 2005b, 2007a, 2007b). Admittedly, there was a certain degree of irony to these undertakings by researchers. Clearly, academics truly convinced themselves that they were breaking new ground by "divulging" relationships that existed between parental family structure and school outcomes, as well as between parental involvement and those same outcomes (Jeynes, 2007a). In reality, American ministers, community leaders, parents, and teachers had been declaring these truths for centuries. The only difference is that academics now had the numbers to support what nearly all Americans already knew via common sense. However, with the rise of marital dissolution and the accompanying decline in the average level of parental involvement, there were now emotional reasons to challenge what nearly all had previously declared was common sense. When one goes through such a trauma as a marital breakup, about the last truth a person wants to acknowledge is that the failure of the marital union has wider implications for others that one loves, especially the children (Wallerstein & Blakeslee, 2003). Indeed, when one experiences such family trauma, one longs or comforting words of assurance that the ramifications of this decision are isolated and transitory (Bengston, 2005; Wallerstein & Blakeslee, 2003). Although that may be naturally what one wants to hear, consistent with previous common sense and the prevailing research, such is clearly not the general case. The fact, however, that many Americans experiencing marital dissolution were in no frame of mind to receive the realities of common sense probably made it necessarily for researchers to rediscover the value of family by presenting numbers from their myriad studies that confirmed what had long been held as widespread societal belief: parental family structure and the involvement of mothers and fathers in raising children were of crucial importance in raising well-balanced youth (Jeynes, 2002a, 2003a, 2005b, 2007b, 2010).

Divorce rates not only surged for the beginning of 1963, but they continued to increase for an unprecedented seventeen consecutive years, topping out and then essentially stabilizing in 1980 (U.S. Census Bureau, 2001). This unyielding upward trend caused concern enough among family scientists. A concurrent trend, however, only added to the concerns of the American public at large and particularly among politicians, ministers, and social workers.

That is, achievement test scores, after about eighty years of stability plummeted during precisely the same 1963–1980 period. It would not be overstating the typical American response at all to say that millions of its citizenry and leaders were alarmed (National Commission on Excellence in Education, 1983; Wirtz, 1977). Suddenly, Americans were concerned that the dissolution of a plethora of American families was about to have monumental implications for its future economic prosperity (National Commission on Excellence in Education, 1983; Wirtz, 1977). The reason is because it is understood by virtually all the political and economic leaders of the world that that the health of a country's school system ultimately has an impact on the Gross Domestic Product (GDP) (National Commission on Excellence in Education, 1983; U.S. Census Bureau, 2006). As one might expect, there is a certain degree of delay in the manifested relationship between the two, but the there is a copious degree of quantifiable data that indicate that the association is much more than mere coincidental juxtaposition (Directorate, 1999; National Commission on Excellence in Education, 1983; Stevenson & Stigler, 1992).

Generally speaking, there is about a ten-year delay between significant changes in the high school achievement of a nation and any changes in its economic output or standard of living (Directorate, 1999; National Commission on Excellence in Education, 1983; U.S. Census Bureau, 2006). This ten-year delay is logical because the high school achievement data covers the age span of approximately fifteen to eighteen years of age. Ten years after this point, at ages twenty-five to twenty-eight, these same individuals are usually active in the workforce and exert a considerable influence on GDP. Therefore, it only makes sense that about a ten-year delay in education's effect on GDP would be plausible. This puissant relationship between educational outcomes and GDP is evident in the educational histories of several major nations and territories including Japan, Korea, Hong Kong, Taiwan, China, and innumerable countries in South America, Africa, and Europe. It therefore should come as no surprise that when American achievement test scores, as measured by a host of both national and state assessments, seemingly fell off the precipice in 1963, that economic growth stalled beginning in 1973 (Directorate, 1999). Most major economists are agreed that the US economy has really never been the same as in 1973 (Geller, 1993; Heal & Chilinisky, 1991; Learsy, 2005). They assert that the nation's standard of living really has not changed since then (Directorate, 1999; National Commission on Excellence in Education, 1983; Learsy, 2005). That is, when one adjusts for inflation, any real increase in American GDP per capita since then has only been a result of the tremendous influx of women into the workforce and the citizenry's obsession with incurring massive amounts of debt in order to procure an unsustainable loan-backed lifestyle (Geller, 1993; Heal & Chilinisky, 1991; Learsy, 2005; U.S. Census Bureau, 2006).

As with myriad other developments in life, the American public became more focused on the family structure and involvement quandary as it became more evident that these family dynamics were having a dramatic impact on the economic conditions of the country (Berrick, 1995; Farley, 1996; National Commission on Excellence in Education, 1983). In the aftermath of the divorce surge of the 1960s and 1970s, welfare rolls swelled, inundated especially with women and children who were there owing either to divorce, or to pre-marital sex resulting in births during the mother's teens (Melody & Peterson, 1999; U.S. Department of Health & Human Services, 1998; U.S. Department of Justice, 1999). Beginning in the 1970s, in particular, an endless litany of research statistics became available providing a large storehouse of information adding credence to the claim that the teeming number of family transitions taking place in the United States was having devastating effects on the state of the economy and creating a new underclass of people inveterately caught in poverty and relegated to living in increasingly numerous enclaves that were worse than most slums, called the inner cities (Berrick, 1995; Edwards & Crain, 2007; Wilson, 1996). Some of the most notable of these statistics included data that most people who were persistently on welfare started there as a result of being an unwed teen with child and that half of all sexually active single males had their first sexual experience by the time they were eleven (U.S. Department of Health and Human Services, 1998; U.S. Department of Justice, 1999).

With this background in mind, new debates emerged in academic and policy-making circles regarding whether the US government was one of the forces inadvertently fostering this new sense of family and child crisis (Hamburg, 1992; Jencks, 1992). In other words, did the attempt under President Lyndon B. Johnson's Great Society and related initiatives to ease economic pressures for those in single parent households actually act as a major catalyst to encourage marital breakups and intercourse out of wedlock (Hamburg, 1992; Jencks, 1992)? That is, was the ostensible removal of many of the economic consequences for engaging in irresponsible relational behavior, including actions that might have provided short-term stimulation for oneself personally, but yielded patent deleterious consequences for the offspring in the long term, actually encouraging the incidence of divorce and premarital intercourse (Hamburg, 1992; Jencks, 1992). At the very minimum, it would be hard to argue that the social welfare proposals of the 1960s buttressed the strength of the family and discouraged behavior harmful to children. There is virtually no one who would argue that the government initiatives helped caregivers or potential caregivers act responsibly in the best interests of intact families and children. Rather, the debate concentrates on the extent of the damage, some averring that the consequences were minimal to nearly nil and others presenting research evidence indicating that the effects were prodigious (Hamburg, 1992; Jencks, 1992).

Research on the Influence of the Family Becomes More Prominent

However one dissects the above debate, it was almost axiomatic that a number of forces work at work in America causing some immense family changes and requiring that children make adjustments to a host of parental transitions that ushered in an era of academics considering the effects of family much more seriously and intently than had previously been the case. Surely, one needed to forget for the moment that the knowledge of academics about family dynamics clearly lagged behind that of the American public who for centuries had experienced the realities of family living on a personal level. But in a very real sense, the fact that the common sense of the public was well ahead of the ivory tower knowledge of America's scholars was almost a moot point (Davis-Kean, 2005; Krivy, 1978; McDonald & Robinson, 2009; Smith, 2009). Clearly, no matter what conclusions the academic world arrived at, Americans were already personally cognizant of the multifarious baleful manifestations that non-intact family structures were creating and nothing that the scholarly world contributed to the debate would change that. Nevertheless, Americans were also keenly aware that the results of university-based research drove government policies that could ultimately affect families.

Many in the American public were poignantly aware that government policies were usually implemented tended to be both tardy and insufficient. With this caveat in mind, however, many Americans were willing to live with these impediments as long as there was eventual government action taken. A salient, although somewhat disconcerting, example is the debate that extended for decades over whether children watching violence on television made it more likely for them to engage in acts of violence (Bandura, 1977). One can certainly intelligently posit that because the debate over whether witnessing acts of violence increased the likelihood of further violence was resolved in classics of religious and philosophical thought such as in the Old Testament and in ancient Greek literature, what emerged as a debate never should have been a debate at all. That is, any person with even the most rudimentary knowledge of religion, philosophy, and history should have been able to resolve this question with the greatest of ease. Nevertheless, because Sigmund Freud (1938) in his theory of catharsis challenged the veracity of this belief, academics were not quickly convinced and in fact usually chose to support Freudian theory and hypotheses rather than the wisdom that had accrued through the ages. In fact, academics sided with Freud so willingly that the issue was not even subject to much debate until a Stanford Professor Albert Bandura (1977) declared his belief that the common sense that had emerged over the ages was indeed correct. Naturally, he did not conceptualize his assertions quite this simply or else he probably would not have been published, but instead propounded a theory called Social Learning Theory, which simply restated this age-old truths that had represented apprehended common sense for most of recorded human history (Bandura, 1977).

Once Bandura propounded his theory a debate ensured for three-and-a-half decades regarding the effect of children watching violence on television. Amazingly, it was not until 1997 that the American Psychological Association finally concluded that after three-and-a-half decades of academic study, youth watching violence on television made it more likely for them to engage in such behavior themselves. It is rather astounding that it took social scientists an interminable length of time to reach a conclusion that had been acknowledged by wider society almost as long as there has been recorded history (Hock, 2005; Salkind, 2006).

It is true that social scientists have frequently trailed the general public in the extent of their understanding of the influences of family factors on youth. Because of this tendency, the general public has become increasingly skeptical about the role of academics in demonstrating any level of sagacity about future sociological trends. Nevertheless, the public often welcomes the involvement of academics in spite of this because they realize that research directs public policy (Davis-Kean, 2005; Krivy, 1978; McDonald & Robinson, 2009; Smith, 2009). As a result, even if they realize that public policy often responds decades after various trends have become entrenched in society, people nevertheless welcome these policy initiatives as a means of preventing a bad situation from becoming worse. Hence, most family scientists, parents, and teachers welcome a more intense study of the family by academics.

What is the relative importance of parental involvement and family structure?

It is unfortunate but true that this question is relatively hard to answer. This is largely because although it is true that research of parental family structure largely presaged the examination of the influence of involvement, rather than fuse into a comprehensive study of the most salient family variables, a dichotomy quickly developed between these two spheres of study. Of particular note is that it was very rare for family structure variables and parental engagement variables to be included in the same study (Jeynes, 2003a, 2005b, 2007b). Consequently, it became very difficult, in most studies, to distinguish between the effects of family structure and those of parental involvement. It was becoming more and more patent that the two variables were inextricably connected. In other words, it is becoming increasingly difficult to discuss the influence of parental involvement without acknowledging that much of what social scientists attribute to the influence of parental engagement is in actuality in part a result of a child coming from an intact family structure (Jeynes, 2010). Similarly, when a study indicates positive effects in coming from an intact parental family structure one manifestation of that advantage is having parents who, on average, are more involved in their children's schooling and upbringing.

Over the past four decades educators have been increasingly concerned about the degree to which parents are involved (or uninvolved) in their children's education. The presence of more parents in the work force, the fast pace of modern society as a whole, and the declining role of the family have all been reasons that some social scientists have suggested to explain an apparent decline in parental involvement in education.

Over the same time span, social scientists have examined the influence of family structure on educational outcomes (Jeynes, 2002a; McLanahan & Sandefur, 1994; Wallerstein & Lewis, 1998). These researchers have determined that coming from a single-parent divorced or widowed family and coming from a never-married single parent family are associated with lower achievement levels (Amato & Keith, 1991; Hetherington, Stanley-Hagan & Anderson, 1989). Additional studies have shown that the introduction of a non-biological parent into a family via parental remarriage and cohabitation lowers academic achievement even further (Hetherington & Jodl, 1994). Research indicates that family structure plays a large role in determining the extent to which parents can spend time with their children (Onatsu-Arvibani & Nurmi, 1997; Riley, 1996). The overall body of research along these lines indicates that: a) a biological parent not living in the home is less likely to be involved in a child's education largely due to accessibility issues and b) if a single parent works, that parent faces certain unique challenges that make it more difficult to be involved in his or her child's education than parents from intact families face (Jeynes, 2002a; McLanahan & Sandefur, 1994; Wallerstein & Lewis, 1998). Most research suggests that the primary reason why parental family structure influences children's academic success is the reduction in the access that a child has to parents and his or her personal resources (Crane, 1996; Morgan, Kitson, & Kitson, 1992).

Social scientists generally agree that family structure clearly influences the degree to which parents can be involved in their children's education (Jeynes, 2002a, Sanders, 1998). However, family structure is almost never included as a component of parental involvement nor is its impact compared to other aspects of parental involvement. Of course parental family structure measures more than merely parental involvement. Nevertheless, it is not logical to measure other aspects of the extent and quality of parental involvement input without considering the reality of this component of parental access. Part of the reason family structure is not examined in parental involvement studies is that, of the research done on parental involvement, only a small percentage of these studies distinguishes between specific aspects of parental involvement.

Although it seems illogical to examine parental involvement without considering whether both parents are even present in the home, the fact that this is rarely done reveals a broader problem in parental involvement research. Social scientists have frequently examined the effects of parental involvement in a general sense, but have only rarely sought to assess the influence of various components of parental involvement.

There is unquestionably a growing body of research that indicates that parental involvement does impact academic achievement in a positive way. Hara (1998) even asserts that increased parental involvement is the key to improving the academic achievement of children. Various studies indicate that parental involvement is salient in determining how well children do in school at both the elementary and secondary school levels (Christian et al., 1998; Mau, 1997; McBride & Lin, 1996; Muller, 1998; Singh et al., 1995). Research by Singh et al. (1995) suggests that the effects of parental involvement may be greater at the elementary school level. The effects of parental involvement manifest themselves in reading achievement (Jeynes, 2003a, 2005b, 2007b; Shaver & Walls, 1998), mathematics achievement (Muller, 1998; Peressini, 1998; Shaver & Walls, 1998), and in other subjects as well (Jeynes, 2003a, 2005b, 2007b; Zdzinski, 1996). The impact of parental involvement is so considerable is that it holds across all level of parental education, ethnicity, and locale (Bogenschneider, 1997; Deslandes et al., 1997; Griffith, 1996; Hampton et al., 1998; Mau, 1997; Villas-Boas, 1998).

In recent years this area of research has matured to a place in which social scientists desire to know more of the specifics about parental involvement. Parental involvement, after all, can be a vague term, which can mean countless different things to different people. In recent years some social scientists have attempted to more clearly define what is meant by parental involvement (Crouter et al., 1999).

Ballantine (1999) notes that there are many aspects of parental involvement and that it would be helpful if researchers would identify which aspects of parental involvement have the greatest benefit on children. Grolnick, Benjet, Kurowski, and Apostoleris (1997) assert that once the academic community knows what parental involvement consists of, it can predict what family and social attributes will contribute most to producing parents that participate in the educational experience of their children. But what aspects of parental involvement help the most? In addition, how does the impact of family structure, which is partially a measure of parental involvement compare with other components of parental involvement?

There is still a great deal of research that needs to be undertaken, regarding which aspects of parental involvement are the most important. In the last few years social scientists have attempted to become more specific in their studies, regarding just what they mean by parental involvement. Hoge, Smit, and Crist (1997) attempted to define parental involvement as consisting of four components: parental expectations, parental interest, parental involvement in school, and family community. They found that of the four components, parental expectations were the most important. Other research either qualifies or disputes these findings. Mau's (1997) findings indicated that while parental expectations were important, parental supervision of homework was very important. Mau also noted some racial differences in the types of parental involvement that parents engaged in. She found that while white parents were more likely to attend school functions than Asian and Asian American parents, the latter parents had higher expectations and their children did more homework. Since Asian and Asian American students generally academically outperformed white students, Mau questioned the importance of parents attending school functions. The small amount of research that has been done on the precise components of parental involvement that are most important suggest that more subtle aspects of parental involvement that involve the extent of contact and expectations are more essential than specific tasks such as attending school functions (Jeynes, 2003a, 2005b, 2007b). To the extent that this is true, family structure would seem to be one important measure of parental involvement. The type of family structure a parent comes from can often affect the amount of time parents spend with children and the quality of that time (Jeynes, 2002a; McLanahan & Sandefur, 1994; Wallerstein & Lewis, 1998).

Part of the reason for the dearth of research about what kinds of parental involvement helps the most stems from the fact that research on parental involvement frequently suffers from one or more of the following limitations: 1) many studies do not use a large nationally representative sample (Bauch & Goldring, 1995; Bronstein et al., 1994; Crouter et al., 1999; McBride & Lin, 1996); 2) the vast majority of studies obtain measures of parental involvement and academic achievement within the same time frame, raising questions about the direction of causality (Bauch & Goldring, 1995; Bronstein et al., 1994; Crouter et al., 1999; McBride & Lin, 1996); 3) the definitions that some studies use for parental involvement are often distinct to the study; and therefore it is difficult to know whether parental involvement, overall, is helpful for students or merely certain aspects of parental involvement (Christian et al., 1998); 4) given that the definitions of parental involvement are often distinct to the study, it is sometimes difficult to draw conclusions regarding which aspects of parental involvement are most helpful (Christian et al., 1998); and 5) some studies examine parental involvement in such a specific context (focusing on either a specific school subject or a specific ethnic group, etc.) that it is difficult to make generalizations to the general population (McBride & Lin, 1996; Muller, 1998; Peressini, 1998).

The only way to logically distinguish between the degree of influence contributed by family structure and that of parental involvement is to include both sets of variables in the same study. Unfortunately, very few studies incorporate both types of variables. Those studies that do incorporate both types of variables indicate that family structure variables appear to be more robust in their size than are parental engagement variables. The analysis included in this chapter will differentiate between family structure and parental involvement variables,

Methods

The population that NELS study draws from includes students who participated in the National Education Longitudinal Survey (NELS) for the years 1990 and 1992. This consisted of 18,726 students total. The U.S. Department of Education's National Center for Statistics sponsored the NELS project. The National Opinion Research Center (NORC) and NORC subcontractors designed the study. The Educational Testing Service (ETS) created the achievement tests used in this study. Of the students sampled 69% were white, 13% were Hispanic, 11% were African American, 6% were Asian, and 1% were Native American. The median family income level was between $40,000 and $50,000. Among the parents, 26% had at least a four-year college degree and 89% had earned a high school diploma.

This study has three purposes: 1) to determine the impact of parental family structure and other aspects of parental involvement on children's academic achievement; 2) to determine the impact of family structure in comparison to the other measures of parental involvement; and 3) to compare the impact of all measures of parental involvement to each other. This study also attempts to address many of the issues that limit one's ability to make specific conclusions about parental involvement, from the results of other studies that have examined this issue. The population that this study draws from includes students who participated in the National Education Longitudinal Survey (NELS) for the years 1990 and 1992. Therefore, this study uses a nationally representative sample and also examines the issue of parental involvement in a more general context. In order to address the issue of causality, the three parental involvement measures were taken from the 1990 (tenth grade) data set and the academic measures were taken from the 1992 (twelfth grade) data set. The family structure variable was taken from the 1992 (twelfth grade) data set. Finally, this study uses a broad set of measures for parental involvement and distinguishes them from one another sufficiently, in order to facilitate making conclusions regarding which aspects of parental involvement are the most helpful to adolescents.

From the NELS questionnaires parental involvement variables were created to be used in GLM regression analysis. For the purposes of this work, family structure will often be referred to as a parental involvement variable, even though it has a broader impact than this. One dummy variable ($PI1$) was created to distinguish between students who were from intact families (= 1) and those who are not. Three sets of dummy variables were created to measure different dimensions of parental involvement. A parental involvement variable ($PI2$) assessed the extent to which a parent was directly involved in helping their child with homework and in their child's social life. Those children whose parents checked their homework, helped with their homework, and knew their closest friends, were coded "yes" for this variable. Another parental involvement ($PI3$) measure was based on the extent to which a child discussed events at school with his or her parents. Those children who discussed school activities, classes, and things studied with parents were coded "yes" for this variable. Another parental involvement variable ($PI4$) measured the extent to which parents were involved in events at school. If parents at least occasionally attended school meetings, school events, and volunteered at school functions, the children were coded with "yes" for this variable.

Academic Achievement Variables

Standardized Tests

Standardized test scores were obtained using tests developed by ETS. IRT scores (Item Response Theory scores) were obtained for the Reading Comprehension Test, the Mathematics Comprehension Test, the Social Studies (History/Citizenship/Geography) Comprehension Test, the Science Comprehension Test, and the Test Composite (Reading and Math test results combined).

Other Independent Variables

Variables Involving Socio-economic Status

The socioeconomic status of a child's family was determined "using parent questionnaire data, when available." Five components composed the socioeconomic status variables: a) father's level of education; b) mother's level of education; c) father's occupation; d) mother's occupation; and e) family income.

The occupational data were recoded using the Duncan SEI (Socio-economic Index) scale, which was also used in the High School and Beyond Survey. If any of the components were missing from the parent questionnaire, equivalent or related questions were used from the student questionnaire to determine SES. Three coded SES variables were used.

Other Variables

Dummy variables were also created for the effect of belonging to each of the various minority races (Black, Hispanic, Asian, and Native American) and gender (female = 1). In this way the effects of each individual race could be compared to being Caucasian, rather than simply having a generic variable for race that would measure the effect of being a member of a variety of racial groups, e.g. non-white. Clearly the effects of being from one race vary from the rest and this method adjusts for this fact.

One missing data variable each was also created for data that was missing for family structure and race. A missing data variable was included for these variables as a means of ascertaining the effect of students whose answers were missing, so as to make the determination of the student's family structure or race impossible. Missing variables were coded with the value 1 when this information was missing; and were coded with the value 0 otherwise.

Models

Two models were used in analyzing the effects of family structure: the SES Model and the No-SES Model. Both models contained the parental involvement variables. Each model also possessed variables for gender and missing data. The SES model possessed variables for SES, while the No-SES Model did not. The use of these models is to obtain overall effects for family structure and to use models that are the most commonly used by social scientists so that the results of this study can be understood in reference to the work that other researchers have done. If controls are used in an educational research study, these are the most common variables used.

Regression analysis was used, using the general linear model, in the analyses. The regression coefficients that emerged were standardized into standard deviation units.

The numbers of children abiding in each family structure (in parentheses) included in this study are: 1) divorced single (1,902); 2) divorced remarried (2,395); 3) widowed single (339); 4) widowed remarried (47); 5) never-married single-parent (394); 6) cohabiting (493); and 7) separated (700). A total of 13,986 students lived in intact families.

Results

The results indicate that family structure and two of the three aspects of parental involvement positively impacted the academic achievement of children. Table 8.1 shows the regression coefficients for family structure variable and each of the other three measures of parental involvement, as well as for the other variables under study, using the No-SES Model. The betas indicate consistently statistically significant effects for parental family structure, parents discussing school with the students, and parent attendance at school events. The aspect of parental involvement that involved checking up on a student's homework and friends did not yield statistically significant effects.

Using the No-SES Model, the betas were largest for family structure for all the measures of academic achievement under study. The regression coefficients for family structure ranged from 0.30 for the Math test, $F(1, 12,983) = 253.88$, $p < 0.0001$, to 0.20 for the Reading test, $F(1, 12,985) = 111.33$, $p < 0.0001$. The regression coefficients for whether parents discussed school events with their child consistently produced the second largest effects. The regression coefficients for this variable ranged from 0.22 for the Reading, $F(1, 12,985) = 51.44$, $p < 0.0001$, and Social Studies tests, $F(1, 12,838) = 49.26$, $p < 0.0001$, to 0.17 for the Science test, $F(1, 12,898) = 31.88$, $p < 0.0001$. The regression coefficients for parents attending school events were weaker. The effects ranged from 0.17 for the Social Studies test, $F(1, 12,838) = 20.02$, $p < 0.0001$, to 0.10 for the Science test, $F(1, 12,898) = 27.17$, $p < 0.0001$. Checking up on a child's homework and friends did not yield statistically significant positive effects. In three cases the betas were not statistically significant and in two cases (the Social Studies and Science tests) the betas yielded statistically significant negative effects. The regression coefficient for the Social Studies test was 0.08, $F(1, 12,838) = 6.14$, $p < 0.05$, and −0.07 for the Science test it was, $F(1, 12,898) = 5.57$, $p < 0.05$.

Table 8.1 Effects (in standard deviation units) for parental involvement in the education of their adolescents for twelfth graders (1992), using the No-SES Model (N = 20,706)

Academic measure	Reading	Math	Social Studies
Intercept	4.79****	5.17****	5.31****
PI1-Family Structure	0.20****a	0.30****a	0.25****b
missing	−0.12***	−0.09***	−0.10***
PI2-Checking Up	−0.04	−0.05	−0.08*
PI3-Discussion	0.22****	0.18****	0.22****
PI4-Attendance	0.11**	0.16****	0.17****
Asian	0.12***	0.34****	0.08*
Hispanic	−0.47****	−0.53****	−0.60****
Black	−0.66****	−0.72****	−0.85****
Native American	−0.57****	−0.60****	−0.61****
Race missing	−0.88****	−0.80****	−0.77****
Gender	0.20****	−0.10****	−0.30****
R^2 for Model	0.12	0.14	0.13
R^2 Model Added by Family Structure Variable	0.03	0.05	0.04

Academic measure	Science	Composite
Intercept	5.53****	4.91****
PI1-Family Structure	0.25****a	0.27****a
missing	−0.11****	−0.11****
PI2-Checking Up	−0.07*	−0.04
PI3- Discussion	0.17****	0.21****
PI4-Attendance	0.10**	0.14***
Asian	0.21****	0.25****
Hispanic	−0.45****	−0.53****
Black	−0.60****	−0.74****
Native American	−0.64****	−0.62****
Race missing	−0.91****	−0.93****
Gender	0.16***	0.05***
R^2 for Model	0.14	0.13
R^2 Model Added by Family Structure Variable	0.04	0.05

Notes
* $p < 0.05$; ** $p < 0.01$; *** $p < 0.001$; **** $p < 0.0001$
a Different from all other parental involvement variables at a statistically significant level.
b Different from all other parental involvement variables, except discussion, at a statistically significant level.

Further statistical analysis using the Scheffe test also indicate that in most cases the effects for parental family structure were larger at a statistically significant level than for all other measures of parental involvement. Although parental family structure is treated as one variable, naturally the various kinds of

Table 8.2 Means and standard deviations for adolescents from the various family structures included in the NELS data set

Academic Measure	Adolescents from an Intact Family	Adolescents from a Divorced Family	Adolescents from a Divorced Remarried Family	Adolescents from a Never-Married Single-Parent Family	Adolescents from a Cohabitation Family	Adolescents from a Widowed Single Parent Family	Adolescents from a Widowed Remarried Family
Standardized Tests							
Math	53.46 (9.65)	51.67 (9.51)	51.04 (9.71)	45.14 (9.67)	47.27 (9.88)	50.64 (9.90)	46.44 (9.76)
Reading	52.68 (9.56)	51.40 (10.10)	51.29 (10.11)	45.25 (10.14)	46.06 (10.01)	50.36 (10.22)	45.03 (10.18)
Science	53.01 (9.64)	51.27 (9.93)	50.81 (10.01)	44.77 (10.05)	47.39 (9.87)	50.36 (9.94)	43.86 (9.97)
Social Studies	53.02 (9.56)	51.27 (10.19)	50.84 (10.15)	46.23 (10.20)	47.34 (10.07)	51.01 (10.22)	44.47 (10.12)
Composite	53.30 (9.57)	51.62 (9.84)	51.21 (9.92)	45.86 (9.88)	47.05 (9.91)	50.44 (9.90)	45.00 (9.88)

non-intact family structures had varying effects on academic achievement. Table 8.2 lists the means and standard deviations for the various kinds of family structure included in the 1992 NELS data set for the five standardized academic measures. The tests results varied considerably, by family structure, across all the standardized measures. Children from intact families obtained the highest test scores in each case, usually around 53 points across the various subjects. Children from never married single parent, widowed remarried, and cohabitation families generally earned the lowest test scores. Children from never-married single parent and widowed remarried families often obtained test scores that were around 45 points.

Table 8.3 lists the regression coefficients for each of the four measures of parental involvement, as well as for the other variables under study, using the SES Model. The addition of the SES variables lowers the absolute values for most of the corresponding regression coefficients, in comparison to those found using the No-SES Model. The additional of the SES variables especially impacted the regression coefficients for parents attending school functions. None of the regression coefficients for this variable were statistically significant. Even with the addition of the SES variables statistically significant effects emerged for all the academic variables for parental family structure and parents discussing school with the students. The regression coefficients for family structure ranged from 0.16 for the Math test, $F(1, 11,414) = 86.58$, p < 0.0001, to 0.08 for the Reading test, $F(1, 11,408) = 19.82$, p < 0.0001. The regression coefficients for whether parents discussed school events with their children ranged from 0.13 for the Reading $F(1, 11,408) = 8.78$, p < 0.0001, to 0.08 for the Science, $F(1, 11,341) = 5.05$, p < 0.01, and 0.08 for the Math, $F(1, 11,414) = 8.04$, p < 0.01, tests. Once again, checking up on a child's homework and friends did not yield statistically significant positive effects. For all five of the academic achievement variables the betas yielded statistically significant negative effects. The regression coefficients were as high as -0.13, $F(1, 12,838) = 17.24$, p < 0.0001, for the Social Studies test. The regression coefficients for parental family structure and parents discussing school with their children were statistically significantly different from the regression coefficients for parents attending school functions and parents checking up on a child's homework and friends.

Most studies that examine parental involvement do not include variables for family structure. Further analysis was therefore undertaken to determine what regression coefficients would emerge for the other three parental involvement variables, if the family structure variables were deleted. Table 8.4 lists the betas that resulted from this action, using the No-SES Model. The regression coefficient values were somewhat higher, once the family structure variables were removed. The regression coefficients for whether parents discussed school events with their child consistently produced the largest effects, once the family structure variables were removed. The regression coefficients for this variable ranged from 0.24 for the Reading, $F(1, 12,985) = 60.75$, p < 0.0001, and Social

Table 8.3 Effects (in standard deviation units) for parental involvement in the education of their adolescents for twelfth graders (1992), using the SES Model (N = 20,706)

Academic Measure	Reading	Math	Social Studies
Intercept	4.31****	4.63****	4.81****
PI1—Family Structure	0.08****b	0.16****a	0.12****b
missing	−0.14	−0.10	−0.11
PI2—Checking Up	−0.09**	−0.11***	−0.08*
PI3—Discussion	0.13****	0.08**	0.13****
PI4—Attendance	−0.02	0.03	0.05
SES Quartile 2	0.28****	0.28****	0.29****
SES Quartile 3	0.49****	0.54****	0.50****
SES Quartile 4	0.95****	1.06****	0.99****
Asian	0.06	0.26****	0.14****
Hispanic	−0.19****	−0.24****	−0.17****
Black	−0.47****	−0.51****	−0.41****
Native American	−0.34***	−0.33***	−0.38****
Race missing	−0.60**	−0.49**	−0.64***
Gender	0.23****	−0.06****	−0.13****
R^2 for Model	0.23	0.25	0.23
R^2 Model Added by Family Structure Variable	0.03	0.04	0.03

Academic Measure	Science	Composite
Intercept	5.05****	4.43****
PI1—Family Structure	0.13****a	0.13****b
missing	−0.11	−0.12
PI2—Checking Up	−0.12****	−0.11***
PI3—Discussion	0.08**	0.11****
PI4—Attendance	−0.02	0.01
SES Quartile 2	0.27****	0.33****
SES Quartile 3	0.48****	0.55****
SES Quartile 4	0.92****	10.07****
Asian	0.02	0.17****
Hispanic	−0.33****	−0.23****
Black	−0.68****	−0.52****
Native American	−0.38****	−0.36****
Race missing	−0.55**	−0.61****
Gender	−0.26****	0.09****
R^2 for Model	0.24	0.25
R^2 Model Added by Family Structure Variable	0.04	0.04

Notes
* $p < 0.05$; ** $p < 0.01$; *** $p < 0.001$; **** $p < 0.0001$
a Different from all other parental involvement variables at a statistically significant level.
b Different from all other parental involvement variables, except discussion, at a statistically significant level.

Table 8.4 Effects (in standard deviation units) for parental involvement in the education of their adolescents for twelfth graders (1992), using the No-SES Model (N = 20,706)

Academic Measure	Reading	Math	Social Studies
PI2—Checking Up	−0.02	−0.03	−0.06
PI3—Discussion	0.24****	0.21****	0.24****
PI4—Attendance	0.13***	0.20****	0.20****

Academic Measure	Science	Composite	
PI2—Checking Up	−0.05	−0.03	
PI3—Discussion	0.19****	0.24****	
PI4—Attendance	0.13***	0.18****	

Notes
* $p < 0.05$; ** $p < 0.01$; *** $p < 0.001$; **** $p < 0.0001$
a Different from all other parental involvement variables at a statistically significant level.
b Different from all other parental involvement variables, except discussion, at a statistically significant level.

Table 8.5 Effects (in standard deviation units) for parental involvement in the education of their adolescents for twelfth graders (1992), using the SES Model (N = 20,706)

Academic Measure	Reading	Math	Social Studies
PI2—Checking Up	−0.08**	−0.10**	−0.12****
PI3—Discussion	0.14****	0.09**	0.13****
PI4—Attendance	−0.01	0.05	0.06

Academic measure	Science	Composite	
PI2—Checking Up	−0.11****	−0.10***	
PI3—Discussion	0.09**	0.12****	
PI4—Attendance	−0.02	0.02	

Notes
* $p < 0.05$; ** $p < 0.01$; *** $p < 0.001$; **** $p < 0.0001$
a Different from all other parental involvement variables at a statistically significant level.
b Different from all other parental involvement variables, except discussion, at a statistically significant level.

Studies tests, $F(1, 12,838) = 59.39$, $p < 0.0001$, to 0.19 for the Science test, $F(1, 12,898) = 40.76$, $p < 0.0001$. The regression coefficients for parents attending school events ranged from 0.20 for the Math, $F(1, 12,983) = 27.59$, $p < 0.0001$, and Social Studies tests, $F(1, 12,838) = 27.68$, $p < 0.0001$, to .19 for the Science test, $F(1, 12,898) = 40.76$, $p < 0.0001$. Checking up on a child's homework and friends did not yield any statistically significant effects in either a positive or negative direction.

Table 8.5 lists the betas for the same three parental involvement variables, once the family structure variable had been removed, using the SES Model. The regression coefficient values were slightly more positive than in the case of using the SES Model with the family structure variable removed. The regression coefficients for parents discussing school with the students ranged from 0.14 for the Reading test, F (1, 11,408) = 19.90, p < 0.0001 to 0.09 for the Science, F (1, 11,341) = 8.48, p < 0.01, and Math, $F(1, 11,414) = 0.60$, p < 0.01 tests. The regression coefficients for parents attending school events did not yield any statistically significant effects. Checking up on a child's homework yielded negative statistically significant results for all five of the academic achievement variables under study. The regression coefficients for this variable ranged from −0.12 for the Social Studies test, $F(1, 11,292) = 14.94$, p < 0.0001 to −0.08 for the Reading test, $F(1, 11,408) = 7.70$, p < 0.01.

In order to address issues of causality, parental involvement variables were used from the tenth grade wave of data. However, in order to make certain that the effects for the various components of parental involvement were not underestimated, analyses were also done using twelfth grade measures of parental involvement. No statistically significant differences emerged between the betas for the twelfth grade measures for parental involvement and the tenth grade measures.

Conclusion

This study supports the notion that coming from an intact family and other measures of parental involvement have a positive impact on academic achievement. In addition, it appears that the adolescents' access to the parents, both in terms of parental availability (as measured by whether a child was from an intact family) and in terms of the extent to which an adolescent discussed school events with parents, had a greater impact on academic achievement than more ostensibly direct parental participation (parental involvement in school functions and keeping up with a student's homework). As noted in the results section, the regression coefficients for parental family structure and parents discussing school with their children were statistically significantly different from the regression coefficients for parents attending school functions and parents checking up on a child's homework and friends, using the SES Model. Sometimes, in fact, parental involvement in the sense of keeping up with an adolescent's homework and social life had a negative impact on academic achievement. This result might have emerged because struggling adolescents need their parents to check on these matters more. Therefore, this particular effect may indicate more about the adolescent than the influence of parental involvement.

The single greatest parental involvement indicator was whether a child came from an intact family. The extent to which parents discussed school issues and attended school functions also had a positive impact on adolescent academic achievement. Although the regression coefficients for each of these facets of parental involvement were not especially large, one must remember that if you add the regression coefficients of the variables for family structure, discussion about school, and attending school functions, the effects for parental involvement actually become quite large. Adding the betas from these three variables would add an average of nearly 0.6 of a standard deviation to the academic outcomes using the No-SES Model. Using the SES Model adding the betas from these three variables would add an average of about 0.25 of a standard deviation to the academic outcomes.

The fact that parental family structure and discussion about school were the most important facets of parental involvement may point to the importance of the communication aspect of parental involvement. Clearly communication with parents is generally going to be higher if there are two parents a child can communicate with rather than one. On average, the presence of two parents will make it easier for children to: a) obtain help with their homework, b) obtain emotional support when needed, c) enjoy a sense of family stability which facilitates performing well academically; and d) grow intellectually as a result of interacting with close adults. Discussing school events with parents also points to the importance of communication. Parents' participation in school events did produce consistent statistically significant effects, but it is apparently consistent parental communication in the form of discussions that is apparently more important. The fact that parental discussion was more important than parental attendance might also indicate that day-by-day parental involvement may be more important than whether parents attend sporadic school events. These results lend some support to an increasing body of literature that points to the importance of family communication in producing emotionally healthy outcomes (Hoge et al., 1997; Unger, McLeod, Brown, & Tressell, 2000).

A fact worth noting is that the inclusion of the SES variables reduced the effects for parental involvement versus those that emerged using the No-SES Model. This is not a surprise, given the fact that past research indicates that there is a high correlation between SES and parental involvement. Highly educated parents, for example, are often more likely to acknowledge the importance of parental support in education (Legutko, 1998; Mulroy et al., 1998; Portes & MacLeod, 1996). Parents with a high level of SES are also likely to acknowledge the primacy of a good education in terms of living a successful adult life (Grayson, 1999; Mulroy et al., 1998; Portes & MacLeod, 1996). Determining the causal relationship between parental involvement and SES is a difficult one. One can argue that some of the same qualities that help make a parent supportive are also likely to produce parents of high SES. For example, a parent who believes trying hard in school is important is more likely than most to be highly educated and is also more likely than most to support his or her children as they pursue education. In addition, a person with a supportive personality is more likely to excel as a boss and is also more likely to excel as an involved parent. One can make the argument that the addition of the SES variables dilutes the effects for parental involvement not because the causal nature of SES so much, as the fact that there are other causal components beyond SES and parental involvement that influence both variables. In terms of SES specifically, a growing number of studies indicate that the level of SES can be a result of various other factors, rather than a primary cause (Gortmaker et al., 1993; Zakrisson & Ekehammer, 1998). Crane (1996) demonstrated that the influence of SES, as a causal variable, could be overestimated if mediating family factors are not taken into account. More research is needed is effectively understand the relationship between parental family structure and SES.

The results of this study should make parents, counselors, and educators more sensitive to the various kinds of parental support that there are, and the extent to which they can contribute to positive academic outcomes for children. Furthermore, the results suggest that some of the more subtle aspects of parental support and involvement, such as communication and parental family structure may impact children's educational outcomes more than some of the more overt typical aspects of parental involvement that are more often regarded as important. The results of this study suggest that although there are numerous single parents involved in their children's education, every person has human limitations. Consequently, it is very difficult for one parent to give children the level of educational benefits that are normally associated with children having two parents. Counselors and educators need to be sensitive to this fact. The fact that family structure and communication are the aspects of parental involvement that, in this study, had the greatest impact on children's educational outcomes suggests that parental availability has a considerable impact on children's achievement. In many respects, these results can be encouraging to many parents. This is because these results suggest that it is more important that parents simply be available and interact with their children about school than rush off to the latest school function or make sure their children have answered every single homework problem.

This chapter has attempted to specifically address what aspects of parental involvement are most important in affecting the academic achievement of adolescents. It is hoped that this chapter will contribute to understanding the importance of intact families and communication as salient aspects of parental involvement. More research is needed to aid in the understanding of why intact families and communication play the major role that they do.

Does Parental Involvement Compensate for the Effects of Divorce (or Single Parenthood)?

Over the past thirty-five years a considerable degree of research has emerged indicating that parental divorce and remarriage generally exert downward pressure on the academic achievement of children (McLanahan & Sandefur, 1994, Wallerstein & Lewis, 1998). Some social scientists believe that the reason for these findings may rest with the fact that children of divorce usually spend less time with both biological parents overall (Wallerstein & Lewis, 1998). As a result, in these families there tends to be less parental involvement in education. Research has consistently indicated that a higher level of parental involvement often produces increases in the academic achievement of children (Deslandes et al., 1997, Mau, 1997, Villas-Boas, 1998). In recent years, family scientists have sought to examine family factors that might neutralize the effects of parental divorce and remarriage. Some social scientists have suggested the parents and/ or stepparents of divorce who are actively involved in school and in the education of their children may not experience the downward effects that divorce and remarriage usually exert on the academic achievement of children (Bronstein et al., 1994, Hetherington, 1992). They believe that if one considers the effects of parental involvement, the effects of parental divorce and remarriage will disappear. The purpose of this study is to examine whether considering the effects of parental involvement on the academic achievement of children will cause the effects of divorce and remarriage to disappear.

The fact that parental divorce and remarriage exert a downward pressure on the academic achievement of children is well documented (Cherlin, 1992; Hetherington & Clingempeel, 1992; Jeynes, 2002a, 2002b, 2002c, 2006b; McLanahan & Sandefur, 1994; Wallerstein, Corbin, & Lewis, 1988). Research on stepfamilies stands at a much less advanced stage than research on single-parent families (Jeynes, 2006b; Wertlieb, 1997). The primary reason for this rests in the fact that relatively few studies on stepfamilies have examined the impact of this family structure on academic achievement (Booth & Dunn, 1994; Emery, 1988; Ganong & Coleman, 1994; Jeynes, 2006b, 2007a; Wertlieb, 1997). Nevertheless, a growing body of research indicates that parental remarriage appears to have somewhat of a negative influence on the academic outcomes of children (Hetherington & Jodl, 1994; Popenoe, 1994; Zill, 1994; Zill & Nord, 1994).

Given that most researchers now acknowledge the effects of parental divorce and remarriage on school outcomes by children, the question that is now commonly debated is why this is the case. Generally, there are three schools of thought that have become the most prominent in explaining the effects of divorce and remarriage on the educational outcomes of children: the "socioeconomic" school of thought, the "non-parental adjustment" school of thought, and the "access to parents" school of thought. Researchers from the socioeconomic school of thought emphasize that non-intact family structures, almost without exception, lower a family's socioeconomic status (Bane & Jargowsky, 1988; McLanahan & Sandefur, 1994; Neighbors, Forehand, & Armistead, 1992; Thomson, Hanson, & McLanahan, 1994). Therefore, when a change in family structure takes place in which the income, employment, and education resources are reduced, the negative effects that are normally associated with coming from a family of lower socioeconomic status are released (Bane & Jargowsky, 1988; McLanahan & Sandefur, 1994). The second school of thought is the "non-parental adjustment" school of thought. Social scientists from this perspective assert that the presence of a caregiver that is not the child's natural parent is a source of stress for most children (Anderson & Rice, 1992; Hetherington & Clingempeel, 1992; Walsh, 1992; Zill & Nord, 1994).

Recent research suggests that all three schools of thought are helpful to some degree in explaining the effects of parental family structure (Jeynes, 2000b; McLanahan & Sandefur, 1994). Nevertheless, if one focuses on issues of causality, it appears that the "access to parents" school of thought probably explains the largest portion of the academic disadvantage that children of divorce face (Allison & Furstenberg, 1989; Furstenberg, 1988; Jeynes, 1998). Therefore, it is this school of thought that will be the focus of this research study. Those that support the "access to parents" school of thought claim that divorce causes the child to have reduced access to a least one parent. These social scientists assert that reduced access to the natural parent has negative and definite impacts on the psychological well being of a child and one way these effects will manifest themselves is in the academic achievement of the child (Cherlin, 1992; Hetherington, 1989; Kelly, 1992). Researchers that adhere to this school of thought generally fall into one of two categories. First, there are those who believe that there are certain advantages that come with living with two natural parents that are very difficult, if not impossible, to duplicate if one of those parents is absent (Cherlin, 1992; Wallerstein & Blakeslee, 1989; Wallerstein et al., 1988; Zill & Nord, 1994). This perspective will be referred to as the "broken home" sub-school of thought. Other researchers believe that if there is still a large degree of access to both parents following the divorce, the disadvantages that one normally associates with parental divorce can be overcome, (Hetherington et al., 1989; Hetherington & Jodl, 1994). This perspective will be referred to as the "compensation" sub-school of thought A number of researchers suggest that parental involvement in education can almost totally overcome the effects that parental divorce generally has on educational outcomes (Hetherington et al., 1989; Mechanic and Hansell, 1989).

There is no question that parental involvement does, on average, increase the academic achievement of children. Hara (1998) even asserts that increased parental involvement is the key to improving the academic achievement of children. Various studies indicate that parental involvement plays an important role in determining how well children do in school at both the elementary and secondary school levels (Christian et al., 1998; Mau, 1997; McBride & Lin, 1996; Muller, 1998; Singh et al., 1995). Research by Singh et al. (1995) suggests that the effects of parental involvement may be greatest at the elementary school level. Deslandes, Royer, Turcott, and Bertrand (1997) reported results that suggest that the parenting style may determine how much of an effect the involvement of parents has at the secondary level. The effects of parental involvement manifest themselves in reading achievement (Jeynes, 2002a; Shaver & Walls, 1998), mathematics achievement (Muller, 1998; Peressini, 1998; Shaver & Walls, 1998), and in other subjects as well (Jeynes, 2002a; Zdzinski, 1996).

The place of parental involvement is sufficiently prominent so that it affects academic achievement no matter what the economic background (Shaver & Walls, 1998) of the student's family and no matter what is the educational level of the parents (Bogenschneider, 1997). The research evidence also indicates that parental involvement positively impacts the academic achievement of children, no matter what the racial heritage is of the children being studied (Mau, 1997; Sanders, 1998; Villas-Boas, 1998). A study by Muller (1998) suggests that parental involvement may help reduce the mathematics achievement gap between boys and girls. Studies done on international children indicate that the positive effects of parental involvement hold for students overseas as well (Deslandes et al., 1997; Mau, 1997; Villas-Boas, 1998). The willingness of parents to participate in the education of their children apparently also transcends the distinction between whether a school is from the inner city or the suburbs (Griffith, 1996; Hampton et al., 1998). Research by Bauch and Goldring (1995) suggests that high levels of parental involvement are more easily achieved when parents have chosen a particular school for their child. Other studies indicate that parental involvement is greatly facilitated if a child comes from an intact family (Onatsu-Arvibani & Nurmi, 1997), when the parents are enthusiastic generally (Zellman & Waterman, 1998), and if the family is religious (Riley, 1996; Sanders, 1998).

Methods

The population that this study draws from includes students who participated in the National Education Longitudinal Survey (NELS) for the years 1988, 1990, and 1992. Therefore, this study uses a nationally representative sample and also examines the issue of parental involvement in a more general context.

In order to address the issue of causality, for the 1992 (twelfth grade) analysis, parental involvement measures were taken from the 1990 (tenth grade) data set and the academic measures were taken from the 1992 (twelfth grade) data set. From the NELS questionnaires family structure variables were created to be used in GLM regression analysis. Family structure dummy variables were created for divorce ("yes" for this dummy variable = 1) and remarriage ("yes" for this dummy variable = 1).

From the NELS questionnaires parental involvement variables were created to be used in GLM regression analysis. Three sets of dummy variables were created to measure different dimensions of parental involvement. The first parental involvement variable assessed the extent to which a parent was directly involved in helping their child with homework and in his or her child's social life. Those children whose parents checked their homework, helped with their homework, and knew their closest friends, were coded "yes" for this variable. The second parental involvement measure was based on the extent to which a child discussed events at school with his or her parents. Those children who discussed school activities, classes, and things studied with parents were coded "yes" for this variable. A third parental involvement variable measured the extent to which parents were involved in events at school. If parents at least occasionally attended school meetings, school events, and volunteered at school functions, the children were coded with "yes" for this variable.

Academic Achievement Variables

Standardized Tests

Standardized test scores were obtained using tests developed by ETS. IRT scores (Item Response Theory scores) were obtained for the Reading comprehension test, the Mathematics comprehension test, the Social Studies (History/Citizenship/Geography) comprehension test, the Science comprehension test, and the Test Composite (Reading and Math test results combined).

Other Independent Variables

Variables Involving Socio-economic Status

The socioeconomic status of a child's family was determined "using parent questionnaire data, when available." Five components composed the socioeconomic status variables: a) father's level of education; b) mother's level of education; c) father's occupation; d) mother's occupation; and e) family income.

The occupational data were recoded using the Duncan SEI (Socio-economic Index) scale, which was also used in the High School and Beyond Survey. If any of the components were missing from the parent questionnaire, equivalent or related questions were used from the student questionnaire to determine SES. Three coded SES variables were used.

Other Variables

Dummy variables were also created for the effect of belonging to each of the various minority races (Black, Hispanic, Asian, and Native American) and gender (female = 1). One missing data variable each was also created for data that was missing for family structure and race.

Models

Two models were used in analyzing the effects of family structure: the SES Model and the No-SES Model. Both models contained the parental involvement variables. Each model also possessed variables for gender and missing data. The SES model possessed variables for SES, while the No-SES Model did not. The use of these models is important for the following reasons:

(a) to obtain overall effects for family structure;
(b) to use models that are the most commonly used by social scientists so that the results of this study can be understood in reference to the work that other researchers have done. If controls are used in a family research study, these are the most common variables used.

Regression analysis was used, using the general linear model, in the analyses.

Results

The results indicate that consistent effects for divorce emerged using the No-SES Model for the eighth grade data set even with the inclusion of the parental involvement variables. Table 9.1 shows the betas for divorce, remarriage, and the other variables under study. For the standardized measures, the effects for divorce showed very little variation from one test to another. In all five cases, the effects for divorce were about one tenth of a standard deviation. The betas were exactly -0.10 for the Math, $F(1, 23,628) = 17.51$, $p < 0.0001$, Science, $F(1, 23,615 = 19.76$, $p < 0.0001$, Test Composite, $F(1, 23,696) = 18.71$, $p < 0.0001$, and Social Studies, $F(1, 23,524) = 17.71$, $p < 0.0001$, tests. For the Reading test the beta was -0.09, $F(1, 23,642) = 14.76$, $p < 0.0001$. In the case of the non-standardized measure, being left back a grade, the effects was larger at 0.16, $F(1, 22,770) = 41.42$, $p < 0.0001$. Although the effects for remarriage all impacted educational outcomes in a slightly negative way, as indicated by the direction of the beta, in only one case was this to a statistically significant degree. This statistically significant effect emerged for the Math test, $F(1, 23,628) = 6.95$, $p < 0.01$. In most case the other betas approached, but did not exceed, statistical significance.

Table 9.1 Effects (in standard deviation units) for divorce and remarriage on the academic achievement of their adolescents for twelfth graders, using the No-SES Model (1988) (N = 25,599)

Academic Measure	Reading	Math	Science	Social Studies	Test Composite
Intercept	4.90****	5.23****	5.37****	5.26****	5.06****
Divorce	−0.09****	−0.10****	−0.10****	−0.10****	−0.10****
Remarriage	−0.02	−0.08**	−0.04	−0.05	−0.05
Missing	0.00	−0.00	0.00	−0.27***	−0.00
PI1—Checking Up	−0.01	−0.06****	−0.02	0.02	−0.04**
PI2—Discussion	0.44****	0.45****	0.40****	0.41****	0.48****
PI3—Attendance	0.07****	0.09****	0.06***	0.09**	0.09****
Asian	0.01	0.25****	0.02	0.07**	0.13****
Hispanic	−0.53****	−0.57****	−0.55****	−0.53****	−0.59****
Black	−0.59****	−0.68****	−0.67****	−0.56****	−0.69****
Native American	−0.64****	−0.61****	−0.71****	−0.66****	−0.68****
Race missing	−0.62****	−0.66****	−0.67****	−0.66****	−0.69****
Gender	0.16****	−0.08****	−0.16****	−0.12****	0.04***

Note
* p < 0.05; ** p < 0.01; *** p < 0.001; **** p < 0.0001

A different pattern of effects arose using the SES Model (see Table 9.2). For the standardized measures, it was the effects for remarriage that were consistently statistically significant rather than the effects for divorce. The betas ranged from −0.11 for the Math test, $F(1, 23,620) = 17.74$, $p < 0.0001$, to −0.06 for the Reading test, F $(1, 23,634) = 4.35$, $p < 0.05$. Nevertheless, for the non-standardized measure, being left back a grade, it was the beta for divorce that was again statistically significant at 0.10, $F(1, 22,765) = 18.98$, p <0.0001, rather than the beta for remarriage. The betas for divorce were not statistically significant for the standardized measures and the effects for remarriage were not statistically significant for being left back a grade.

Using both the No-SES and the SES Models, the aspect of parental involvement that impacted academic achievement the most was a child discussing school events with his or her parents. The effects for this variable were much larger for the standardized measures than the non-standardized measure. The effects for the discussion variable were over four-tenths of a standard deviation using the No-SES Model and two-tenths of a standard deviation using the SES Model. The effects were only about one-tenth of a standard deviation for the non-standardized measure of being left back a grade. In a supplementary analysis in which family structure was used as a variable, rather than parental divorce and remarriage, the discussion variable was second in absolute value only to the family structure variable. The family structure variable in this supplementary analysis was determined by whether a student resided in an intact family.

Table 9.2 Effects (in standard deviation units) for divorce and remarriage on the academic achievement of their adolescents for twelfth graders, using the SES Model (1988) (N = 25,599)

Academic Measure	Reading	Math	Science	Social Studies	Composite
Divorce	0.02	0.02	−0.00	0.00	0.02
Remarriage	−0.06*	−0.11****	−0.07**	−0.09**	−0.09***
Missing	−0.00	−0.00	0.00	−0.02	−0.04
PI2—Checking Up	0.01	−0.04	−0.00	−0.00	−0.01
PI3—Discussion	0.32****	0.32****	0.29****	0.23****	0.34****
PI4—Attendance	−0.01	0.00	−0.01	−0.00	−0.00
SES Quartile 2	0.27****	0.25****	0.23****	0.29****	0.28****
SES Quartile 3	0.48****	0.45****	0.43****	0.49****	0.50****
SES Quartile 4	0.88****	0.95****	0.81****	0.88****	0.99****
Asian	−0.02	0.24****	0.01	0.06*	0.11****
Hispanic	−0.30****	−0.33****	−0.34****	−0.31****	−0.34****
Black	−0.42****	−0.50****	−0.51****	−0.39****	−0.50****
Native American	−0.50****	−0.45****	−0.59****	−0.52****	−0.51****
Race missing	−0.46****	−0.50****	−0.53****	−0.50****	−0.52***
Gender	0.19****	−0.05****	−0.13****	−0.09****	0.07****

Note
* p < 0.05; ** p < 0.01; *** p < 0.001; **** p < 0.0001

Table 9.3 Effects (in standard deviation units) for divorce and remarriage on the academic achievement of their adolescents for twelfth graders, using the No-SES Model (1992) (N = 20,706)

Academic Measure	Reading	Math	Science	Social Studies	Composite
Intercept	5.04****	5.21****	5.34****	5.26****	5.13****
Divorce	−0.08****	−0.14****	−0.11****	−0.11****	−0.11****
Remarriage	0.08	−0.05	−0.06	−0.03	−0.05
Missing	−0.27****	−0.29***	−0.29****	−0.27***	−0.30****
PI1—Checking Up	−0.04	0.05	−0.01	−0.02	−0.02
PI2—Discussion	0.40****	0.43****	0.38****	0.39****	0.44****
PI3—Attendance	0.11****	0.15****	0.09****	0.08***	0.14***
Asian	0.03	0.33****	0.03	0.15****	0.19****
Hispanic	−0.49****	−0.54****	−0.61****	−0.47****	−0.56****
Black	−0.68****	−0.77****	−0.89****	−0.64****	−0.77****
Native American	−0.60****	−0.62****	−0.62****	−0.69****	−0.65****
Race missing	−0.70****	−0.64****	−0.65****	−0.90****	−0.73****
Gender	0.17****	−0.13****	−0.34****	−0.19****	0.02

Note
* p < 0.05; ** p < 0.01; *** p < 0.001; **** p < 0.0001

Table 9.3 lists the betas for divorce, remarriage, and the other variables under study using the No-SES Model for the twelfth grade data set. For the standardized measures, the effects for divorce were somewhat larger than they were using

Table 9.4 Effects (in standard deviation units) for divorce and remarriage on the academic achievement of their adolescents for twelfth graders, using the SES Model (1992) (N = 20,706)

Academic Measure	Reading	Math	Science	Social Studies	Composite
Intercept	4.52****	4.63****	4.83****	4.71****	4.54****
Divorce	0.02	−0.03	−0.02	−0.01	−0.00
Remarriage	−0.09**	−0.12****	−0.12****	−0.09**	−0.11***
Missing	−0.08	−0.02	−0.10	−0.00	−0.04
PI2—Checking Up	0.04	−0.03	0.00	−0.01	0.01
PI3—Discussion	0.27****	0.29****	0.25****	0.26****	0.30****
PI4—Attendance	0.03	0.06**	0.02	−0.00	0.05
SES Quartile 2	0.30****	0.29****	0.28****	0.30****	0.32****
SES Quartile 3	0.49****	0.55****	0.48****	0.51****	0.56****
SES Quartile 4	0.93****	1.05****	0.92****	0.97****	1.06****
Asian	0.01	0.27****	0.00	0.12***	0.15****
Hispanic	−0.22****	−0.26****	−0.34****	−0.20****	−0.26****
Black	−0.49****	−0.55****	−0.70****	−0.45****	−0.56****
Native American	−0.37****	−0.36****	−0.39****	−0.45****	−0.39****
Race missing	−0.44**	−0.42**	−0.45**	−0.65****	−0.48***
Gender	0.20****	−0.09****	−0.28****	−0.15****	0.06****

* $p < 0.05$; ** $p < 0.01$; *** $p < 0.001$; **** $p < 0.0001$

the eighth grade data set. The largest regression coefficient in absolute value, −0.14, emerged for the Math test, $F(1, 14,182) = 33.86$, $p < 0.0001$. The regression coefficients for the Science, $F(1, 14,079) = 22.15$, $p < 0.0001$, Test Composite, $F(1, 14,212) = 23.76$, $p < 0.0001$, and Social Studies tests, $F(1, 14,010) = 22.15$, $p < 0.0001$, were all −0.11. For the Reading test the beta was −0.08, $F(1, 14175) = 10.09$, $p < 0.01$. The regression coefficients for the twelfth grade non-standardized measures were −0.08 for being left back a grade, $F(1, 18,960) = 13.07$, $p < 0.001$ and −0.08 for the Basic Core set of courses, $F(1, 17,099) = 11.57$, $p < 0.001$.

The pattern of regression coefficients was again different using the SES Model (see Table 9.4). For the standardized measures, the effects for remarriage were again consistently statistically significant rather than the effects for divorce. The betas ranged from −0.12 for the Math, $F(1, 12,329) = 15.55$, $p < 0.0001$, and Science, $F(1, 12,247) = 15.91$, $p < 0.0001$ tests to −0.09 for the Reading, $F(1, 12,317) = 8.43$, $p < 0.01$, and Social Studies, $F(1, 12,192) = 8.46$, $p < 0.01$, tests. However, in contrast to the effects that emerged for being left back a grade, for the eighth grade, the remarriage variable and not the divorce variable produced the statistically significant effects at −0.08 of a standard deviation, $F(1, 15,122) = 7.67$, $p < 0.01$. The effects for remarriage came close, but did not exceed statistical significance. The divorce variable did not produce any statistically significant effects.

Once again, the effects for children discussing school with their parents was the parental involvement variable that produced the largest regression coefficients in terms of their absolute values.

Discussion

The results of this study indicate that children of divorce trail their counterparts in intact families in terms of academic achievement, even when considering variables for parental involvement. In other words parental involvement does not explain all the effects for parental divorce and remarriage on academic success. In addition, high degrees of parental involvement on the part of single parent divorced parents is not sufficient to remove the academic disadvantage faced by children of divorce. The results do suggest that depending on whether or not one controls for SES, the pattern of regression coefficients does change. Using the No-SES Model, the variable for divorce, more than the variable for remarriage, exerts the downward pressure on academic success. Using the SES Model, the remarriage variable produces larger betas than the divorce variable. These results are not surprising and are consistent with other studies that show this same pattern (Amato and Ochiltree, 1987; Jeynes, 2002a, 2006b). These findings emerge because the act of remarriage generally raises the family SES level, especially the income component of SES. Concurrently, according to this study and various longitudinal studies, the act of remarriage apparently does not raise and may even reduce the educational outcomes of adolescents. These results therefore indicate that considering the increased level of SES that remarriage produces, one would expect that academic achievement would also rise. The negative regression coefficients that emerge using the SES Model simply reflect the fact that given the increased level of family SES that remarriage causes, there is no expected rise and even a slight decline in academic achievement.

Given that the regression coefficients used in this study are additive, this raises some concerns regarding the academic success of divorced reconstituted families. The act of parental remarriage does not help the already depressed levels of academic success experienced by children from divorced single-parent families.

Nevertheless, one should note that parental involvement does have an impact on academic achievement and it does in fact somewhat compensate for the downward pressure that is exerted by parental divorce and remarriage, on the academic success of adolescents. The variable for children discussing school events with their parents especially influenced academic success. In supplementary analyses in which family structure (i.e. whether a student resided in an intact family) was used as a variable, rather than parental divorce and remarriage, the discussion variable was second in absolute value only to the family structure variable. All the results taken together point to two prominent conclusions that emerge from this study. First, parental divorce and remarriage are significant enough events so that, as important as parental involvement is, the latter cannot totally compensate for the impact that parental divorce and remarriage have on academic achievement. Second, parental involvement does impact the academic success of children. Therefore parents from divorced and reconstituted families should be encouraged to be as involved as possible in their children's education. The results of this study primarily support the "broken home" school of thought of those who believe that there are certain advantages that come with living with two natural parents that are very difficult, if not impossible, to duplicate if one of those parents is absent (Cherlin, 1992; Wallerstein & Blakeslee, 1989; Wallerstein, et al., 1988; Zill & Nord, 1994).

The question arises as to why parental involvement does not totally compensate for the effects of divorce and remarriage. There are several possibilities. However, some of the most prominent involve drawing from the theories mentioned earlier. First, those theorists who espouse the "broken home" perspective as opposed to the "compensation" perspective argue that there are a lot of unseen benefits of living in an intact family that parental involvement cannot eliminate. The mere presence of a parent encourages an atmosphere of love, support, and stability that many researchers argue cannot be underestimated (Wallerstein & Lewis, 1998; Zill & Nord, 1994). Second, socioeconomic theory probably accounts for some of the difference as well. However, it should be noted that the effects for remarriage remained even after SES variables were included in the analysis. Third, the non-parental adjustment school of thought probably helps explain why the effects for remarriage remained even after the SES variables were included in the analysis. Researchers are gaining a greater appreciation for the fact that there are a large number of adjustments that children need to make to the introduction of a non-biological parent in the household (Hetherington & Jodl, 1994; Popenoe, 1994; Zill, 1994; Zill & Nord, 1994).

The results of this study suggest that parental involvement by parents of divorce is not in itself sufficient to eliminate the downward impact of parental divorce and remarriage on the academic achievement of adolescents. This study does not in any way contradict the notion that parents of divorce should seek to become involved in the educational experiences of their children. Rather, it may point to the fact that the reduced access to the non-custodial parent, which nearly always accompanies a divorce, may make it difficult for a biological parent or a stepparent to compensate for that loss. A myriad of psychological factors may play a role in this as well. These results may also encourage family therapists and educators to help families of divorce avoid unrealistic expectations of what the effects of parental involvement by single or remarried parents can produce in the academic lives of children. Future research should focus on the dynamics of why parental involvement cannot overcome the effects of parental divorce and remarriage.

Success and Parental Involvement and What Can Be Done to Enhance Parental Involvement

Human beings have more of a propensity to think more about the moment, the immediate, and the near term than they have a propensity to develop feasible long-term strategies. Additionally, most people, unless they have dedicated their lives to do otherwise, focus on addressing their own concerns before the needs of others (Leary, 2008; Ratelle et al., 2005). That being the case, instructors need to help parents arise above their own concerns and stresses and focus on the future of their children (Leary, 2008; Ratelle et al., 2005).

Parents Should Become Involved Early

There is something to be said for schools offering classes in parenting so that family members can become engaged in their children's education at as early an age as possible (Salkind, 2006; Saracho, 1986). The present strategy of inviting family members to participate beginning in kindergarten is an ill-advised orientation that developed more as a knee jerk reaction rather than as any proactive strategy that was constructive and forward thinking (Jeynes, 2010; Mapp et al., 2010).

The reality of the matter is that most psychologists and family scientists believe that learning takes place with the greatest rapidity in the first five years of a child's life. Therefore, parents should be prepared to be actively engaged with a child's learning processes at a far younger age than kindergarten. Rather, without causing undue stress for the child, the parent ought to be actively engaged as soon as possible (Salkind, 2006). As has been affirmed, the general trend is that the earlier and more thoroughly one becomes involved in the son or daughter's education, the greater the positive influence on children (Jeynes, 2010, in press, Kennedy, 2001). That being the case, it should come as no surprise that regularly interacting with the child before its birth is the most appropriate entry point for parental involvement (Farrelly, 2009). Those children whose parents interact with them while they are in the womb are more likely to speak earlier and experience faster brain development than parents who do not interact with their babies while they are in the womb (Farrelly, 2009). Although this fact appears quite intuitive, the fact remains that few parents engage in this type of behavior (Farrelly, 2009).

Parents can talk and sing to the child in the womb. Research indicates that babies can recognize a parent's voice after being in the womb for about eighteen weeks (Beckwith & Geisler, 1991; Farrelly, 2009; Tallack, 2006; Vaughan, 1996). In addition, there is evidence to suggest that traumatic events experienced by the mother can influence the child (Slater & Henderson, 2003; Tallack, 2006; Vaughan, 1996). Moreover, to whatever extent the mother engages in emotional outbursts, this too can influence the child (Slater & Henderson, 2003; Tallack, 2006; Vaughan, 1996). The reality is that an innumerable number of parental attitudes and behaviors frequently impact the development of the child (Slater & Henderson, 2003; Tallack, 2006; Vaughan, 1996). Parents would be wise if they understood these facts and then acted on them (Jeynes, 2010).

It is unfortunate that: 1) more is not taught on the salience of prenatal experience in the lives of children and 2) Americans are often distracted with other responsibilities and priorities so that their sons and daughters are frequently shortchanged. First, considering the impressive array of results supporting the notion that children can learn and develop a great deal in the womb, there is usually little teaching to help parents become cognizant of these realities. It would be advisable for schools, churches, and hospitals to offer classes and films about these truths offering this information would likely electrify mothers and fathers about the opportunity to make such an impact on the child's life even before family can view the baby's face. It will also help them ease into the role of parents and internalize both the responsibilities of the joys of this reality at more of an incipient stage than would otherwise be the case. Clearly raising children is a formidable responsibility and the sooner that society can facilitate parents adapting to this new lifestyle, the better, it will be for all the members of the family (Baumrind, 1971; Brooks & Goldstein, 2001). Additionally, the more parents procure insight about the almost unfathomable potential that is often latent in each stage of development, the greater will be the realization of the full gamut of the resplendent childhood experiences (Brooks & Goldstein, 2001; Jeynes, 1999a).

Second, the point that Americans are often distracted with other responsibilities and priorities so that their sons and daughters are frequently shortchanged. Often Americans esteem people based on their productivity (Goldberg, 2008; Van Luijk, 2004; Wempe & Donaldson, 2004). That is, the more productive a person is, at least potentially, the greater than individual is valued (Goldberg, 2008, Van Luijk, 2004; Wempe & Donaldson, 2004). Consequently, Americans tend to value adolescents, young adults and middle-aged people the most and esteem the least the youngest and oldest individuals in the populace (Myers, 2000; Noll, 2002). The result of this orientation is that youth below the age of thirteen are regarded almost as half citizens and often are not even introduced when adults greet one another. One is fully aware of the debate regarding the value of a child in the womb to know that Americans vary regarding how much value they believe that this life has (Myers, 2000; Noll, 2002). The reality of the matter is that the divergent views on this topic have caused people to think in terms of viability rather than in terms of taking the steps necessary to help children in the womb develop so that they can realize their full potential both by the time they are born and afterward. It is unedifying and a disservice to American schooling and families, when the nation's leaders and citizenry become steeped in the quagmire of debate so completely, that they cease to offer priceless advice that could help families have more productive children who are more likely to realize their full potential.

The reality of the matter is that parents can take actions to benefit the long-term potential of their children in the womb. These children are living beings that after fifteen weeks in the womb suck their thumbs and try to escape when they feel endangered (Farrelly, 2009, Tallack, 2006; Vaughan, 1996). Parents should talk and sing to these babies in the womb so that they can reach their fullest potential (Farrelly, 2009).

The Child as a Baby

The first year or two of a child's life is probably its most important. During this period the child develops a foundational outlook on life that forms the foundation for the rest of its days (Bronfenbrenner, 1979; Salkind, 2006). During this time the quality and quantity of about loving interaction with that child will play a pivotal role in determining when that youngster will walk and talk (Bronfenbrenner, 1979; Salkind, 2006). Various studies have indicated that providing a loving, stimulating, and interactive environment is vital if a child is to discover and then unleash his or her full potential (Bronfenbrenner, 1979; Salkind, 2006). For example, such practices as regular loving hugs and other expressions of compassionate contact are associated with subsequent higher levels of achievement and satisfaction with life by the youth (Koenig, 1999; Post, 2006; Snyder & Lopez, 2009). In addition, the extent to which parents interact with youngsters and use a broad range of vocabulary is a good predictor of when the child will speak his or her first word as well as subsequent educational achievement (Brazelton, 1992; Johnson, 1994; Salkind, 2006). Parents who are well educated are much more likely to exhibit high levels of loving interaction and stimulation. This is one of the reasons why people who are highly educated and of high socioeconomic status tend to produce children of the same orientation (Jeynes, 2002a, 2002b). That is, those who are highly educated tend to produce an atmosphere in their home that is stimulating and that encourages reaching one's fullest potential, self-discipline, and high levels of morality (Jeynes, 2002a, 2002b). Myriad American parents are simply unaware of the vital role that such home teaching can play in increasing the propensity for student success in virtually and kind of environment (Jeynes, 2006a, 2010). It is incumbent upon the instructors, ministers, community leaders, and society at large to enlighten those who are less aware of what it takes for their children to succeed. These techniques should not be applied only by the more educated classes, because they are more conversant with these techniques owing to the fact they witnessed their parents apply then successfully. However, given that myriad family scientists agree that the most vital time for a parent to be involved in the life of his or her children is during the first five years, ministers, community leaders, and educators should help parents live up to their full potential during this period (Bronfenbrenner, 1979; Jeynes, 2010, in press; Salkind, 2006). In fact, the first five years are so important that one can often predict how well a child is going to do in school and in life as a whole by how academically advanced a child is when he or she enters kindergarten (Bronfenbrenner, 1979; Salkind, 2006). Therefore, it is only logical that schools encourage mothers and fathers to participate in their children's schooling well before kindergarten begins (Bronfenbrenner, 1979; Salkind, 2006).

There is no question that if instructors encourage parents involving themselves in the lives of their sons and daughters beginning at kindergarten or early elementary school, this is a practice that will doubtlessly yield some positive scholastic effects (Bronfenbrenner, 1979; Salkind, 2006). Research results appear to suggest this result (Jeynes, 2006a). Nevertheless, to whatever extent that research indicates that children develop the most in their first years upon this planet it would appear of utmost important for parents to become fairly intensely engaged in those five years.

As much as social scientists have determined that parental involvement is often a vital prerequisite to student success, educators will do a disservice to the educational future of the country if they do not advise family members to become actively engaged in their children's lives well before the school years begin (Bronfenbrenner, 1979; Salkind, 2006). Two of the reasons why it is so key to take actions along these lines are because studies show that the actively engaged parent has more influence during the first five years of a child's life than during any other proportional period (Bronfenbrenner, 1979; Salkind, 2006). Second, if family members have been active participants during a child's first years of life, it will be relatively facile for teachers to encourage them to become engaged at later points in a child's development including naturally when school begins (Jeynes, 2006a).

Why Social Scientists Do Not Focus on Pre-K Analysis

Moreover, to the extent that educators are concerned with maximizing the scholastic accomplishments of youth they should actively inspire mothers and fathers to participate in their children's schooling as early as possible. Nearly all the primary studies on parental investment in their offspring focuses on the elementary or secondary school years (Lamb, 1997). Almost none of the writings on parental participation focus on the preschool years. Rather the subject is almost never discussed prior to the elementary school years (Jeynes, 2007a). Although, encouraging parental involvement at the earliest possible age appears logical, it is clearly understandable why academics have not engaged in that much quantitative research examining the effects of parental participation on preschool children. It is far easier to assess academic outcomes at the elementary and secondary school level than it is for the preschool age group (Salkind, 2006; Saracho, 1986). If one can even design assessments for these youngsters who are two, three, four, and five years old, it is not patent just what one would be measuring (Jeynes, 2006a; Salkind, 2006; Saracho, 1986).

Various social scientists have pointed out that on myriad occasions one is really not measuring such variables as the ability to sit still for a long period of time, the understanding that such sit-down exams are important, or a child's level of self-discipline (Jeynes, 2006a; Salkind, 2006; Saracho, 1986).

There is one truism about young children that can hardly be avoided. That is, the younger that a child is the more difficult it is to identify what a given means of assessment actually measures (Jeynes, 2006a). The clearest cases of this principle are in new born and other infant assessments such as Bayley's Scales and Gesell's Developmental Schedules. Some psychological and child development experts have made the mistake of equating the results of these tests to intelligence (Johnson, 1994). Many physicians used to believe that if a child looked around at his or her surroundings shortly after birth, this was an early sign of intelligence (Johnson, 1994). There may or may not be some nebulous relationship between these two factors, but it is not a reliable one (Johnson, 1994).

In spite of the problems associated with measuring the intelligence of preschoolers, scholars need to exhibit some common sense and exhort parents to become more involved in the lives of their younger children (Jeynes, 2010; Saracho, 1986). One does not have to possess reliable and valid measures of assessment to conclude the obvious (Jeynes, 2007a; 2010). To deny the vital nature of parental participation based on a technicality would be exceedingly unwise. It would be much like not encouraging infants to play with rattles and infant toys simply because adequate intelligence measurements cannot be formalized.

Encouraging Parents to Become Involved in the Early Childhood Years

If ever parents, especially young ones, are to become engaged in their children's development and education it is an action that should be taken early and it is key that these parents learn to emerge out of their focus on themselves and instead redirect a substantial degree of their energy onto their own children. This is particularly a challenge in this generation because the instant nature of the availability of technology has caused many Americans to live in a self-centered bubble (Leary, 2008). Sociologists have often described this generation as rude and self-centered, thinking little about holding up lines at stores and tuning out others to tend to cell phone calls and text messaging. Parents need to be helped by teachers to emerge out of this bubble to help their children realize their potential (Leary, 2008).

The Need for Support

One of the most difficult challenges for educators in relation to parental involvement is that they quickly realize that those children who need the involvement the most often receive it the least (Brown et al., 2007; Casanova et al., 2005; Cross & Slater, 2000; Davis-Kean, 2005; Delgado-Gaitan, 2004; Hara, 1998). To the extent that this is the case teachers need to try to do all that they can to draw parents into the school community and into the depths of their children's lives (Henderson & Mapp, 2002; Hoover-Dempsey et al., 2002; Kay & Fitzgerald, 1997). It is vital that educators become cognizant of the interests of these parents and think of creative ways to make act more as team members in their children's lives. In Britain the project Sure Start has drawn mothers in via aerobic classes and trailblazed a unique approach to drawing in men by offering martial arts classes (Potter & Carpenter, 2008). This is especially laudable because many schools offer aerobics classes, which are viewed by many as appealing to women and which do in fact attract women far more than men (Potter & Carpenter, 2008). And indeed, most schools do a far better job of reaching out to mothers than they do of reaching out to fathers (Jeynes, 2005f; Potter & Carpenter, 2008). The fact that this program reaches out to fathers is particularly impressive.

Parental Involvement, and Student Behavior

Increasingly social scientists have grown in sensitivity to the fact that parental engagement affects far more than student achievement (Jeynes, 2008a). It also has a profound effect on student behavior (Jeynes, 2005b; 2007b). At a symposium sponsored by the Harvard Family Research Project, Harvard University invited four speakers to declare, in a united voice, the need for a broadening of research on parental involvement to include its influence on many components of youth behavior, attitudes, and psychological well being (Jeynes, Henderson, Hoover-Dempsey, & Epstein, 2005). Partially as a result of this Harvard symposium, social scientists have initiated a number of different studies that incorporate an examination of the effects of parental involvement on a much more comprehensive level than was previously the case (Jeynes et al., 2005).

Since this time various studies have been done that indicate that parental involvement is associated with having children who are less likely to engage in substance abuse, be discriminated against, or be involved in acts of violence (Jeynes, 2008a). There is no question that this particular facet of research will continue to expand and the research community will continue to apprehend what parents have known for centuries, that the ultimate effects of parental involvement are broad and considerable.

The Perceptions of College Students

The vast majority of parental involvement studies that have been undertaken obtained data on the extent of parental involvement based on either observations, parental, teacher, or student input (Jeynes, 2003a; Ratelle et al., 2005). Each of these approaches has its advantages and disadvantages. The one common Achilles heal that all these measures possess is that they all examine parental engagement using a relatively short span of time. One recent study, however, sought to ask college students to evaluate their mother and father's engagement across the life span and deduce certain conclusions (Jeynes, 2008a). Of course even this approach possesses some shortcomings, most notably that the college students are asked to respond thinking retrospectively and that their memories may or may not be accurate. Nevertheless, it can also be argued that because the college students are older and more mature individuals, they can assess the degrees of parental involvement and other issues in a more accurate way than they could during their youth. It is on this latter basis that it would be wise to respond to the results of these studies quite seriously.

Retroactively, therefore, it is conceivable that these college students may have forgotten the extent to which their parents were engaged in their lives and schooling. In spite of these potential weaknesses the results of this study were quite enlightening. The extent of parental involvement generally, and high parental expectations specifically, were highly correlated with elevated levels of academic achievement (Jeynes, 2008a). In addition, parental family structure was also associated with higher levels of scholastic performance among the children (Jeynes, 2008a). All these findings together appear reasonable and facilitate the procurement of a broad understanding about the potential benefits of parental involvement. Research indicates that the expectations of the mother and father may be the most vital component of parental involvement. The findings of this study confirm the salience of these expectations.

Parental Involvement's Resurrection after the Days of John Dewey

As was noted earlier in the book, parental involvement declined after Dewey propounded his ideas about teachers being the schooling specialists, now that the industrial revolution was in place. However, one of the most poignant lessons one can garner from the research on parental involvement is that the industrial model that was advocated first by John Dewey is dated and no longer appropriate for the information age. This model, which Dewey first advocated around the turn of the twentieth century, began to be implemented slowly in the 1920s, but was not fully in place until the 1960s. He averred that the industrial age necessitated that all people function as specialists (Dupuis, 1966, Egan, 2002). Moreover, he declared that teachers were the educational specialists and needed to supplant parents as the most salient instructors (Dupuis, 1966, Egan, 2002). That shift in orientation caused parents to be sidelined in the teaching process in favor of schooling employees all in the name of industrial efficiency and professionalism (Gatto, 2001; Giarelli, 1995; Wallace, 1995).

Whether or not Dewey was correct in his conclusions regarding his era of the late 1800s and early 1900s has less relevance now because Americans now live in the twenty-first century. With regards to the twenty-first century, the nation no longer abides in the industrial age, but in the information age (Bossidy, Charon & Burch, 2004, Gates, 1995, Jarvis, 2009; Meyer, 2003; Yoffle, 1997). In complete contrast to the industrial age in which there was increased distinguishing between functions and specialization, there is now increased integration of previously separate specializations (Gates, 1995; Jarvis, 2009; Johnson, 1997; Meyer, 2003; Yoffle, 1997). The degree of overlap in relatively specialized corporations and job descriptions is causing a refusing of previously separate disciplines (Gates, 1995; Jarvis, 2009; Meyer, 2003; Yoffle, 1997).

For example, two decades ago, Americans primarily associated Apple Computer with MacIntosh computers (Gillam, 2008; Imbimbo, 2009). It was a chief competitor of corporations such as IBM, Microsoft, and Dell. As time has passed, however, various technologies have become inter-related (Gates, 1995; Jarvis, 2009; Gillam, 2008; Imbimbo, 2009; Meyer, 2003; Yoffle, 1997). CEOs and technological wizards have realized that in order to stand at the forefront of technological innovation certain technologies and platforms must be integrated (Gillam, 2008; Imbimbo, 2009). The boundaries of computer hardware, software, and telecommunications are no longer so ostensible and at some levels it is not even clear the extent to which they exist. Distinctions that used to help one differentiate between various types of technology companies are now not only blurred and often debatable, but companies who definitely describe themselves as one type or the other are often seen as limiting their growth potential by their own rigidity (Bossidy et al., 2004; Bunnell & Brate, 2000).

The number of technological companies that have redefined themselves by fusing or interrelating technologies is constantly growing. Not only this, but what is especially impressive is that those corporations that are expanding their reach in this manner are generally the fastest growing major companies in America. Apple computer, for example, used to be a computer company. However, the nations' adolescents now generally associate Apple with the iPod and its prodigious music software business (Gillam, 2008; Imbimbo, 2009; Jarvis, 2009). In addition the leading business people now associate Apple with the iPhone (Gillam, 2008; Imbimbo, 2009). Currently, most stock analysts believe that the company's largest potential for growth rests in its iPhone business (Gillam, 2008; Imbimbo, 2009). In its iPhone, Apple has unleashed the ultimate expression of interrelating technologies. The iPhone integrates computer technology, the telephone, the Internet, texting, and so forth into one device. Its users love the iPhone and to no one's surprise it ranks first in customer satisfaction. Americans realize that the most integrative device on the face of the earth is also the most effective (Bunnell & Brate, 2000; Gillam, 2008; Imbimbo, 2009; Meyer, 2003; Yoffle, 1997).

Google is another company that is developing beyond its original rubric (Battelle, 2005, Jarvis, 2009, Stross, 2008). Google used to be regarded purely as an Internet search engine. It has now, however, expanded its reach to include among other contraptions a rival to the iPhone (Bunnell, 2000, Gillam, 2008, Jarvis, 2009). It is interesting to note that both in terms of stock—and earnings—performance Google has well outperformed its long-time rival Yahoo largely because it has more completely adapted to the realities of the information age by seeking to harness its clout across a variety of technological applications (Bossidy et al., 2004, Bunnell, 2000, Gillam, 2008, Jarvis, 2009). In contrast to Google's insistence on integrating technologies rather than remaining centered on a particular specialty, Yahoo has rebuffed Microsoft's plethora of attempts to buy the company and become a company whose influence extends across a variety of technologies (Jarvis, 2009, Stross, 2008). Yahoo's insistence on remaining a specialist and not adapting to the times has raised the ire of business commentators, crushed its stock price, and caused a number of experts to call for the resignation of its CEO (Jarvis, 2009, Stross, 2008).

The list of high technology companies that have sought to produce integrative technologies is almost as great as the NASDAQ stock index itself, which possesses an abundance of technology companies (Bossidy et al., 2004; Meyer, 2003; Yoffle, 1997). For example, Cisco Systems has gone from a company that Value Line listed as a "computer peripherals" company to one focused on producing "telecommunications equipment" (Bunnell & Brate, 2000). Cisco, led by CEO John Chambers, has always been a networking company (Bunnell & Brate, 2000). Before it went public, Stanford University professors believed it was imperative that computers effectively communicate with one another (Bunnell & Brate, 2000). Over the years, as Cisco has grown, it has become widely known for being a company that constantly integrated more and more technologies so that it became increasingly dominant in its field (Bossidy et al., 2004; Bunnell & Brate, 2000; Meyer, 2003; Yoffle, 1997).

Smaller American companies, as well as foreign manufacturers have also increased their degree of integration in order to make improved products. Research in Motion Palm, Sony, and Samsung has engaged in integrating various technologies in order to produce cutting edge products.

On the basis of the rise of the information age, one could argue that schools need a new instructional rubric that goes beyond Dewey's antiquated industrial model. One may well argue that Dewey's call to change education because of the development of the industrial revolution may well be reasonable, even if one does not accept the paradigm that he proposed. If one adheres to the line of thinking that one should adapt to the technological realities of one's time, then it is only logical that the United States should dispose of an antiquated industrial model that embraces the notion of teachers as specialists and parents as outsiders looking into school practices (Gates, 1995; Meyer, 2003; Yoffle, 1997). Rather, American society needs to adopt a more integrative approach consistent with the information age. This paradigm, which is integrative in nature, would encourage parental involvement and restore it to its rightful place in the education establishment.

If one examines the last forty-five years, there is probably no time in the nation's history in which the public school system has been subjected to so much censure. The seventeen consecutive years of decline in the nation's average SAT scores indubitably propelled the initial trepidation. The scores remained depressed for so long that the SAT had to be removed in 1995 in order to give the American people the impression that SAT scores were a good deal higher than they actually were (Feinberg, 1995; Gillam, 2008; Jarvis, 2009; Young, 1995).

Although there are quite a number of reasons (some scholastically related and some not) why academic achievement, most notably SAT scores, declined and remained below there 1963 levels, the fact that during the 1963–1980 period many schools did not encourage parental engagement certainly did not help (Jeynes, 2007a; Wirtz, 1977). In fact, the College Board's meticulous examination of the achievement test score decline concluded that the family was one of the most prominent reasons for the plummeting scores (Wirtz, 1977).

Parents play too vital a role in both the development and education of a child to be at best tolerated and at worst excluded from the schooling process. Children need both their parents and teachers involved in their learning experiences and if teachers do not more aggressively invite the input and participation of parents, teachers run the risk of simultaneously appearing both arrogant and ignorant (Gatto, 2001). Teachers want to be respected for their expertise and this is understandable. Nevertheless, parents want to be respected as well (Jeynes, 2006a, 2007a, 2010). Moreover, just as teachers have rights, so do parents (Jeynes, 2006a, 2007a, 2010).

The Need for Parents and Teachers to be Partners

The research presented in this book clearly demonstrates that parental engagement aids considerably in youth reaching their full academic potential. Teachers and parents need to partner together in helping children reach their full potential. Teachers can take several steps to help ensure that their relationship with the parents is indeed a partnership and not an adversarial one. First, the child is the parents' offspring and not that of the teachers. It is extremely important for the teacher to humbly acknowledge that the teacher is coming alongside the parent to aid in the development of the child and not the other way around (Jeynes, 2005b, 2007b). Second, with the first truth in mind, the teacher should realize that although he or she has a certain expertise in inculcating children with certain truths the teacher should not regard himself or herself as the education specialist. To maintain such an attitude disrespects the role of the parent (Jeynes, 2006a, 2010). Although the teacher does have a good deal of knowledge about educating children in general the parent possesses expertise about the education and development of that child in particular (Jeynes, 2006a, 2010). Therefore, if one chooses to be objective for a moment one might be able to build a stronger argument that it is the parent who is the specialist in educating the child rather than stating that it is the teacher who is.

In addition, research has shown quite consistently support for the intuitive notion that intact families are associated with higher levels of parental engagement (Jeynes, 1999a, 2003b, 2006b). This naturally only makes sense because parents are human beings just like everyone else. The reality of the matter is that it is easier for two parents to tend to the needs of child than for one to make such an attempt (Jeynes, 2003b). This statement is not designed to offend the many single parents who attempt to tend to the needs of their children as well as they possibly can (McLanahan & Sandefur, 1994). Instead, the purpose of this declaration is to point out the rather patent notion that it is easier for two people to minister to the needs of their children than it is for one parent to complete the same task (Jeynes, 2003b, 2005b, 2007b). One parent also possesses twenty-four hours in which to tend to his or her child while the two-parent family has potentially forty-eight hours to care for and watch over the child.

Two-Parent Intact Families and Parental Engagement

To whatever extent there are advantages that accrue to a child from abiding in an intact two-parent family, it is in the best interests of the citizenry of this country to promote two-parent families. This is not merely a matter of supporting government policies that promote the family, but undertaking personal actions that support families under stress and that in no way encourage the destruction or fragmentation of the family. If one diminishes the prominence of sacredness of the family in one's heart and mind one is more likely to engage in activities that can directly or potentially undermine the health of the family (Jeynes, 2002a). Such actions may be as direct and deleterious as committing adultery and thereby devastating not only one's own family, but also the family of one's partner in intercourse. Indirect activities may include disparaging remarks toward another person's husband or wife or by acting cold and distant toward one of the spouses in order to embarrass him or her in a public setting. American society needs to become more actively engaged in promoting the intact two-parent family. It does not begin as many might opine with supporting a particular mode of government policy. Rather the strengthening of the family begins with each individual.

Chapter 11

What Do We Know and What Do We Still Need to Know?

What We Do Know: Accomplishments to Date

1. We Now Understand the Breadth of the Influence of Parental Involvement

Nearly every study examining the effects of parental involvement concludes it considerably influences the lives and education of children (Spera, 2005; Wallace & Walberg, 1993), regardless of race, gender, and socioeconomic status (Jeynes, 2003a, 2007b). The fact that a myriad of analyses, examining this practice from many perspectives, show such consistent patterns is important (Griffith, 1996; Hampton et al., 1998). In addition to this consistency, recent meta-analyses reveal that most of the components of parental involvement have statistically significant effects (Fan & Chen, 2001; Jeynes, 2003a, 2005b). Types of parental involvement such as parental expectations, communication, parents reading with their children, and parental style each markedly influence student educational outcomes in their own right (Afifi & Olson, 2005; Englund et al., 2004; Jeynes, 2005b). Other facets of parental involvement such as checking homework and attending school functions have less consistent influences (Jeynes, 2003a, 2005b). Nevertheless, it is noteworthy that so many aspects of parental support have an effect.

The impact of multifarious aspects of parental engagement is not only apparent in meta-analyses, but also in a long list of studies on specific types of parental involvement that show statistically significant results, such as parental expectations, communication, and checking homework (Afifi & Olson, 2005; Braden, 1999, Davis-Kean, 2005; Jeynes, 2005f). However, although individual components of involvement demonstrate discrete merit (Jeynes, 2005b, 2005f; Wallace & Walberg, 1993), meta-analyses on parental involvement indicate that, as one might expect, it has its greatest impact through the interaction of many components (Jeynes, 2003a, 2005b).

The meta-analyses and nationwide data set analyses included in this book indicate that some of the most potent aspects of parental involvement are some of the subtlest. Yes, it is true that family attendance and laying down home-based guidelines have some ameliorative value. Nevertheless, given that meta-analyses in essence quantitatively summarize the existing body of research, it is patent that subtle aspects of parental engagement such as maintaining high expectations, possessing a free flow of communication between parent and child about school and life in general, and practicing a child-rearing approach that is inundated with genuine love and yet provides wise structure in which youth can grow.

Regarding parental expectations, it is clear from the analyses in this book that one can do more damage by aiming disparaging remarks toward children than one can ever neutralize by the limited redemptive actions of attending a few school functions. Such remarks as "you're so stupid" can be so caustic as to emasculate boys and demoralize girls. The high expectations that were associated with elevated levels of academic outcomes were not those of an authoritarian nature in which a father or mother bellowed, "You will go to Harvard or Yale." Rather, these expectations are often more unspoken than they are spoken. It is a general understanding that is a product of a potent work ethic, a strong faith regarding the future, and a pleasantly tenacious spirit.

Parental style is another subtle, albeit important, component of parental participation. The parental style that was associated with school success to the greatest degree was one that was concurrently associated with a high degree of love and care towards one's children and a strong degree of structure. To a considerable degree, this finding is in accordance with Baumrind's (1971) theory regarding approaches to parenting and also contemporary thinking by some family theorists that an atmosphere of love and structure must exist simultaneously in any given home (Dobson, 1970). And that beyond this axiom, one of the greatest acts of kindness that a parent can show to a child is a loving form of discipline (Dobson, 1970). In the short term, it may even hurt the parent to apply the use of loving discipline, but in the long term the child must internalize a certain degree of self-discipline in order to prevent undertaking actions that could be deleterious either to oneself or to others (Dobson, 1970).

Communication between parents and children is also imperative if one is to foster constructive parental engagement. It is rare indeed for there to be a dearth of communication in the household and for academic success to follow. Communication provides life to any close relationship, whether it be a marital relationship or one that exists between parents and their children. To the extent that there is a free flow of positive communication, mothers and fathers will be able to act knowledgably regarding school and other aspects of a child's life. In contrast, a lack of communication causes misunderstandings to burgeon and then accrue, which in and of themselves can lead to all kinds of miscommunications and mishaps (Brooks & Goldstein, 2001). Eventual lack of communication can also result from negative exchanges that preceded it, so that at least one person in the parent–child relationship does not wish to communicate (Afifi & Olson, 2005). This being the case, one can see how the presence of affirmative communication can make an abetting contribution to family involvement.

2. We Know that Programs Designed to Increase Parental Involvement Often Work

As it became clear that parental involvement influenced school outcomes, educators and other practitioners initiated numerous programs across the country to encourage mothers and fathers to become more active participants in the schooling of their children (Schwartz, 1996; Shaver & Walls, 1998). Churches and university research groups have been some of the most active sponsors of these programs (Hoover-Dempsey, 2005). Among the most publicized programs have been Robert Slavin's "Success for All" and Houston's Project Reconnect (Bryant, 1996; Slavin, 2002). Others have founded program centers designed to foster parental involvement and develop theories about parental engagement in their children's schooling. These efforts include endeavors by Joyce Epstein (2001) and Kathryn Hoover-Dempsey and colleagues (2002).

Reports attesting to the success of these various programs have been encouraging. Objective assessments and anecdotal testimonies regarding the efficacy of many of these initiatives have consistently been reported (Epstein, 2001; Hoover-Dempsey et al., 2002). Based on these assessments, most social scientists currently believe parental involvement programs generally work (Henderson & Mapp, 2002). In addition, all the meta-analyses of programs indicate that, on average, they tend to be quite effective (Jeynes, 2003a, 2005b, 2007b). Although one research synthesis indicated that parental involvement programs did not have an impact, this study failed to combine statistically the studies included, as a meta-analysis does (Mattingly et al., 2002). In addition, the research synthesis did not include a number of published studies included in the meta-analyses; while the meta-analyses included all the studies in the Mattingly research synthesis (Jeynes, 2005b, 2007b; Mattingly et al., 2002).

Those who have sponsored parental involvement programs have also shared that parents and community organizations, such as churches and other civic groups, have demonstrated a willingness to participate actively in these programs (Hoover-Dempsey, 2005). This is a key development in order to increase the likelihood that the programs will be successful. One concern among researchers is the extent to which the effects of parental involvement from programs with compulsory components compare to those of parents who voluntarily participate in their children's education (Mattingly et al., 2002). Nevertheless, the fact that parents in programs are excited about these initiatives is a good sign.

3. The Idea of Parent–Teacher Partnerships May Not Always be Welcomed by Educators

Although practitioners and theorists have started a number of initiatives that exhort and direct parents to become more involved in their children's school, these efforts depend on schools and teachers willing to partner with parents

(Ford, Follmer & Litz, 1998; Sanders & Epstein, 2000). Few would debate the reality that most schools and teachers are not very open to such partnerships.

Today, teachers have become professionals and regard themselves as such (Lindle, 1990; Peressini, 1998). This movement toward "professionalization" began with Horace Mann's efforts in the 1830s and 1840s and has continued ever since (Gatto, 2001; Tyack, 1974). Although most would portray this as a positive historical development, it does pose certain challenges for the parental involvement movement. That is, many teachers are reluctant to partner with parents because teachers view themselves as professionals who know considerably more about education than do parents (Lindle, 1990; Peressini, 1998). Numerous teachers recognize the value of parental involvement as a concept but view the actual process of partnering with parents as parental meddling (Lindle, 1990; Peressini, 1998). Those programs currently in place must devote considerable effort to find schools willing to participate in their program (Kay & Fitzgerald, 1997), and because of the sheer number of schools in America, those promoting the programs generally find willing schools (Kay & Fitzgerald, 1997).

However, the fact still remains teachers are not always eager to participate in such programs, but there are a number of reasons why their protestations against parental involvement lack merit. First, in the case of doctors and lawyers (other professionals to whom teachers often compare themselves), those who hire them can provide critical information to understanding a situation and taking appropriate action (Peressini, 1998). If a doctor is not willing to listen to his or her patient, the consequences can be dire. Similarly, an attorney can also gain greater insight into a case if he or she chooses to apply information supplied by the client. In each case, if the medical or legal process is one in which the patient or client is relegated to a position of outsider, the process suffers. It follows that if teachers educate children without parental involvement in the process, instruction will also suffer.

Second, unlike other professions, nearly all parents are involved in the instruction of their children (Bauch & Goldring, 1995; Jeynes, 2006a). This is particularly true in the preschool years, but also extends throughout the various stages of a child's development. A parent functions far less as a doctor and lawyer at home, and far more as a teacher (Peressini, 1998). Consequently, one would expect that parents would desire to give input considerably more with teachers than they would with doctors, lawyers, and other professionals.

Parents are in fact so much a part of their children's education that most children still regard their parents as their most salient teachers (Bauch & Goldring, 1995; Borruel, 2002; Peressini, 1998). After all, most parents train their children for many years. In contrast, most teachers instruct a given child only nine months (Boyer, 1995). This is one of the main reasons why people today still debate whether parents or schools are primarily responsible for educating children (Boyer, 1995).

In order for teachers to welcome the involvement of parents and for parents to acknowledge the professionalism of teachers, there needs to be a mutual respect. Parents need to acknowledge that in the vast majority of cases teachers know more about educating than parents do. Similarly, teachers need to realize that in nearly every case parents know more about their children than teachers do. Only in this climate of mutual respect can more teachers eagerly invite greater parental participation in education and can parents enjoy the experience of heightened involvement. As it stands now, many textbooks instruct preservice teachers on how to win parental support. However, few of these textbooks address how to act as a parental advocate. This reflects the resistance among many teachers to the parents' perspective and desire to be involved in school.

Of course, parent–teacher friction over education is nothing new. Surveys suggest that when parents and teachers are asked what steps can be taken to improve student educational outcomes, the two groups give entirely different answers (Boyer, 1995). Parents claim the key is hiring better teachers, and teachers tend to assert that parents need to be more involved (Boyer, 1995). Despite such rhetoric, many educators simply do not welcome the idea of parent–teacher partnerships (Lindle, 1990; Peressini, 1998). By comprehending this reality, sponsors of parental involvement programs can develop partnership plans that consider the threats to professionalism that teachers often fear, and yet nevertheless attempt to heighten the extent of parental involvement.

Summarizing Thoughts

Unquestionably, the past three decades of research in parental involvement have produced some substantial breakthroughs in our knowledge base of this discipline. However, as is often the case in the social sciences, these advances have also yielded new and stimulating questions that researchers need to address in the future.

One of the accomplishments of this research is that it has given us a greater appreciation of the breadth of parental involvement's influence. We now have a fuller understanding that the influence of parental involvement holds across race and gender and that it has a myriad of components, nearly all of which contribute to its overall impact on educational and psychological outcomes (Davis-Kean, 2005; Jeynes, 2005b, 2007b). As salient and useful as this information is, one pressing question is whether this same trend holds for parental involvement programs. Likewise, we now know of the more subtle aspects of parental involvement that have the most influence. Does this same trend hold for parental involvement programs?

The current body of research is vitally important for more reasons than just the knowledge that it provides. First, informative previous studies can help social scientists ask the right questions for future research. For example, without insight about what types of parental involvement are most important generally, practitioners would have little guidance about what features of parental involvement would be most likely to make a program successful. Second, the current body of research can give us insight into just how important some of these questions are. In this sense, the findings of various studies act much like a jigsaw puzzle. They not only fill in previous gaps, but they also provide a sense of the relative importance of the remaining gaps—what we do not know about parental involvement is likely more crucial than what we do know.

What We Need to Learn

1. Do the Same Qualities of Parental Involvement that are the Most Influential in Everyday Life Resemble Those that are Also the Most Salient in Parental Involvement Programs?

In the minds of sponsors of parental involvement programs, this is probably the most important question. It seems logical that the order of influence would be nearly identical. However, closer examination reveals reasons why they could be considerably different (Jeynes, 2005b, 2007b). First, let us examine the possibility that the order of influence of parental involvement traits would be nearly identical or at least very similar. One can argue that parental involvement, whether it is voluntary or involuntary and inherent or extrinsically motivated, possesses the same dynamics and influence. For example, one could aver that parental expectations will influence children's school outcomes across a variety of situations, some involving programs and others not, because of the inherent value of parental expectations. That is, whether parental expectations already reside in the caregivers or whether program sponsors teach such practices, parental expectations are important determinants of educational outcomes. Similarly, one can also argue that parents reading with their children from a young age, parent–child communication about school, and other facets of parental involvement are puissant parts of parental involvement whether they are inherent to a parent's nature or whether program practitioners have taught parents the practice of these virtues.

Nevertheless, one can also argue that the order of influence of types of parental involvement could be quite different in a parental involvement program versus the type of parental participation manifested in every day life. This assertion would be based on the notion that certain aspects of parental involvement are easier to teach and learn than others (Afifi & Olson, 2005). Consequently, the aspects of parental involvement that would have the greatest impact in programs would be those that combine the most influential, easiest to teach, and easiest to learn. Under this scenario, there would likely be some degree of overlap between parental involvement traits with the greatest impact in life versus in programs. Nevertheless, because of the added components of teaching and learning, one would expect some differences in the two lists.

Resolving this issue is important, because the present body of research has provided a good deal of insight into what facets of parental involvement have the greatest impact in everyday life. However, it is imperative that we know how much guidance these results can give practitioners who sponsor parental involvement programs (Mattingly et al., 2002; Jeynes, 2010).

This issue can also be addressed at another level. Are the types of parental involvement that most raise achievement among the general population also the same qualities that have the greatest impact on students no matter what a child's gender, race, or class might be? Although meta-analytic studies indicate the influence of *overall* parental involvement holds across race, gender, and class, one should not assume the *types* of parental involvement that most effect academic outcomes are identical across racial, class, gender, and cultural background. It is conceivable, for example, that the overall effect size for parental involvement might be quite consistent across students of different races and classes but for entirely distinct reasons. That is, it is possible that the underlying contributing aspects of parental involvement might show a different pattern for each group, although the combined impact of the aggregated components of parental involvement might be the same. Whether the impact of parental involvement programs and specific components of parental participation within these programs differs by race, gender, and class is also a topic worthy of considerable study.

2. Are the Subtle Aspects of Parental Involvement as Easy to Teach as the More Overt Expressions of Involvement?

As previously mentioned, meta-analyses indicate that some of the most subtle types of parental involvement are most strongly related to scholastic outcomes. What is unclear however, whether one refers to programs or simply a less formal means of counseling parents, is if these more subtle aspects of parental involvement are more difficult to teach than others (Afifi & Olson, 2005; Davalos et al., 2005).

One might hypothesize that the more subtle aspects of parental involvement based on personality more than intentional action might be more difficult to teach. For example, it seems plausible that it would prove more difficult to teach parents to communicate about school with their children and hold high expectations for their children than it would be to encourage parents to attend school functions and to establish productive household rules.

Clearly we do not know for certain that the more subtle types of parental involvement are more difficult to teach than the more overt expressions of family participation in education (Jeynes, 2005b). However, it is vital that social scientists determine whether this is true. If the more subtle aspects are more challenging to teach then in order to formulate programs we cannot totally rely on the results of previous studies that suggest that subtle aspects of parental involvement have the greatest impact on achievement. This is because in order to inaugurate effective parental involvement programs, the sponsors of these programs must successfully instruct parents to implement various components of parental involvement (Epstein, 2001; Henderson & Mapp, 2002). Even if certain subtle traits are the most vital aspects of family involvement, if they cannot be easily taught, this is problematic. The success of parental involvement programs depends on the extent to which it is facile to teach parents to incorporate the most essential aspects of family engagement. This means that the potential efficacy of the best parental involvement programs depends on the ability to instruct parents to internalize and practice the subtlest facets of parental involvement. Just how easy or difficult it is to teach these subtle aspects is something that the research community has yet to determine (Jeynes, 2006a, 2010).

Second, if a present way of teaching subtle aspects of parental involvement does not work particularly well, then social scientists need to discover more efficacious means of instruction. In order words, even if a particular study finds that subtle types of parental involvement are challenging to teach and therefore are not as effective as those expressed by parents in every day situations, it does not mean that one should assume that it must remain that way. Instead, one should look at alternative ways of inculcating involvement that will produce superior results.

Family and educational researchers have a pretty good sense of what facets of parental involvement have the greatest effects on achievement when exercised in every day life. However, few programs distinguish between different types of parental involvement. Consequently, social scientists know far less about the types of parental involvement that yield the greatest results in programs than they do about the relative influence of various kinds of parental involvement in everyday life.

3. We Need to Understand More Fully the Relationship between Family Structure and Parental Involvement

Many separate studies examine the relationship between family structure and school outcomes and between parental involvement and these outcomes (Jeynes, 1999a, 2003b). However, little research examines the influence of family structure on parental involvement (Jeynes, 2002a, 2006b). There are probably three reasons for this. First, few social scientists study both parental involvement and family structure. Second, many people assume that non-intact family structures negatively impact parental involvement. Third, there is among some researchers a reluctance to engage in research that makes non-intact families look bad (McLanahan & Sandefur, 1994). These reasons may be understandable, but consequently little is known about the relationship between specific family structures, parental involvement, and academic outcomes (Jeynes, 2002a; Jeynes, 2010).

The academic community knows very little, for example, about the influence of parental remarriage on parental involvement (Jeynes, 2002a; Jeynes, 2010). How involved are most stepparents in their children's education? Does parental remarriage typically reduce the amount of time the biological parent spends with the child? Are men and women living in a cohabiting relationship less likely to be involved in a child's education than intact families? What parental involvement programs have been specifically designed with single parents in mind? What types of these programs have been the most successful? The academic community really does not know the answers to these questions. Given that most American children today will spend some time in a single parent family, it is imperative that educators and family researchers know the answers to these questions. Moreover, it is important for school leaders to know how to develop programs with family situations in mind.

4. We Need to Identify What Creative Actions are Most Likely to Attract Parents to Become Involved

Undoubtedly, parents face many hurdles in becoming involved in their children's education (Epstein, 2001; Slaughter-Defoe, 2001). It is also undeniable that teachers often confront resistant parents (Lindle, 1990; Peressini, 1998). Given these challenges, educational leaders must identify the creative actions most likely to attract parental involvement.

During the nineteenth and the first two-thirds of the twentieth century school leaders did not have to use unique techniques to encourage parental involvement. During this period, parental attendance at school functions was high (Jeynes, 2005b, 2007b). School officials were not surprised when parents did show up. Rather, they were surprised when parents did not show up. However, parents today face challenges educators need to be sensitive to if they expect parents to increase their level of involvement.

First, parents face many time pressures, such as two parents working, the high cost of living, and long commute times, among others. Over the last thirty years, two parents working outside the home has become the usual employment configuration in the American family (United States Census Bureau, 2004). When only one of two parents works outside the home, it is easier for one parent to attend school functions (McLanahan & Sandefur, 1994; Wallerstein & Blakeslee, 1989). Time is also an issue for single parents who must fulfill the roles usually associated with two parents (McLanahan & Sandefur, 1994; Wallerstein & Blakeslee, 1989; Jeynes, 2002b).

Second, the high cost of living causes many parents to work longer hours than they otherwise would. Moreover, even families with two parents working feel little economic benefit because they overextend, such as the purchase of costlier homes. Consequently, people work two or more jobs or excessive overtime hours in order to make ends meet. This means many parents have inflexible schedules in which to participate in their children's education.

Third, many parents do not speak English as their first language (U.S Department of Education, 2002). Not surprisingly, research shows that the main factor determining whether ESL parents involve themselves in their children's education is whether they speak English (Keith & Lichtman, 1994). Cognizant of the hurdles these parents face, teachers need to show creative ways to reach out to and involve these parents.

Fourth, low-income parents in particular lack financial resources. Many times school events involve the payment of money. Examples of this include bake sales and fund raisers. In these situations, some parents feel awkward in attending unless they purchase something.

Fifth, parents also sometimes feel intimidated because of friction they or their children experience with the teacher. Consequently, parents believe that school leaders almost always take the side of the teacher (Baker, 2001).

Naturally, many factors inhibit parental involvement, and the presence of these issues means educators cannot assume parents will attend the standard parent–teacher meetings and the typical assemblies. Nevertheless, educators need to identify unique actions they can take to attract parents who struggle with these issues. Various schools have initiated programs to address these parental challenges (Hoover-Dempsey et al., 2002; Mattingly et al., 2002). Unfortunately, we do not yet know which of these programs work best.

For parents with time management issues due either to job-related or cost of living-related issues, teachers may need to meet them in the evenings or on the weekends. In order to reach ESL parents, teachers may need to become skilled at least to some degree in a second language or use an interpreter. Parental involvement generally might also be increased if a class has a parent of the week program in which parents come in and share about their occupations, their interests, their hobbies, or their culture. Schools might also offer evening meals to commuters on the go. Offering food is an undeniably effective means of drawing parents into schools.

Any or all these programs may be effective ways of encouraging parents to become more involved. However, the research community does not yet know which of these efforts would be the most effective. Moreover, social scientists also do not know how the effectiveness of these programs might vary among different types of schools.

What We Need to Do With What We Know

In order for academic success to be heightened it is important not only that knowledge be maximized, but that there be a determination to apply wisely that knowledge that has already been obtained. Few would gainsay the assertion that it is very important to engage parents in the educating of their children. In spite of this awareness, there are still a plethora of teachers that in the name of professionalism do not welcome the participation of parents. This resistant attitude is often held by instructors, pointing to Dewey's declaration that, as a result of industrialization, teachers are now the education specialists. Congruent with this orientation, although Dewey constantly mentions teachers in his references to education, he almost never mentions parents (Dewey, 1902, 1910, 1915; Egan, 2002). Increased education specialization may or may not have been the appropriate response to the fact of industrialization. However, the reality of the matter is that we are now in the information age rather than in the industrial age. In this information age, the trend is not increased specialization, but the reverse (Jarvis, 2009; Meyer, 2003; Yoffle, 1997). Presently, technologies are converging. Companies that used to be computer hardware companies, such as Apple, in recent years have been depending on profit growth in music software, iPods, and iPhones (Gillam, 2008; Imbimbo, 2009). Cisco Systems has gone from a computer peripherals company to a focus on telecommunication equipment manufacturing and service (Bunnell & Brate, 2000). Google has emerged as a company competing with Apple's iphone after becoming known primarily as an Internet search engine giant. Truly, the trend in the information age is one of convergence rather than specialization. More than ever in the information age, convergence is needed so that parents are not longer relegated to the fringe of the educational process, but rather they are welcomed as partners in the schooling of their children. The reality is that parents and teachers need to work together in order to maximize educational outcomes. And teachers need to work to help satisfy the needs of the parents and their children, not so much the other way around.

These are the realities of family living and the information age. Parental involvement is one of the keys to ensuring educational success. It is not enough to enjoy the fact that increasingly more is known about the advantages of parental involvement. American society must act on this increased knowledge. To do otherwise is to run the risk of possessing much knowledge, but only a small amount of wisdom.

Concluding Thoughts

A nation is only as strong as the families that constitute that nation. Therefore, it is essential that the United States develop policies that strengthen families rather than weaken them (Jeynes, 1999a, 2003b). This being the case it is of utmost importance that the nation foster policies that encourage rather than discourage parental involvement. It is unconscionable for any nation to encourage practices that undermine the strength of the family. And yet by adhering to an educational philosophy that espouses a rubric based on specialization, the United States may be doing just this. Beyond this, if the American education system is to be strong, parents need to be engaged in helping educate their children. To act to relegate parents to a secondary role to that of teachers is not respectful toward the vital role that they play. The results of the meta-analyses and nationwide data sets included in this book indicate that parental involvement is associated with higher academic outcomes. These findings apply to youth of various races and both genders. They also apply to parental involvement programs, although the effect sizes are smaller than in situations in which the parental involvement is voluntary.

It is also clear that the impact of parental engagement is so pervasive and deep that several of the primary components of this involvement have statistically significant effects even in and of themselves. Aspects of parental involvement such as expectations, parental style, communication, reading aloud to children, and other components, have a tangible and well-defined relationship with educational outcomes. Although some of these findings were based on correlations that did not address the issue of causality, most of the studies included in the study did address issues of causality, so that in the majority of the studies the direction of causality was clear. Also, in the case of parental involvement programs, one cannot argue that student academic achievement influenced whether a parent was in the experimental or control group of this study because whether a youth was included in the experimental group was based on random assignment. Therefore the direction of causality in this case was quite clear.

The research presented in this book also indicates that the call to increased parental involvement is not an exhortation to do something that is foreign. Parental participation is an activity that has roots going back to the days of the Pilgrims and Puritans (Eavey, 1964). Beginning with this period, parental involvement became a practice that was inextricably connected with the American conception of the family and it remained that way for more than three centuries. With this in mind, it is therefore important to comprehend that the call for the American public to become more engaged as parents in the educational and behavioral development of their children is hardly new. Academics are not at the cutting edge of this debate, but rather simply calling Americans back to their previous practices.

The combination of history, quantitative analysis, and examining its relationship to issues of diversity and family structure serves as a reminder to the American people such involvement is foundational if one is to expect high levels of achievement among children. The quantitative analysis provides support for why parental involvement was such an important part of American family practices for so many years. The integration of history and the analysis of the relationship between involvement and family structure also enables Americans to apprehend why the increased incidence of single parent families likely spawned increased calls for parental engagement. Clearly, there is a concern among many Americans that the nation's children have been suffering as a result of recent family trends in terms of marital dissolution, family work practices, and the degree of parental engagement in the educational and behavioral development of their children.

The revived interest in parental involvement is a positive development in American society. What the significance is of this renewed interest in parental participation has yet to be totally understood. Nevertheless, any development that in essence calls for more love and time invested in those that one loves would seem to be healthy (Pestalozzi, 1916). Whether this increased interest is simply out of recognition that adults have often been insensitive or somewhat oblivious to the needs of their children or whether it constitutes a turning point in American history in which the needs of children play a more prominent role in American thinking, is yet to be determined. Nevertheless, it is patent that there is a growing awareness on the part of the American public and academics that parents play certain roles in the lives of their children that cannot be replicated by any other person in society, no matter how well meaning that succor may be. Therefore, it is vital that educators encourage and not discourage the involvement of parents in children's schooling, whether or not a teacher personally welcomes such participation. The research presented in this book is a reminder that the academic prowess of youth will be maximized when parents and teachers work together as partners.

The research in this book also serves to give guidance to both parents and educators regarding the most salient components of parental involvement. Even if people acknowledge the importance of parental involvement, they want to have direction about what specific actions they can take that will yield the greatest benefit for their children. Countless parents want nothing but the best for their children, but do not believe they do possess the necessary information to become engaged in their children's lives in the most ameliorative way possible. The information provided in this book should provide more valuable information to parents and teachers than ever before about how to maximize the efficacy of parental involvement. To the extent that this added knowledge will produce more loving environments in which children can grow, these analyses and research will have been well worth the effort.

References

Chapter I

Albrecht, S. L., & Heaton, T. B. (1984). Secularization, higher education, and religiosity. *Review of Religious Research, 26* (1), 43–58.

Amano, I. (1990). *Education and Examination in Modern Japan.* Tokyo: University of Tokyo Press.

Bagley, W. C. (1915). Editorial. *School and Home Education, 35,* 4–5.

Ballantine, J. H. (1999). Figuring in the father factor. *Childhood Education, 76* (2), 104–105.

Barth, G. P. (1980). *City people: The Rise of Modern City Culture in Nineteenth-Century America.* New York: Oxford University Press.

Bartlett, R. (1978). *The Faith of the Pilgrims.* New York: United Church Press.

Beckner, W. (1983). *The Case for the Smaller School.* Bloomington, IN: Phi Delta Kappa Educational Foundation.

Bender, T. (1975). *Toward an Urban Vision: Ideas and Institutions in Nineteenth-Century America.* Lexington: University Press of Kentucky.

Big List of Korean Universities (web page) (2002). Durham, NC: Duke University. www. duke.edu/`myhan/c_biku.html, accessed 1 May 2003.

Blinderman, A. (1976). *Three Early Champions of Education: Benjamin Franklin, Benjamin Rush, and Noah Webster.* Bloomington: Phi Delta Kappa Educational Foundation.

Bourne, W. O. (1870). *History of the Public School Society.* New York: Wood.

Boyer, E. (1985). High School. In Beatrice & Ronald Gross (Eds.), *The Great School Debate.* New York: Simon & Schuster.

Carlsmith, L. (1964). Effect of early father absence on scholastic aptitude. *Harvard Educational Ereview, 34* (1), 3–21.

Carlsmith, L. (1973). Some personality characteristics of boys separated from fathers during World War II. *Ethos, 1* (4), 466–477.

CBS News. WBBM Radio. Chicago, Illinois. August 28,1994.

Chauncy, C. (1655). Charles Chauncy on Liberal Learning. In Smith, W. (Ed.) (1973), *Theories of Education in Early America.* (pp. 15–23). Indianapolis, IN: Bobbs-Merrill Company.

Cherlin, A. J. (1978). Remarriage as an incomplete institution. *American Journal of Sociology, 84* (30, 634–650.

Clarke, J. (1730). John Clarke's Classical Program of Studies. In Wilson Smith, (Ed.)

(1973). *Theories of Education in Early America* (pp. 38–45). Indianapolis, IN: Bobbs-Merrill Company.

Coleman, J. S. (1988). "Social capital" and schools: One reason for higher private school achievement. *Education Digest, 53,* 6–9.

Coleman, J., Hoffer, T., & Kilgore, S. (1982). *High School Achievement: Public, Catholic, and Private Schools Compared.* New York: Basic Books.

Cornog, E. (1998). *The Birth of Empire: DeWitt Clinton, & the American Experience, 1769–1828.* New York: Oxford University Press.

Cremin, L. A. (1977). *Traditions of American Education.* New York: Basic Books.

Cubberley, E. (1920). *The History of Education.* Boston, MA: Houghton Mifflin.

Cubberley, E. (Ed.). (1934) *Readings in Public Education in the United States: A Collection of Sources and Readings to Illustrate the History of Educational Practice and Progress in the United States.* Cambridge, MA: Riverside Press.

D'Andrea, A. (1983). Joint custody as related to parental involvement and paternal self-esteem. *Conciliation Courts Review, 21* (2), 81–87.

Dewey, J. (1902). *The Child and the Curriculum.* Chicago: University of Chicago Press.

Dewey, J. (1915). *The School and Society.* Chicago: University of Chicago Press.

Dewey, J. (1964). *John Dewey's Impressions of Soviet Russia and the Revolutionary World: Mexico-China-Turkey, 1929.* New York: Teachers' College Press.

Dewey, J. (1978). *John Dewey: The Middle Works, 1899–1924, Volume 5: 1908,* Boydston, J. (Ed.). Carbondale: Southern Illinois University Press.

Dewey, J. (1990). *The School and Society/The Child and the Curriculum.* Chicago: University of Chicago Press.

Downs R. B. (1978). *Friedrich Froebel.* Boston: Twayne.

Duberman, L. (1975). *The Reconstituted Family: A Study of Remarried Parents and their Children.* Chicago: Nelson Hall Publishers.

Durst, P. L., Wedemeyer, N. V., & Zurcher, L. A. (1985). Parenting partnerships after divorce: Implications for practice. *Social Work, 30* (5), 423–428.

Eavey, C. B. (1964). *History of Christian Education.* Chicago: Moody Press.

Epstein, J. (2001). *School, Family, and Community Partnerships.* Boulder: Westview Press.

Erikson, E. (1964). *Identity, Youth & Crisis.* New York: Norton.

Fagan, J. (2000). African American and Puerto Rican American parenting styles, paternal involvement and Head Start children's social competence. *Merrill-Palmer Quarterly, 46* (4), 592–612.

Feinberg, L. (1995). A new center for the SAT. *College Board Review, 174,* 8–13, 31–32.

Filler, L. (1965). *Horace Mann on the Crisis in Education.* Yellow Springs, Ohio: Antioch Press.

Fitzpatrick, E. A. (1969). *The Educational Views and Influence of DeWitt Clinton.* New York: Arno Press.

Fraser, J. W. (2001). *The School in the United States.* Boston, MA: McGraw Hill.

Gangel, K. O., & Benson, W. S. (1983). *Christian Education: Its History and Philosophy.* Chicago: Moody.

Gatto, J. G. (2001). *The Underground History of American Education.* New York: Oxford Village Press.

GeographyIQ. (2006). *Rankings: Literacy.* GeographyIQ.com. www.geographyiq.com/ranking/ranking_Literacy

Gordam, C. J. (1961). *Parents and Religion: A Preface to Christian Education*. Philadelphia: Westminster Press.

Greaves, R. L. (1969). *The Puritan Revolution and Educational Thought: Background for Reform*. New Brunswick, NJ, Rutgers University Press

Griffith, J. (1996). Relation of parental involvement, empowerment, and school traits to student academic performance. *Journal of Educational Research*, 90 (1), 33–41.

Gump, P. V., & Barker, R. G. (1964). Overview and prospects. In Barker, R. G., & Gump, P. V. (Eds.), *Big School, Small School: High School Size and Student Behavior*. Stanford, CA: Stanford University Press.

Gutek, G. L. (1968). *Pestalozzi and Education*. New York: Random House.

Heafford, M. (1967). *Pestalozzi: His Thought and its Relevance Today*. London: Methuen.

Henderson, A. T., & Mapp, K. L. (2002). *A New Wave of Evidence: The Impact of School, Family, and Community Connections on Student Achievement*. Austin, TX: Southwest Educational Development Laboratory.

Hetherington, E. M., & Clingempeel, W. G. (1992). Coping with marital transitions: A family systems perspective. *Monographs of the Society for Research in Child Development*, 57(1).

Hetherington, E. M., & Jodl, K. M. (1994). Stepfamilies as settings for child development. In A. Booth and J. Dunn (Eds.), *Stepfamilies: Who Benefits? Who Does Not?* (pp. 55–79). Hillsdale, NJ: Erlbaum Associates.

Hiner, N. R. (1988). The cry of Sodom enquired into: Educational analysis in seventeenth century New England. *The Social History of American Education*. Urbana, IL: University of Illinois Press.

Hoffer, T., Greeley, A. M., & Coleman, J. S. (1987). Catholic High School effects on achievement growth. In Haertel, E. H., James, T., & Levin, H. (Eds.), *Comparing Public and Private Schools* (pp. 67–88). New York: Falmer Press.

Holy Bible. (1973). Grand Rapids, MI: Zondervan.

Hood, C. (2001). *Japanese Education Reform: Nakasone's Legacy*. Routledge: London.

Hoover-Dempsey, K. V., Walker, J. M., & Jones, K. P. (2002). Teachers involving parents (TIP): Results from an in-service teacher education program for enhancing parental involvement. *Teacher and Teacher Education*, 18 (7), 843–867.

Horne, H. H. (1923). *Idealism in Education or First Principles of Making Men and Women*. New York: Macmillan.

Horne, H. H. (1931). *This New Education*. New York: Abingdon.

Horne, H. H. (1932). *The Democratic Philosophy of Education: Companion to Dewey's Democracy and Education*. New York: Macmillan.

Huffman, L., Mehlinger, S., & Kerivan, A. (2000). *Off to a Good Start*. Chapel Hill: Child Mental Health Foundation & Agencies Network.

Husband, J., & O'Loughlin, J. (2004). *Daily Life in the Industrial United States, 1870–1900*. Westport, CT: Greenwood Press.

Jacob, M. C. (1997). *Scientific Culture and the Making of the Industrial West*. New York: Oxford University Press.

Jeynes, W. (1999a). The effects of religious commitment on the academic achievement of black and Hispanic children. *Urban Education*, 34 (4), 458–479.

Jeynes, W. (2000b). The effects of several of the most common family structures on the academic achievement of eighth graders. *Marriage and Family Review*, 30 (1/2), 73–97.

Jeynes, W. (2002a). *Divorce, Family Structure, and the Academic Success of Children.* Binghamton, New York: Haworth Press.

Jeynes, W. (2003a). A meta-analysis: the effects of parental involvement on minority children's academic achievement. *Education & Urban Society, 35* (2), 202–218.

Jeynes, W. (2003b). The effects of black and Hispanic twelfth graders living in intact families and being religious on their academic achievement. *Urban Education, 38* (1), 35–57.

Jeynes, W. (2004). Immigration in the United States and the golden age of education: Was Ravitch right? *Educational Studies, 35* (3), 248–270.

Jeynes, W. (2005a). A meta-analysis: Parental involvement and secondary student educational outcomes. *Evaluation Exchange of the Harvard Family Research Project, 10* (4), 6.

Jeynes, W. (2005b). A meta-analysis of the relation of parental involvement to urban elementary school student academic achievement. *Urban Education, 40* (3), 237–269.

Jeynes, W. (2005c). Parental involvement in East Asian schools. In Hiatt-Michael, D. (Ed.). *International Perspectives on Parental Involvement* (pp. 153–179). Greenwich, CT: Information Age Press.

Jeynes, W. (2006a). Standardized tests and the true meaning of kindergarten and pre-school. *Teachers' College Record, 108* (10), 1,937–1,959.

Jeynes, W. (2007a). *American Educational History: School, Society & the Common Good.* Thousand Oaks, CA: Sage.

Jeynes, W. (2007b). The relationship between parental involvement and urban second-ary school student academic achievement: A meta-analysis. *Urban Education, 42* (1), 82–110.

Jeynes, W. (2009). *A Call to Character Education and Prayer in the Schools.* Westport, CT: Praeger.

Jeynes, W. (2010). The salience of the subtle aspects of parental involvement and encour-aging that involvement: implications for school-based programs. *Teachers' College Record, 112* (3), 747–774.

Kaestle, C. (1973). *Joseph Lancaster & the Monitorial School Movement.* New York: Teachers' College Press.

Keenleyside, H. L., & Thomas, A. F. (1937). *History of Japanese Education and Present Educational System.* Tokyo: Hokuseido Press.

Keith, P. B., & Lichtman, M. V. (1994). Does parental involvement influence the aca-demic achievement of Mexican–American eighth-graders? Results from the National Education Longitudinal Study. *School Psychology Quarterly, 9* (4), 256–273.

Kliebard, H. M. (1969). *Religion and Education in America.* Scranton, PA: International Textbook Company.

Lawson, D., & Lean, A. E. (1964). *John Dewey and the World View.* Carbondale, IL: Southern Illinois University Press.

Levine, R. A., & White, M. (1986). Human conditions: The cultural basis of educational development. New York: Rutledge.

Lewy, G. (1996). *Why America Needs Religion.* Grand Rapids: Eerdmanns.

Lilley, I. M. (1967). *Friedrich Froebel: A Selection from his Writings.* Cambridge: Cambridge University Press.

Lindle, J. C. (1990). Five reasons to prepare your staff for parental involvement. *School Administrator, 47* (6), 19–22, 24.

Mann, H. (1839). *Second Annual Report.* Dutton & Wentworth.

Mann, H. (1845). *Eighth Annual Report.* Dutton & Wentworth.

Mann, H. (1846). *Ninth Annual Report.* Dutton & Wentworth.

Mann, H. (1849). *Twelfth Annual Report.* Dutton & Wentworth.

Mann, H. (1957). *The Republic and the School: Horace Mann on the Education of Free Men.* New York: Teachers' College, Columbia University.

Mann, H. (1969). *Lectures on Education.* New York: Arno.

Mann, M. P. (Ed.) (1907). *Life of Horace Mann.* Washington, D.C.: National Education Association.

Martin, J. (2002). *The Education of John Dewey: A Biography.* New York: Columbia University Press.

Mather, C. (1708). A Master in Our Israel. In Smith, W. (1973). *Theories of Education in Early America* (pp. 9–24). Native Americanapolis: Bobbs-Merrill Company.

McLanahan, S., & Sandefur, G. (1994). *Growing Up with a Single Parent: What Hurts, What Helps.* Cambridge: Harvard University Press.

McClellan, E. B., & Reese, W. J. (1988). *The Social History of American Education.* Urbana: University of Illinois Press.

Messerli, J. (1972). *Horace Mann: A Biography.* New York, Knopf.

Morgan, J. (1986). *Godly Learning: Puritan Attitudes Towards Religion, Learning, and Education.* New York: Cambridge University Press.

National Center for Education Statistics. (1989). *Trends in International Mathematics and Science Study, 1988.* Washington, D.C.: National Center for Education Statistics.

National Center for Education Statistics. (1993). *120 Years of American Education.* Washington, D.C.: U.S. Department of Education.

National Commission on Excellence in Education. (1983). *A Nation at Risk.* Washington, D.C.: National Commission on Excellence in Education.

Peressini, D. D. (1998). The portrayal of parents in the school mathematics reform literature: Locating the context for parental involvement. *Journal for Research in Mathematics Education, 29* (5), 55–582.

Pestalozzi, J. (1801). *Leonard and Gertrude.* Philadelphia: Groff.

Pestalozzi, J. (1898). *How Gertrude Teaches her Children: An Attempt to Help Mothers to Teach their Own Children and an Account of the Method.* Trans. Lucy Hoilland & Francis Turner, Syracuse: Bardeen.

Pestalozzi, J. (1916). How a child is led to God through maternal love. In Green, J. A. (Ed.), *Pestalozzi's Educational Writings.* London: Edward Arnold.

Popenoe, D. (1994). The evolution of marriage and the problem of stepfamilies: A biosocial perspective. In A. Booth and J. Dunn (Eds.) *Stepfamilies: Who Benefits? Who Does Not?* (pp. 55–79). Hillsdale, New Jersey: Erlbaum Associates.

Pulliam, J. D., & Van Patten, J. J. (1999) *History of Education in America.* Merrill/Prentice Hall: Upper Saddle River, New Jersey.

Ravitch, D. (1974). *The Great School Wars.* New York: Basic Books.

Rippa, S. A. (1997). *Education in a Free Society.* White Plains: Longman.

Rury, John L. (2002). *Education and Social Change: Themes in the History of American Schooling.* Mahwah, NJ: Erlbaum Associates.

Rush, B. (1785). *Plan of Education.* Carlisle, PA: Dickinson College.

Rush, B., letter to Richard Price, May 25, 1786, in Butterfield, L. H. (Ed.) (1951). *Letters of Benjamin Rush, Vol. 1.* Princeton, NJ: Princeton University Press, pp. 388–389.

Sah-Myung, H. (1983). The Republic of Korea. In Thomas, R. M., & Postlethwaite, T. N. (Eds.), *Schooling in East Asia.* Oxford: Pergamon Press, (pp. 204–235).

Shimizu, K. (1992). Shido: Education and selection in Japanese middle school. *Comparative Education, 28* (2), 114–125.

Simons, R. L. (1994). The impact of mothers' parenting involvement by nonresidential fathers and parental conflict on the adjustment of adolescent children. *Journal of Marriage & the Family, 56* (2), 356–374.

Smith, W. (1973). *Theories of Education in Early America.* Indianapolis: Bobbs-Merrill Company.

Spodek, B. (2003). *Handbook of Research on the Education of Young Children.* New York: Macmillan.

Spring, J. (1997). *The American School 1642–1996.* New York: Longman.

Stipek, D., & Seal, K. (2001). *Motivated Minds: Raising Children to Love Learning.* New York: Holt & Co.

Tharp, L. H. (1953). *Until Victory: Horace Mann and Mary Peabody.* Boston: Little, Brown.

Tyack, D. (1974). *The One Best System: A History of American Urban Education.* Cambridge: Harvard University Press.

Ulich, R. (1957). *Three Thousand Years of Educational Wisdom.* Cambridge: Harvard University Press.

Ulich, R. (1968). *A History of Religious Education.* New York: New York University Press.

U.S. Census Bureau. (2001). *Census 2000.* Washington, D.C.: U.S. Census Bureau.

U.S. Department of Education. (2005). *Digest of Education Statistics.* Washington, D.C.: United States Department of Education.

U.S. Department of Education. (1990). *1989 Education Indicators.* Washington, D.C.: U.S. Department of Education.

U.S. Department of Justice. (1983). *Report to the Nation on Crime and Justice.* Washington, D.C.: U.S. Department of Justice.

Urban, W., & Wagoner, J. (2000). *American Education: A History.* Boston: McGraw Hill.

Wallerstein, J. S., & Blakeslee, S. (1989). *Second Chances: Men, Women, and Children a Decade after Divorce.* New York: Ticknor and Fields.

Weber, M. (1958). *The Protestant Ethic and the Spirit of Capitalism.* Trans. Talcott Parsons. New York: Charles Scribner's Sons.

Webster, N. (1793). *Effects of Slavery on Morals and Industry.* Hartford: Hudson & Goodwin.

Webster, N. (1834). *The Value of the Bible, and the Excellence of the Christian Religion: For use of families and schools.* New Haven: Durrie & Peck.

White, D. F. (1989). *The Urbanists, 1865–1915.* New York: Greenwood Press.

Williams, B. M., Wright, D., & Rosenthal, D. (1983). A model for intervention with latency-aged children of divorce. *Family Therapy, 10* (2), 111–124.

Willison, G. F. (1966). *Saints and Strangers.* London: Longmans.

Wirtz, W. (1977). *On Further Examination.* New York: College Entrance Examination Board.

Young, J. W. (1995). Recentering the SAT score scale. *College & University, 70* (2), 60–62.

Yulish, S. M. (1980). *The Search for a Civic Religion.* Washington, D.C.: University Press of America.

Zill, N. (1994). Understanding why children in stepfamilies have more learning and behavior problems than children in nuclear families. In A. Booth & J. Dunn (Eds.), *Stepfamilies: Who Benefits? Who Does Not?* (pp. 109–137). Hillsdale: Erlbaum.

Zill, N., & Nord, C. W. (1994). *Running in Place.* Washington, D.C.: Child Trends.

Chapter 2

Bandura, A. (1977). *Social Learning Theory.* Englewood Cliffs, NJ: Prentice Hall.

Baumrind, D. (1971). Current patterns of parental authority. *Developmental Psychology, 4*(1), 1–103.

Blanshard, P. (1963). *Religion and the Schools.* Boston: Beacon Press.

Bo, I. (1995). The sociocultural environment as a source of growth among 15–16 year old boys. *Children's Environment, 12*(4), 469–478.

Boehnke, K., Scott, W. A., & Scott, R. (1996). Family climate as a determinant of academic performance. East Asian and Euro–American cultures compared. In Pandey, J., & Sinha, D. (Eds.), *Asian Contributions to Cross-Cultural Psychology* (pp. 119–137). Thousand Oaks: Sage Publications.

Borruel, T. W. (2002). The ten p's of parent communication. A strategy for staff development. *Child Care Information Exchange, 143*(1), 54–57.

Bronfenbrenner, U. (1979). *The Ecology of Human Development.* Cambridge, MA: Harvard University Press.

Brooks, R. B., & Goldstein, (2001). *Raising Resilient Children: Fostering Strength, Hope, and Optimism in Your Child.* Lincolnwood, IL: Contemporary Books.

Brooks, R. B., & Goldstein, S. (2001). *Raising Resilient Children: Fostering Strength, Hope, and Optimism in Your Child.* Lincolnwood, IL: Contemporary Books.

Brown, B. B., Bakken, J. P., Nguyen, J., & Von Bank, H. G. (2007). Sharing information about peer relations: Parents and adolescent opinions and behaviors in Hmong and African American families. In Brown, B. B., & N. S. Mounts (Eds.), *Linking Parents and Family to Adolescent Peer Relations: Ethnic and Cultural Considerations* (pp. 67–82). San Francisco: Jossey Bass.

Carleton, D. (2002). *Landmark Congressional Laws on Education.* Westport, CT: Greenwood Press.

Casanova, P., Garcia-Linares, C., de la Torre, M., & Carpio, d. (2005). Influence of family and socio-demographic variables on students with low academic achievement. *Educational Psychology, 25*(4), 423–435.

Cherlin, A. J. (1978). Remarriage as an incomplete institution. *American Journal of Sociology, 84*(3), 634–650.

Cohen, D. K. (1973). The price of community control. In C. Greer (Ed.), *The Solution as Part of the Problem* (pp. 42–65). New York: Harper & Row.

Conciatore, J. (1990). Nation's report card shows little progress, black students close gap. *Black Issues in Higher Education, 6*(22), 30–31.

Crews, F. C. (1998). *Unauthorized Freud: Doubters Confront a Legend.* New York: Viking.

Cross, T., & Slater, R. B. (2000). The alarming decline in the academic performance of African–American men. *Journal of Blacks in Higher Education, 27*, 82–87.

Cubberley, E. (1920). *The History of Education.* Boston: Houghton Mifflin.

Davalos, D. B., Chavez, E. L., & Guardiola, R. J. (2005). Effects of perceived parental school support and family communication on delinquent behaviors in Latinos and white non-Latinos. *Cultural Diversity & Ethnic Minority Psychology, 11*(1), 57–68.

Davis-Kean, P. E. (2005). The influence of parent education and family income on child achievement: The indirect role of parent expectations and the home environment. *Journal of Family Psychology, 19* (2), 294–304.

Delgado-Gaitan, C. (2004). *Involving Latino Families in Schools: Raising Student Achievement through Home–School Partnerships.* Thousand Oaks: Sage.

Dewey, J. (1902). *The Child and the Curriculum.* Chicago: University of Chicago Press.

Dewey, J. (1910). *The Influence of Darwin on Philosophy.* New York: Holt.

Dewey, J. (1915). *The School and Society.* Chicago: University of Chicago Press.

Dewey, J. (1920). *Reconstruction in Philosophy.* New York: Holt.

Dewey, J. (1990). *The School and Society/The Child and the Curriculum.* Chicago: University of Chicago Press.

Doinick, E. (1998). *Madness on the Couch: Blaming the Victim in the Heydey of Psychoanalysis.* New York: Simon & Schuster.

Domina, T. (2005). Leveling the home advantage: Assessing the effectiveness of parental involvement in elementary school. *Sociology of Education, 78* (3), 233–249.

Dunn, J. (1955). *Retreat from Learning.* New York: David McKay.

Egan, K. (2002). *Getting It Wrong from the Beginning.* New Haven: Yale University Press.

Englund, M. M., Luckner, A. E., Whaley, G. J., & Egeland, B. (2004). Children's achievement in early elementary school: Longitudinal effects of parental involvement, expectations and quality of assistance. *Journal of Educational Psychology, 96* (4), 723–730.

Epstein, J. (2001). *School, Family, and Community Partnerships.* Boulder: Westview Press.

Etzioni, A. (1964). *Social Change: Sources, Patterns & Consequences.* New York: Basic Books.

Freud, S. (1938). *The Basic Writings of Sigmund Freud.* New York: Modern Library.

Friedman, H., & Schustock, M. W. (2001). *Readings in Personality: Classic Theories in Modern Research.* Boston: Allyn & Bacon.

Fromkin, V. (1973). *Speech Errors as Linguistic Evidence.* The Hague, Netherlands: Mouton.

Garbers, C., Tunstill, J., & Allnock, D. (2006). Facilitating access to services for children and families: Lessons for Sure Start local programmes. *Child & Family Social Work, 11* (4), 287–296.

Goldberg, J. (2008). Exit stage right. *National Review, 60* (22). 1 December, 8–12.

Green, C. L. Walker, J. M. T., & Hoover-Dempsey, K. V. (2007). Parents' motivations for involvement in children's education: An empirical test of a theoretical model of parental involvement. *Journal of Educational Psychology, 99* (3), 532–544.

Green, L. R., Blasik, K., Hartshorn, K., & Shatten-Jones, E. (2000). Closing the achievement gap in science: A program to encourage minority and female students to participate and succeed. *ERS Spectrum, 18,* 3–13.

Green, S. R. (2001). Closing the achievement gap: Lessons learned and challenges ahead. *Teaching and Change, 8,* 215–224.

Hamburg, D. A. (1992). *Today's Children: Creating a Future for a Generation in Crisis.* New York: Times Books.

Hara, S. R. (1998). Parent involvement: The key to improved student achievement. *School Community Journal, 8* (2), 9–19.

Haycock, K. (2001). Closing the achievement gap. *Educational Leadership, 58* (6), 6–11.

Hedges, L. V., and Nowell, A. (1999). Changes in the black–white gap in achievement test scores. *Sociology of Education, 72,* 111–135.

Henderson, A. T., & Mapp, K. L. (2002). *A New Wave of Evidence: The Impact of School, Family, and Community Connections on Student Achievement.* Austin, TX: Southwest Educational Development Laboratory.

Hetherington, E. M., & Jodl, K. M. (1994). Stepfamilies as settings for child development. In A. Booth and J. Dunn (Eds.), *Stepfamilies: Who Benefits? Who Does Not?* (pp. 55–79). Hillsdale, New Jersey: Erlbaum Associates.

Hiner, N. R., & Hawes, J. M. (1985). Growing Up in America: Children in Historical Perspective. Urbana: University of Illinois Press.

Hoover-Dempsey, K. V., Walker, J. M., & Jones, K. P. (2002). Teachers involving parents (TIP): Results from an in-service teacher education program for enhancing parental involvement. *Teacher and Teacher Education, 18* (7), 843–867.

Jencks, C. (1992). *Rethinking Social Policy: Race, Poverty & the Underclass.* Cambridge, MA: Harvard University.

Jeynes, W. (1999a). The effects of religious commitment on the academic achievement of black and Hispanic children. *Urban Education, 34* (4), 458–479.

Jeynes, W. (1999b). The effects of remarriage following divorce on the academic achievement of children. *Journal of Youth and Adolescence, 28* (3), 385–393.

Jeynes, W. (2000a). Assessing school choice: A balanced perspective. *Cambridge Journal of Education, 30* (2), 223–241.

Jeynes, W. (2000b). The effects of several of the most common family structures on the academic achievement of eighth graders. *Marriage and Family Review, 30* (1/2), 73–97.

Jeynes, W. (2001a). The effects of recent parental divorce on their children's consumption of alcohol. *Journal of Youth and Adolescence, 30* (3), 305–319.

Jeynes, W. (2001b). The effects of recent parental divorce on their children's consumption of marijuana and cocaine. *Journal of Divorce and Remarriage, 35* (3/4), 43–65.

Jeynes, W. (2001c). The effects of recent parental divorce on their children's sexual attitudes and behavior. *Journal of Divorce and Remarriage, 35* (1/2), 115–133.

Jeynes, W. (2002a). *Divorce, Family Structure, and the Academic Success of Children.* Binghamton, New York: Haworth Press.

Jeynes, W. (2002b). Does widowhood or remarriage have the greater impact on the academic achievement of children? *Omega: Journal of Death and Dying, 44* (3), 319–343.

Jeynes, W. (2002c). The challenge of controlling for SES in social science and education research. *Educational Psychology Review, 14* (2), 205–221.

Jeynes, W. (2002d). The Relationship between the Consumption of Various Drugs by Adolescents and their Academic Achievement. *American Journal of Drug and Alcohol Abuse, 28* (1), 1–21.

Jeynes, W. (2003a). A meta-analysis: the effects of parental involvement on minority children's academic achievement. *Education & Urban Society, 35* (2), 202–218.

Jeynes, W. (2003b). The effects of black and Hispanic twelfth graders living in intact families and being religious on their academic achievement. *Urban Education, 38* (1), 35–57.

Jeynes, W. (2005a). A meta-analysis: Parental involvement and secondary student educational outcomes. *Evaluation Exchange of the Harvard Family Research Project, 10* (4), 6.

Jeynes, W. (2005b). A meta-analysis of the relation of parental involvement to urban elementary school student academic achievement. *Urban Education, 40,* (3), 237–269.

Jeynes, W. (2005c). Parental involvement in East Asian schools. In Hiatt-Michael, D. (Ed.). *International Perspectives on Parental Involvement* (pp. 153–179). Greenwich, CT: Information Age Press.

Jeynes, W. (2006a). Standardized tests and the true meaning of kindergarten and preschool. *Teachers' College Record, 108* (10), 1,937–1,959.

Jeynes, W. (2006b). The impact of parental remarriage on children: A meta-analysis. *Marriage and Family Review, 40* (4), 75–102.

Jeynes, W. (2007a). *American Educational History: School, Society & the Common Good.* Thousand Oaks, CA: Sage.

Jeynes, W. (2007b). The relationship between parental involvement and urban secondary school student academic achievement: A meta-analysis. *Urban Education, 42* (1), 82–110.

Jeynes, W. (2008a). A meta-analysis of the relationship between phonics instruction and minority elementary school student academic achievement student. *Education & Urban Society, 40* (2), 151–166.

Jeynes, W. (2008b). Factors that reduce or eliminate the achievement gap. Speech given at Harvard University Conference on the Achievement Gap in Cambridge, Massachusetts, February.

Jeynes, W. (2008c). The academic contributions of faith-based schools. Speech given at the White House Conference on inner city children and faith based schools in Washington, D.C., April.

Jeynes, W. (2009). *A Call to Character Education and Prayer in the Schools.* Westport, CT: Praeger.

Jeynes, W. (2010). The salience of the subtle aspects of parental involvement and encouraging that involvement: implications for school-based programs. *Teachers' College Record, 112* (3), 747–774.

Jeynes, W., & Littell, S. (2000). A meta-analysis of studies examining the effect of whole language instruction on the literacy of Low-SES students. *Elementary School Journal, 101* (1), 21–33.

Johnson, P. (1997). *A History of the American People.* New York: Harper Collins.

Jones, L. V. (1984). White–black achievement differences: The narrowing gap. *American Psychologist, 39,* 1,207–1,213.

Kay, P., & Fitzgerald, M. (1997). Parents + teachers + action research = real involvement. *Teaching Exceptional Children, 30* (1), 8–14.

Kirsh, S. J. (2006). *Children, Adolescents and Media Violence.* Thousand Oaks: Sage Publications.

Kliebard, H. M. (1969). *Religion and Education in America.* Scranton, PA: International Textbook Company.

Kozol, J. (1991). *Savage Inequalities.* New York: Crown Publishers.

Krivy, L. (1978). *Falling Off the Ivory Tower: Common Sense Commentaries on Schools and Schooling.* Lahaska, PA: New Hope Publishers.

Lamb, M. (1997). *The Role of the Father in Child Development.* New York: Wiley.

Leary, D. (2008). *Why We Suck: A Feel Good Guide to Staying Fat, Loud, Lazy, and Stupid.* New York: Viking.

Lightfoot, S. L. (1978). *Worlds Apart: Relationships between Families and Schools.* New York: Basic Books.

Logsdon, J. M., & Launius, R. D. (2000). *Reconsidering Sputnik: Forty Years since the Soviet Satellite.* Sydney, Australia: Harward Academic.

Mapp, K. L., Johnson, V. R., Strickland, C. S., & Meza, C. (2010). High school family centers: Transformative spaces linking schools and families in support of student learning. In W. Jeynes (Ed.), *Family Factors and the Educational Success of Children,* (pp. 336–366). New York: Routledge.

McCluskey, N. G. (1958). *Public Schools and Moral Education.* New York: Columbia University.

McDonald, L. G., & Robinson, P. (2009). *A Colossal Failure of Common Sense.* New York: Crown.

McLanahan, S., & Sandefur, G. (1994). *Growing Up with a Single Parent: What Hurts, What Helps.* Cambridge: Harvard University Press.

Melody, M. E., & Peterson, L. M. (1999). *Teaching America about Sex.* New York: New York University Press.

Michaelsen, R. (1970). *Piety in the Public School.* London: Macmillan.

Micklethwart, J., & Woodridge, A. (2009). *God is Back: How the Global Revival of Faith is Changing the World.* New York: Penguin.

Moynihan, P. (1965). *The Moynihan Report.* Washington, D.C.: U.S. Department of Labor.

National Commission on Excellence in Education. (1983). *A Nation at Risk.* Washington, D.C.: National Commission on Academic Excellence.

Orfield, G., Kahlenberg, R. D., Gordon, E. W., Genessee, F., Slocumb, P. D., & Payne, R. K. (2000). The new diversity. *Principal, 79* (5), 6–32.

Osborne, J. W. (1999). Unraveling underachievement among African American boys from an identification with the academics perspective. *Journal of Negro Education, 68,* 555–565.

Paik, S. J. (2007). Conclusion and recommendations. In S. J. Paik, & H. J. Walberg (Eds.). *Narrowing the Achievement Gap* (pp. 185–193). New York: Springer.

Pong, S., Dronkers, J., & Hampden-Thompson, G. (2003). Family policies and children's school achievement in single- versus two-parent families. *Journal of Marriage & the Family, 65,* 681–699.

Popenoe, D. (1994). The evolution of marriage and the problem of stepfamilies: A biosocial perspective. In A. Booth and J. Dunn (Eds.) *Stepfamilies: Who Benefits? Who Does Not?* (pp. 55–79). Hillsdale, New Jersey: Erlbaum Associates.

Ratelle, C. F., Larose, S., & Guay, F. (2005). Perceptions of parental involvement and support as predictors of college students' persistence in science curriculum. *Journal of Family Psychology, 19* (2), 286–293.

Ravitch, D. (1974). *The Great School Wars.* New York: Basic Books.

Reglin, G. L. (1993). *At Risk "Parent and Family" School Involvement Strategies for Low Income Families and African American Families of Unmotivated and Underachieving Students.* Springfield, IL: Charles Thomas.

Rimm-Kaufman, S. E., & Pianta, R. C. (2005). Family–school communication in preschool and kindergarten in the content of a relationship-enhancing intervention. *Early Education Development, 16* (3), 287–316.

Roach, R. (2001). In the academic and think-tank world, pondering achievement-gap remedies take center stage. *Black Issues in Higher Education, 18* (1), 26–27.

Rodgers, K. B., & Rose, H. A. (2002). Risk and resiliency factors among adolescents who experience marital transitions. *Journal of Marriage & the Family, 64,* 1,024–1,037.

Rumberger, R. W., & Willms, J. D. (1992). The impact of racial and ethnic segregation on the achievement gap in California high schools. *Educational Evaluation and Policy Analysis, 14*, 377–396.

Roscigno, V. J. (1998). Race, institutional languages, and the reproduction of educational disadvantage. *Social Forces, 76*, 1,033–1,061.

Salkind, N. J. (2006). *Encyclopedia of Human Development.* Thousand Oaks, CA: Sage Publications.

Sikorski, R. (1993). *Controversies in Constitutional Law.* New York, Garland.

Simpson, C. (1981). Classroom organization and the gap between minority and non-minority student performance levels. *Educational Research Quarterly, 6* (3), 43–53.

Slavin, R., & Madden, N. (2006). Reducing the gap: Success for All and the achievement of African American students. *Journal of Negro Education, 75* (3), 389–400.

Smith, H. L. (2009). *Taking Back the Tower: Simple Solutions to Saving Higher Education.* Westport, CT: Praeger.

So, A. Y., & Chan, K. S. (1984). What matters? The relative impact of language background and socioeconomic status on reading achievement. *NABE: Journal for the National Association for Bilingual Education, 8* (3), 27–41.

Spring, J. (1997). *The American School 1642–1996.* New York: Longman.

Stevenson, H. W., & Stigler, J. W. (1992). *The Learning Gap.* New York: Summit Books.

Thompson, G. L. (2007). Improving the schooling experience of African American students. In S. J. Paik, & H. L. Walberg (Eds.), *Narrowing the Achievement Gap* (pp. 153–170). New York: Springer.

Troen, S. K. (1988). Popular education in nineteenth century St. Louis. In E. McClellan, & W. J. Reese (1988). *The Social History of American Education* (pp. 119–136). Urbana: University of Illinois.

Ulich, R. (1968). *A History of Religious Education.* New York: New York University Press.

U.S. Department of Education. (2005). *Digest of Education Statistics.* Washington, D.C.: United States Department of Education.

U.S. Center for Education Statistics. (1966). *Equality of Educational Opportunity.* Washington, D.C.: U.S. Center for Education Statistics.

U. S. Department of Education. (2005). *Digest of Education Statistics.* Washington, D.C.: United States Department of Education.

U. S. Department of Education. (2008). *Digest of Education Statistics.* Washington, D.C.: United States Department of Education.

U.S. Department of Health & Human Services. (1998). *Statistical Abstract of the United States.* Washington, D.C.: U.S. Department of Health & Human Services.

U.S. Department of Justice. (1999). *Age-specific Arrest Rate and Race-specific Arrest Rates for Selected Offenses, 1965–1998.* Washington, D.C.: U.S. Department of Justice.

Wallerstein, J. S., & Blakeslee, S. (1989). *Second Chances: Men, Women, and Children a Decade after Divorce.* New York: Ticknor and Fields.

Wallerstein, J. S., & Lewis, J. (1998). The long-term impact of divorce on children: A first report from a 25-year study. *Family and Conciliation Courts Review, 36* (3), 368–383.

Wentzel, K. R. (2002). Are effective teachers like good parents? Teaching styles and student adjustment in early adolescence. *Child Development, 73* (1), 287–301.

White, M. (1987). *The Japanese Educational Challenge: A Commitment to Children.* New York: Free Press.

Wirtz, W. (1977). *On Further Examination.* New York: College Entrance Examination Board.

Yewchuk, C. R., & Schlosser, G. (1995). Characteristics of the parents of eminent Canadian women. *Roeper Review, 18* (1), 78–83.

Chapter 3

*Study was included in the meta-analysis.

*Allen, J. J. (1991). An assessment of parental involvement in student homework in Dodds Elementary Schools in Spain and Turkey. (Doctoral dissertation, University of Nevada-Reno). *Dissertation Abstracts International,* 53/03, 713.

*Austin, C. A. (1988). Homework as a parental involvement strategy to improve the achievement of first grade children (Doctoral dissertation, Memphis State University). *Dissertation Abstracts International,* 50/03, 622.

*Bal, S. A., & Goc, J. D. (1999). *Increasing Parental Involvement to Improve Achievement in Reading and Math.* Chicago: Xavier University.

Ballantine, J. H. (1999). Getting involved in our children's education. *Childhood Education, 75* (3), 170–171.

*Bermudez, A. B., & Padron, Y. N. (1990). Improving language skills for Hispanic students through home–school partnerships. *Journal of Educational Issues of Language Minority Students, 6* (1), 33–43.

Bronstein, P., Stoll, M. F., Clauson, J., Abrams, C. L., & Briones, M. (1994). Fathering after separation or divorce: Factors predicting children's adjustment. *Family Relations, 43* (4), 469–479.

*Brutsaert, H. (1998). Home and school influences on academic performance. State and Catholic elementary schools in Belgium Compared. *Educational Review, 50* (1), 37–43.

*Buchanan, A. E., Hansen, P. J., & Quilling, M. R. (1969). *Effects of Increased Home–School Contact on Performance and Attitudes in Mathematics.* Madison: University of Wisconsin Research and Development Center for Cognitive Learning.

Christian, K., Morrison, F. J., & Bryant, F. B. (1998). Predicting kindergarten academic skills: Interactions among child care, maternal education, and family literacy environments. *Early Childhood Research Quarterly, 13* (3), 501–521.

*Clarke, C. (1993). *Project Familia: Final Evaluation Report, 1992–1993.* Brooklyn: New York City Board of Education. Office of Research, Evaluation, and Assessment.

*Collazo-Levy, D., & Villegas, J. (1984). *Project Parents: Awareness, Education, and Involvement. O.E.E. evaluation report, 1982–1983.* Brooklyn: New York City Board of Education.

Deslandes, R., Royer, E., & Turcotte, D. (1997). School achievement at the secondary level: Influence of parenting style and parent involvement in schooling. *McGill Journal of Education, 32* (3), 191–207.

Eccles, J. S., & Harold, R. D. (1993). Parent–school involvement during the early adolescent years. *Teachers' College Record, 94,* 568–587.

Epstein, J. (2001). *School, Family, and Community Partnerships.* Boulder: Westview Press.

Fan, X., & Chen, M. (2001). Parental involvement and students' academic achievement: A meta-analysis. *Educational Psychology Review, 13* (1), 1–22.

*Fantuzzo, J. W., Davis, G. Y., & Ginsburg, M. D. (1995). Effects of parental involvement in isolation or in combination with peer tutoring on student self-concept and mathematics achievement. *Journal of Educational Psychology, 87,* (2), 272–281.

*Fuligni, A. S. (1995). Effects of parental involvement and family context on the academic achievement of third- and fourth-grade children (Doctoral dissertation, University of Michigan). *Dissertation Abstracts International*, 56/04, 2,350.

*Georgiou, S. N. (1999). Parental attributions as predictors of involvement and influences on child achievement. *British Journal of Educational Psychology*, 69 (3), 409–429.

*Gilmore, J. (1985). Improving the attendance of primary children by involving parents in their education. Practicum Report. Nova University, Fort Lauderdale.

Glass, G. V., McGaw, B., & Smith, M. L. (1981). *Meta-analysis in Social Research*. Beverly Hills: Sage.

Green, L. R., Blasik, K., Hartshorn, K., & Shatten-Jones, E. (2000). Closing the achievement gap in science: A program to encourage minority and female students to participate and succeed. *ERS Spectrum*, 18, 3–13.

Green, S. R. (2001). Closing the achievement gap: Lessons learned and challenges ahead. *Teaching and Change*, 8 (2), 215–224.

Greenhouse, J. B., & Iyengar, S. (1994). Sensitivity analysis and diagnosis. In H. Cooper & S. Iyengar (Eds.), *Handbook of Research Synthesis* (pp. 383–398). New York: Russell Sage Foundation.

*Griffith, J. (1996). Relation of parental involvement, empowerment, and school traits to student academic performance. *Journal of Educational Research*, 90 (1), 33–41.

*Griffith, J. (1997). Linkages to school structure and socio-environmental characteristics to parental satisfaction with public education and student academic achievement. *Journal of Applied Social Psychology*, 27 (2), 156–186.

Grolnick, W. S., Benjet, C. Kurowski, C. O., & Apostoleris, P. H. (1997). Predictors of parental involvement in children's schooling. *Journal of Educational Psychology*, 89 (3), 538–548.

*Grolnick, W. S., & Slowiaczek, M. L. (1994). Parents' involvement in children's schooling: A multidimensional conceptualization and motivational model. *Child Development*, 65 (1), 237–252.

*Hampton, F. M., Mumford, D. A., & Bond, L. (1998). Parental involvement in inner city schools: The project FAST extended family approach to success. *Urban Education*, 33 (3), 410–427.

Hara, S. R. (1998). Parent involvement: The key to improved student achievement. *School Community Journal*, 8 (2), 9–19.

Hedges, L. (1981). Distribution theory for Glass's estimate of effect size and related estimators. *Journal of Educational Statistics*, 6 (1), 107–128.

Hedges, L. V., & Cooper, H. (Eds.) (1994). *The Handbook of Research Synthesis*. New York: Russell Sage Foundation.

Henderson, A. T., & Mapp, K. L. (2002). *A New Wave of Evidence: The Impact of School, Family, and Community Connections on Student Achievement*. Austin, TX: Southwest Educational Development Laboratory.

*Hess, R. D., Holloway, S. D., Dickson, W. P., & Price, G. G. (1984). Maternal variables as predictors of children's school readiness and later achievement in vocabulary and mathematics in sixth grade. *Child Development*, 55 (5), 1,902–1,912.

*Hoge, D. R., Smit, E., & Crist, J. T. (1997). Four family process factors predicting academic achievement for sixth and seventh grade. *Educational Research Quarterly*, 21 (2), 27–42.

Hoover-Dempsey, K., & Sandler, H. (1997). Why do parents become involved in their children's education? *Review of Educational Research*, 67 (1), 3–42.

Jeynes, W. (1999a). The effects of religious commitment on the academic achievement of black and Hispanic children. *Urban Education, 34* (4), 458–479.

Jeynes, W. (2002a). *Divorce, Family Structure, and the Academic Success of Children.* Binghamton, New York: Haworth Press.

Jeynes, W. (2002b). The challenge of controlling for SES in social science and education research. *Educational Psychology Review, 14* (2), 205–221.

Jeynes, W. (2003b). The effects of black and Hispanic twelfth graders living in intact families and being religious on their academic achievement. *Urban Education, 38* (1), 35–57.

Jeynes, W. (2004). Immigration in the United States and the golden age of education: Was Ravitch right? *Educational Studies, 35* (3), 248–270.

Jeynes, W. (2005d). Effects of parental involvement on African American children's academic achievement. *Journal of Negro Education, 74* (3), 260–274.

*Koskinen, P. S., Blum, I. H., Bisson, S. A., Phillips, S. M., & Creamer, T. S. (2000). Book access, shared reading and audio models: the literacy learning of linguistically diverse students in school and at home. *Journal of Educational Psychology, 92* (1), 23–336.

*Lipman, M.A.R. (1985). Parental involvement in mathematics homework: A comparison of mothers of fifth and sixth grade students in single-parent households to dual-parent households (Doctoral dissertation, Temple University). *Dissertation Abstracts International,* 55/12, 112.

*Long, A. L. (1991, December). Parental involvement and achievement of fourth grade students. Unpublished doctoral dissertation, Purdue University, West Lafayette.

*Luchuck, U. L. (1998). The effects of parental involvement on student achievement. Unpublished master's thesis. Salem-Teikyo University, Salem, West Virginia.

*Mantzicopoulos, P. Y. (1997). The relationship of family variables to Head Start children's preacademic competence. *Early Education and Development, 8* (4), 357–375.

*Marcon, R. A. (1993, March). Parental involvement and early school success: Following the "class of 2000" at year five. Paper presented at the Biennial Meeting of the Society for Research in Child Development, New Orleans.

*Marcon, R. A. (1999a, March). Impact of parental involvement on children's development and academic performance: A three cohort study. Paper presented at the meeting of the Southeastern Psychological Association, Savannah, Georgia.

*Marcon, R. A. (1999b). Positive relationships between parent school involvement and public school intercity preschoolers' development and academic performance. *School Psychology Review, 28* (3), 395–412.

Mattingly, D. J., Prislin, R., McKenzie, T. L., Rodriguez, J. L., & Kayzar, B. (2002). Evaluating evaluations: The case of parental involvement programs. *Review of Educational Research, 72* (4), 549–576.

Mau, W. (1997). Parental influences on the high school students' academic achievement: A comparison of Asian immigrants, Asian Americans, and white Americans. *Psychology in the Schools, 34* (3), 267–277.

*McKinney, J. A. (1975). The development and implementation of a tutorial program for parents to improve the reading and mathematics achievement of their children (ERIC Document No. 113 703).

McLanahan, S., & Sandefur, G. (1994). *Growing Up with a Single Parent: What Hurts, What Helps.* Cambridge: Harvard University Press.

*Miliotis, D., Sesma, A., & Masten, A. S. (1999). Parenting as a protective process for school success in children from home less families. *Early Education and Development, 10* (2), 111–133.

*Miedel, W. T., & Reynolds, A. J. (1999). Parent involvement in early intervention for disadvantaged children: Does it matter? *Journal of School Psychology, 37* (4), 379–402.

Muller, C. (1998). Gender differences in parental involvement and adolescents' mathematics achievement. *Sociology of Education, 71* (4), 336–356.

*Nesbitt, G. K. (1993). The effects of three school-to-home parental involvement communication programs on reading achievement, conduct, homework habits, attendance, and parent–student–school interaction (Doctoral dissertation, Georgia State University). *Dissertation Abstracts International, 54/11,* 3993.

*Offenberg, R. M., Rodriguez-Acosta, C., & Epstein, B. (1979). *Project PACT (Parents and Children Together): Evaluation for the Second Year, 1978–79.* Philadelphia: Philadelphia School District, Office of Research and Evaluation.

Peressini, D. D. (1998). The portrayal of parents in the school mathematics Reform literature: Locating the context for parental involvement. *Journal for Research in Mathematics Education, 29* (5), 55–582.

*Revicki, D. A. (1981). The relationship among socioeconomic status, home environment, parental involvement, child self-concept, and child achievement (Doctoral dissertation, University of North Carolina—Chapel Hill). *Dissertation Abstracts International,* 42/6, 2484.

*Reynolds, A. J. (1992). Comparing measures of parental involvement on their effects on academic achievement. *Early Childhood Research Quarterly, 7* (3), 441–462.

Rosnow, R. L., & Rosenthal, R. (1996). Computing contrasts, effect sizes, and counter-nulls on other people's published data: General procedures for research consumers. *Psychological Methods, 1* (4), 331–340.

Sanders, M. G. (1998). The effects of school, family, and community support on the academic achievement of African American adolescents. *Urban Education, 33* (3), 385–409.

*Schwartz, S. S. (1996). *Focus on First Graders.* El Paso, Texas: El Paso Independent School District.

*Shaver, A. V., & Walls, R. T. (1998). Effect of Title I parent involvement on student reading and mathematics achievement. *Journal of Research and Development in Education,* 31 (2), 90–97.

*Taylor, L. C, Hinton, I. D., & Wilson, M. N. (1995) Parental influences on academic performance in African–American students. *Journal of Child and Family Studies, 4* (3), 93–302.

*Uguroglu, M. E., & Walberg, H. J. (1986). Predicting achievement and motivation. *Journal of Research and Development in Education, 19* (3), 1–12.

*Villas-Boas, A. (1998). The effects of parental involvement in homework on student achievement in Portugal and Luxembourg. *Childhood Education, 74* (6), 367–371.

*Williams, V. (1999). The influence of parenting practices on ethnic identity and social and academic outcomes (Doctoral dissertation, Florida Atlantic University). *Dissertation Abstracts International,* 60/07, 3,599.

*Woods, C., Barnard, D. P., & TeSelle, E. (1974). *The Effect of Parental Involvement Programs on Reading Readiness Scores.* Mesa, Arizona: Mesa Public Schools.

*Yap, M., & Enoki, D. Y. (1995). In search of the elusive magic bullet: Parental involvement and student outcomes. *School Community Journal, 5* (2), 97–106.

*Zellman, G. L., & Waterman, J. M. (1998). Understanding the impact of parent school involvement on children's educational outcomes. *Journal of Educational Research, 91* (1), 146–156.

Chapter 4

*Asterisks indicate studies included in the meta-analysis.

*Aeby, V. G., Thyer, B. A., & Carpenter-Abey, T. (1999). *Comparing Outcomes of an Alternative School Program Offered With and Without Intensive Family Involvement.* U.S. Department of Education, Washington, D.C.

Ballantine, J. H. (1999). Getting involved in our children's education. *Childhood Education, 75* (3), 170–171.

Bauch, P. A., & Goldring, E. B. (1995). Parent involvement and school responsiveness. Facilitating the home–school connection in school of choice. *Educational Evaluation & Policy Analysis, 17,* 1–21.

*Bermudez, A. B., & Padron, Y. N. (1990). Improving language skills for Hispanic students through home–school partnerships. *Journal of Educational Issues of Language Minority Students, 6* (1), 33–43.

Bronstein, P., Stoll, M. F., Clauson, J., Abrams, C. L., & Briones, M. (1994). Fathering after separation or divorce: Factors predicting children's adjustment. *Family Relations, 43* (4) 469–479.

*Brown, J. D., & Madhere, S. (1996). Post-secondary achievement: How prepared are our children? Presented at the National Black Family Summit at Hilton Head, S.C. April 4.

*Brownell, A. B. (1995). *Determinants and Consequences of Parental Involvement in Education.* Northwestern University: Evanston, Illinois.

*Cardenas-Rivera, N. G. (1994). A study of acculturation, parenting style and adolescents' academic achievement in a group of low socioeconomic status Mexican American families. Dissertation Texas A&M.

Christian, K., Morrison, F. J., & Bryant, F. B. (1998). Predicting kindergarten academic skills: Interactions among child care, maternal education, and family literacy environments. *Early Childhood Research Quarterly, 13* (3), 501–521.

*Cooper, H., Lindsay, J. J., & Nye, B. (2000). Homework in the home: How student, family, and parenting-style differences relate to the homework process. *Contemporary Educational Psychology, 25* (4), 464–487.

Crane, J. (1996). Effects of home environment, SES, and maternal test scores on mathematics achievement. *Journal of Educational Research, 89* (5), 305–314.

Crouter, A. C., Helms-Erickson, H., Updegraff, K., & McHale, S. M. (1999). Conditions underlying parents' knowledge about children's daily lives in middle childhood. Between- and within- family comparisons. *Child Development, 70* (1), 246–259.

*Desimone, L. M. (1996). Comparing the relationship of parent involvement and locus of control to adolescent school achievement: An analysis of racial/ethnic and income differences. Dissertation for the University of North Carolina at Chapel Hill.

*Deslandes, R., Royer, E., & Turcotte, D. (1997). School achievement at the secondary level: Influence of parenting style and parent involvement in schooling. *McGill Journal of Education, 32* (3), 191–207.

*Eagle, E. (1989). Socioeconomic status, family structure and parental involvement: The correlates of achievement. Paper presented at the Annual Meeting of the American Educational Research Association in San Francisco on March 27–31, 1989.

*Epstein, J. L., Herick, S. C., & Coates, L. (1996). Effects of summer home learning packets on student achievement in language arts in the middle grades. *School Effectiveness & School Improvement, 7*(4), 383–410.

*Fehrmann, P. G., Keith, T. Z., & Reimers, T. H. (1987). Home influence on school learning: Direct and indirect effects of parental involvement on high school grades. *Journal of Educational Research, 80*(6), 330–337.

*Fletcher, A. (1994). Parental and Peer influence on the academic achievement of African American adolescents. Doctoral Dissertation. Temple University.

Gortmaker, S. L., Must, A., Perrin, J. M., Sobol, A. M. et al. (1993). Social and economic consequences of overweight in adolescence and young adulthood. *New England Journal of Medicine, 329*(14), 1008–1012.

Grayson, P. J. (1999). Who goes to university and why? *Education Canada, 39* (2), 37–39.

Grolnick, W. S., Benjet, C., Kurowski, C. O., & Apostoleris, P. H. (1997). Predictors of parental involvement in children's schooling. *Journal of Educational Psychology, 89*(3), 538–548.

*Grolnick, W. S., & Slowiaczek, M. L. (1994). Parents' involvement in children's schooling: A multidimensional conceptualization and motivational model. *Child Development, 65*(1), 237–252.

*Hampton, F. M., Mumford, D. A., & Bond, L. (1998). Parental involvement in inner city schools: The project FAST extended family approach to success. *Urban Education, 33* (3), 410–427.

Hara, S. R. (1998). Parent involvement: The key to improved student achievement. *School Community Journal, 8* (2), 9–19.

Hedges, L. (1981). Distribution theory for Glass's estimate of effect size and related estimators. *Journal of Educational Statistics, 6*(1), 107–128.

*Heiss, J. (1996). Effects of African American family structure on school attitudes on school attitudes and performance. *Social Problems, 43*(3), 246–267.

*Hoge, D. R., Smit, E., & Crist, J. T. (1997). Four family process factors predicting academic achievement for sixth and seventh grade. *Educational Research Quarterly, 21*(2), 27–42.

Jeynes, W. H. (1998). Examining the effects of divorce on the academic achievement of children: How should we control for SES? *Journal of Divorce and Remarriage, 29* (3/4), 1–21.

*Jeynes, W. H. (2000). Effects of parental involvement on the academic achievement of adolescents. Paper presented at the annual conference of the American Psychological Association in Washington, D.C. in August, 2000.

Jeynes, W. (2002a). *Divorce, Family Structure, and the Academic Success of Children.* Haworth Press: Binghamton, New York.

*Jeynes, W. (2002e) Does parental involvement eliminate the effects of parental divorce on the academic achievement of adolescents? *Journal of Divorce and Remarriage, 37* (1/2), 101–115.

*Keith, T. Z., Keith, P. B., Quirk, K. J., Cohen-Rosenthal, E., & Franzese, B. (1996). Effects of parental involvement on achievement for students who attend school in rural America. *Journal of Research in Rural Education, 12*(2), 55–67.

*Keith, T. M., Keith, P. B., Bickley, P. G., & Singh, K. (1992, April). Effects of parental involvement of eighth grade achievement: LISREL analysis of NELS-88 data. Paper presented at the Annual Meeting of the American Educational Research Association, San Francisco.

*Keith, T. Z., Keith, P. B., Troutman, G. C., Bickley, P. G., Trivette, P. S., & Singh, K. (1993). Does parental involvement affect eighth-grade student achievement? Structural analysis of national data. *School Psychology Review, 22* (3), 474–496.

*Keith, T. M., Keith, P. B., Sperduto, J., Santillo, S., & Killings, S. (1998) Longitudinal effects of parental involvement on high school grades: similarities and differences across gender and ethnic groups. *Journal of School Psychology 36* (3), 335–363.

*Keith, P. B., & Lichtman, M. (1994). Does parental involvement influence the academic achievement of Mexican American eighth graders? Results from the National Education Longitudinal Study. *School Psychology Quarterly, 9* (4), 256–272.

*Keith, P. B., & Lichtman, M. (1992, April). Testing the influences of parental involvement on Mexican–American eighth grade students' academic achievement: A structural equations analysis. Paper presented at the Annual Meeting of the American Educational Researcher's Association in San Francisco, California.

*Keith, T. Z., Reimers, T. M., Fehrmann, P. G., Pottebaum, S. M., & Aubey, L. W. (1986). Parental involvement, homework, and TV time: Direct and indirect effects on high school achievement. *Journal of Educational Psychology 78*(5), 373–80.

Legutko, R. S. (1998). Family effect on rural high school students' postsecondary decisions. *Rural Educator, 20* (2), 11–14.

*Ma, X., (1999). Dropping out of advanced mathematics: The effects of parental involvement. *Teachers' College Record, 101*(1), 60–81.

Mattingly, D. J., Prislin, R., McKenzie, T. L., Rodriguez, J. L., & Kayzar, B. (2002). Evaluating evaluations: The case of parental involvement programs. *Review of Educational Research, 72* (4), 549–576.

*Mau, W. (1997). Parental influences on the high school students' academic achievement: A comparison of Asian immigrants, Asian Americans, and white Americans. *Psychology in the Schools, 34* (3), 267–277.

McBride, B. A., & Lin, H. (1996). Parental involvement in prekindergarten at-risk programs: Multiple perspectives. *Journal of Education for Students Placed at Risk, 1* (4), 349–372.

*McNeal, R. B. (1999). Parental involvement as social capital: Differential effectiveness on science achievement, truancy, and dropping out. *Social Forces, 78* (1), 117–144.

*Melby, J. N., & Conger, R. D. (1996). Parental behaviors and adolescent academic performance: A longitudinal analysis. *Journal of Research on Adolescence, 6* (1), 113–137.

Muller, C. (1998). Gender differences in parental involvement and adolescents' mathematics achievement. *Sociology of Education, 71* (4), 336–356.

Mulroy, M. T., Goldman, J., & Wales, C. (1998). Affluent parents of young children: Neglected parent education audience. *Journal of Extension, 36* (1), 15–30

*O'Reilly, M. E. (1992). The involvement of parents of high school students in a positively-oriented seminar directed at academic achievement. Doctoral dissertation. Loyola University, Chicago, Illinois.

*Paulson, S. E. (1994a). Parenting Style and Parental Involvement: Relations with adolescent achievement. *Mid-Western Educational Researcher 7* (1), 6–11.

*Paulson, S. E. (1994b). Relations of parenting style and parental involvement with ninth grade Students' achievement. *Journal of Early Adolescence, 14* (2), 250–267.

*Peng, S. S., & Wright, D. (1994). Explanation of Academic Achievement of Asian American students. *Journal of Educational Research, 87*(6), 346–352.

Peressini, D. D. (1998). The portrayal of parents in the school mathematics reform literature: Locating the context for parental involvement. *Journal for Research in Mathematics Education*, 29 (5), 55–582.

Portes, A., & MacLeod, D. (1996). Educational progress of children and immigrants: The roles of class, ethnicity, and school context. *Sociology of Education*, 69 (4), 255–275.

*Russell, S., & Elder, G. H. (1997). Academic success and rural America: Family background and community integration. *Childhood*, 4 (2), 169–181.

*Sanders, M. G. (1996). *School–Family Community Partnerships and the Academic Achievement of African American, Urban adolescents*. Center for Research on the Education of Students Placed at Risk. Baltimore, MD.

*Shanham, T., & Walberg, W. (1985) Productive influences on high school student achievement. *Journal of Educational Research*, 78 (6), 357–363.

*Simich-Deudgeon, C. (1993). Increasing student achievement through teacher knowledge about parental involvement. In Chavkin, N. (Ed.). *Families and Schools in a Pluralistic Society*. Albany, New York: SUNY.

*Singh, K., Bickley, P. G., Trivette, P., Keith, T. Z., Patricia, P. B., & Anderson, E. (1995). The effects of four components of parental involvement on eighth-grade student achievement: structural analysis of NELS-88 data. *School Psychology Review*, 24 (2), 219–317.

*Steinberg, L., Lamborn, S. D., Dornbusch, S. M., & Darling, N. (1992). Impact of parenting processes on adolescent achievement: authoritative parenting, school involvement, and encouragement to succeed. *Child Development*, 63 (5), 1,266–1,281.

*Steinberg, L., Elmen, J. D., & Mounts, N. S. (1989). Authoritative parenting, psychological social maturity, and academic success among adolescents. *Child Development*, 60 (6), 1,424–1,436.

*Stevenson, D.L., & Baker, D. P. (1987). The family–school relation and the child's school performance. *Child's Development*, 58 (5), 1,348–1,357.

*Sui-Chu, E. H., & Willms, J. D. (1996). Effects of parental involvement on eighth-grade achievement. *Sociology of Education*, 69 (2), 126–147.

*Taylor, L. C., Hinton, I. D., & Wilson, M. N. (1995) Parental influences on academic performance in African–American Students *Journal of Child and Family Studies*, 4 (3), 93–302.

*Taylor, R. D. (1996). Adolescent perceptions of kinship support and family management practices. Association with adolescent adjustment in African American families. *Developmental Psychology*, 32 (4), 687–695.

*Uguroglu, M. E., & Walberg, H. J. (1986). Predicting achievement and motivation. *Journal of Research and Development in Education*, 19 (3), 1–12.

*Unger, D. G., McLeod, C. E., Brown, M. B., & Tressell, P. A. (2000). The role of family support in interparental conflict and adolescent academic achievement. *Journal of Child and Family Studies* (2), 191–202.

*Veneziano, R. A. (1996). Perceived paternal warmth, paternal involvement, and youths' psychological adjustment in a rural, biracial southern community. Dissertation for University of Connecticut.

*Williams, V. (1999). The influence of parenting practices on ethnic identity and social and academic outcomes. Doctoral dissertation. Florida Atlantic University in Boca Raton, FL, August.

*Wise, J. H. (1972). Parent participation reading clinic—A research demonstration project: Final report. Washington, D.C.: Children's Hospital of the District of Columbia.

*Yan, W. (1999). Successful African American students. *Journal of Negro Education, 68* (1), 5–22.

*Yap, M., & Enoki, D. Y. (1995). In search of the elusive magic bullet: Parental involvement and student outcomes. *School Community Journal, 5* (2), 97–106.

Zakrisson, I., & Ekehammer, B. (1998). Social attitudes and education: Self-selection or socialization? *Scandinavian Journal of Psychology, 39* (2), 117–122.

*Zdzinski, S. F. (1992). Relationships among parental involvement, music aptitude, and musical achievement of instrumental music students. *Journal of Research in Music Education, 40* (2), 114–125.

Zellman, G. L., & Waterman, J. M. (1998). Understanding the Impact of Parent School Involvement on Children's Educational Outcomes. *Journal of Educational Research, 91* (1), 146–156.

Chapter 5

*Asterisks indicate studies included in the meta-analysis

*Austin, C. A. (1988). Homework as a parental involvement strategy to improve the achievement of first grade children. Dissertation for Memphis State University in Memphis, Tennessee.

Balli, S. J. (1998). When mom and dad help: Student reflections on student involvement with homework. *Journal of Research and Development in Education, 31*(3), 142–146.

Balli, S. J., Demo, D. H., & Wedman, J. F. (1998). Family involvement with children's homework: An intervention in the middle grades. *Family Relations, 47* (2), 149–157.

Bauch, P. A., & Goldring, E. B. (1995). Parent involvement and school responsiveness. Facilitating the home–school connection in school of choice. *Educational Evaluation & Policy Analysis, 17,* 1–21.

Bermudez, A. B., & Padron, Y. N. (1990). Improving language skills for Hispanic students through home–school partnerships. *Journal of Educational Issues of Language Minority Students, 6* (1), 33–43.

Bogenschneider, K. (1997). Parental involvement in adolescent schooling: A proximal process with transcontextual validity. *Journal of Marriage and the Family, 59* (3), 718–733.

*Brown, J. D., & Madhere, S. (1996). Post-secondary achievement: How prepared are our children. Presented at the National Summit at Hilton Head, South Carolina, April 4.

*Cardenas-Rivera, N. G. (1994). A study of acculturation, parenting style and adolescents' academic achievement in a group of low socioeconomic status Mexican American families. Dissertation for Texas A & M University in College Station, Texas.

Christian, K., Morrison, F. J., & Bryant, F. B. (1998). Predicting kindergarten academic skills: Interactions among child care, maternal education, and family literacy environments. *Early Childhood Research Quarterly, 13* (3), 501–521.

Coleman, J. S., & Hoffer, T. (1987). *Public & Private High Schools: The Impact of Communities.* New York: Basic Books.

Conciatore, J. (1990). Nation's report card shows little progress, black students close gap. *Black Issues in Higher Education, 6* (22), 30–31.

Crane, J. (1996). Effects of home environment, SES, and maternal test scores on mathematics achievement. *Journal of Educational Research, 89* (5), 305–314.

Cross, T., & Slater, R. B. (1995). A first view of the academic performance of African Americans at three highly ranked colleges. *Journal of Blacks in Higher Education, 7*(1), 76–79.

Cross, T., & Slater, R. B. (2000). The alarming decline in the academic performance of African–American men. *Journal of Blacks in Higher Education, 27,* 82–87.

Deslandes, R., Royer, E., Turcott, D., & Bertrand, R. (1997). School achievement at the secondary level: Influence of parenting style and parent involvement in schooling. *McGill Journal of Education, 32* (3), 191–207.

Dixon, C.S. (1994). An examination of income adequacy for single women two years after divorce. *Journal of Divorce & Remarriage, 22* (1/2), 55–71.

*Fletcher, A. (1994). Parental and peer influence on the academic achievement of African American adolescents. Doctoral dissertation. Temple University in Philadelphia, Pennsylvania. AT 9512675.

*Georgiou, S. N. (1999). Parental attributions as predictors of involvement and influences on child development. *British Journal of Educational Psychology, 69* (3), 409–429.

Gordon, M. T. (1976). A different view of the IQ–achievement gap. *Sociology of Education, 49*(1), 4–11.

Gortmaker, S. L., Must, A., Perrin, J. M., Sobol, A. M., et al. (1993). Social and economic consequences of overweight in adolescence and young adulthood. *New England Journal of Medicine, 329* (14), 1,008–1,012.

Grayson, P. J. (1999). Who goes to university and why? *Education Canada, 39* (2), 37–39.

Green, L. R., Blasik, K., Hartshorn, K., & Shatten-Jones, E. (2000). Closing the achievement gap in science: A program to encourage minority and female students to participate and succeed. *ERS Spectrum, 18,* 3–13.

Green, S. R. (2001). Closing the achievement gap: Lessons learned and challenges ahead. *Teaching and Change, 8,* 215–224.

Griffith, J. (1996). Relation of parental involvement, empowerment, and school traits to student academic performance. *Journal of Educational Research, 90* (1), 33–41.

Griffith, J. (1997). Linkages to school structure and socio-environmental characteristics to parental satisfaction with public education and student academic achievement. *Journal of Applied Social Psychology, 27* (2), 156–186.

*Hampton, F. M., Mumford, D. A., & Bond, L. (1998). Parental involvement in inner city schools: The project FAST extended family approach to success. *Urban Education, 33* (3), 410–427.

Hara, S. R. (1998). Parent involvement: The key to improved student achievement. *School Community Journal, 8* (2), 9–19.

Haycock, K. (2001). Closing the achievement gap. *Educational Leadership, 58* (6), 6–11.

Hedges, L. V., & Nowell, A. (1999). Changes in the black–white gap in achievement test scores. *Sociology of Education, 72,* 111–135.

Hess, R. D., Holloway, S. D., Dickson, W. P., & Price, G. G. (1984). Maternal variables as predictors of children's school readiness and later achievement in vocabulary and mathematics in sixth grade. *Child Development, 55* (5), 1,902–1,912.

Hetherington, E. M., & Jodl, K. M. (1994). Stepfamilies as settings for child development.

In A. Booth and J. Dunn (Eds.), *Stepfamilies: Who Benefits? Who Does Not?* (pp. 55–79). Hillsdale, New Jersey: Erlbaum Associates.

Jackson, J. (1978). In pursuit of equity, ethics, and excellence: The challenge to close the gap. *Phi Delta Kappan, 60* (3), 191s–193s.

Jeynes, W. H. (1998). Examining the effects of divorce on the academic achievement of children: How should we control for SES? *Journal of Divorce and Remarriage, 29* (3/4), 1–21.

Jeynes, W.H. (2002a). *Divorce, Family Structure & the Academic Success of Children.* Binghamton, NY: Haworth Press.

Jeynes, W. H. (2002b) Does parental involvement eliminate the effects of parental divorce on the academic achievement of adolescents? *Journal of Divorce and Remarriage, 37* (1/2), 101–115.

Jeynes, W. (2002c). Examining the effects of parental absence on the academic achievement of adolescents: the challenge of controlling for family income. *Journal of Family and Economic Issues, 23* (2), 189–210.

Jeynes, W. (2002d). The challenge of controlling for SES in social science and education research. *Educational Psychology Review, 14* (2), 205–221.

Jeynes, W. (2003a). A meta-analysis: the effects of parental involvement on minority children's academic achievement. *Education & Urban Society, 35* (2), 202–218.

Jeynes, W. (2003b). The effects of black and Hispanic twelfth graders living in intact families and being religious on their academic achievement. *Urban Education, 38* (1), 35–57.

Jeynes, W. (2005b). A meta-analysis of the relation of parental involvement to urban elementary school student academic achievement. *Urban Education, 40,* (3), 237–269.

Jeynes, W. (2005e). Effects of parental involvement and family structure on the academic achievement of adolescents. *Marriage and Family Review, 37* (3), 99–117.

Jeynes, W. (2006a). Standardized tests and the true meaning of kindergarten and pre-school. *Teachers' College Record, 108* (10), 1,937–1,959.

Jeynes, W. (2007b). The relationship between parental involvement and urban secondary school student academic achievement: A meta-analysis. *Urban Education, 42* (1), 82–110.

Jeynes, W. (2010). The salience of the subtle aspects of parental involvement and encouraging that involvement: implications for school-based programs. *Teachers' College Record, 112* (3), 747–774.

Jones, L. V. (1984). White–black achievement differences: The narrowing gap. *American Psychologist, 39,* 1,207–1,213.

Juliusdottir, S. (1997). An Icelandic study of five parental lifestyles: Conditions of fathers without custody and mothers without custody. *Journal of Divorce & Remarriage, 26*(3/4), 87–103.

*Keith, P. B., & Lichtman, M. (1992, April). Testing the influences of parental involvement on Mexican-American eighth grade students' academic achievement: A structural equations analysis. Paper presented at the Annual Meeting of the American Educational Researchers' Association, San Francisco, California.

*Keith, P. B., & Lichtman, M. (1994). Does parental involvement influence the academic achievement of Mexican American eighth graders? Results from the National Education Longitudinal Study. *School Psychology Quarterly, 9* (4), 256–272.

Legutko, R. S. (1998). Family effect on rural high school students' postsecondary decisions. *Rural Educator, 20* (2), 11–14.

*Marcon, R. A. (1999a, March). Impact of parental involvement on children's development and academic performance: A three cohort study. Paper presented at the meeting of the Southeastern Psychological Association in Savannah, Georgia.

*Mau, W. (1997). Parental influences on the high school students' academic achievement: A comparison of Asian immigrants, Asian Americans, and white Americans. *Psychology in the Schools, 34* (3), 267–277.

McBride, B. A., & Lin, H. (1996). Parental involvement in prekindergarten at-risk programs: Multiple perspectives. *Journal of Education for Students Placed at Risk, 1* (4), 349–372.

Muller, C. (1998). Gender differences in parental involvement and adolescents' mathematics achievement. *Sociology of Education, 71* (4), 336–356.

Mulroy, M. T., Goldman, J., & Wales, C. (1998). Affluent parents of young children: Neglected parent education audience. *Journal of Extension, 36* (1), 15–30.

*Nesbitt, G. K. (1993). The effects of three school-to-home parental involvement communication programs on reading achievement, conduct, homework habits, attendance, and parent–student–school interaction (Doctoral dissertation for Georgia State University, 1993). *Dissertation Abstracts International,* AAG 54/11 3993.

Nurmi, J., & Onatsu-Arvibani, T. P. (1997). Family background and problems at school in society: The role of family compositional, emotional atmosphere, and parental education. *European Journal of Psychology of Education, 13* (2), 315–330.

Orfield, G., Kahlenberg, R. D., Gordon, E. W., Genessee, F., Slocumb, P. D., & Payne, R. K. (2000). The new diversity. *Principal, 79* (5), 6–32.

Peressini, D. D. (1998). The portrayal of parents in the school mathematics reform literature: Locating the context for parental involvement. *Journal for Research in Mathematics Education, 29* (5), 55–582.

Portes, A., & MacLeod, D. (1996). Educational progress of children and immigrants: The roles of class, ethnicity, and school context. *Sociology of Education, 69* (4), 255–275.

Revicki, D. A. (1981). The relationship among socioeconomic status, home environment, parental involvement, child self-concept, and child achievement (Doctoral dissertation, University of North Carolina, 1981). *Dissertation Abstracts International,* AAG, 42/06 2484.

*Reynolds, A. J. (1992). Comparing measures of parental involvement on their effects on academic achievement. *Early Childhood Research Quarterly, 7* (3), 441–462.

Riley, R. W. (1996). Promoting family involvement in learning. *Professional Psychology: Research and Practice, 27* (1), 3–4.

Roach, R. (2001). In the academic and think-tank world, pondering achievement-gap remedies take center stage. *Black Issues in Higher Education,* 18 (1), 26–27.

Ross, S. M., Smith, L. J., & Casey, J. P. (1999). "Bridging the gap": The effects of the Success for All Program on elementary school reading achievement as a function of student ethnicity and ability level. *School Effectiveness and School Improvement, 10* (2), 129–150.

Rumberger, R. W., & Willms, J. D. (1992). The impact of racial and ethnic segregation on the achievement gap in California high schools. *Educational Evaluation and Policy Analysis, 14,* 377–396.

*Sanders, M. G. (1996). *School-Family Community Partnerships and the Academic Achievement of African American, Urban Adolescents.* Center for Research on the Education of Students Placed at Risk, Baltimore, Maryland.

Sanders, M. G. (1998). The effects of school, family, and community support on the academic achievement of African American adolescents. *Urban Education, 33* (3), 385–409.

Shaver, A. V., & Walls, R. T. (1998). Effect of Title I parent involvement on student reading and mathematics achievement. *Journal of Research and Development in Education, 31,* 90–97.

Simpson, C. (1981). Classroom organization and the gap between minority and nonminority student performance levels. *Educational Research Quarterly, 6* (3), 43–53.

Singh, K., Bickley, P. G., Trivette P., Keith, T. Z., Keith, P. B., & Anderson, E. (1995). The effects of four components of parental involvement on eighth grade student achievement. *School Psychology Review, 24* (2), 299–317.

Slater, R. B. (1999). Ranking the states by the Black–White scoring gap. *Journal of Blacks in Higher Education, 26,* 105–110.

Slavin, R., & Madden, N. (2006). Reducing the gap: Success for All and the achievement of African American students. *Journal of Negro Education, 75* (3), 389–400.

So, A. Y., & Chan, K. S. (1984). What matters? The relative impact of language background and socioeconomic: Status on reading achievement. *NABE: Journal for the National Association for Bilingual Education, 8* (3), 27–41.

Stevenson, H. W., & Stigler, J. W. (1992). *The Learning Gap.* New York, New York: Summit Books.

*Strage, A., & Brandt, T. S. (1999). Authoritative parenting and college students' academic adjustment and success. *Journal of Educational Psychology, 91* (1), 146–156.

*Taylor, L. C., Hinton, I. D., & Wilson, M. N. (1995). Parental influences on academic performance in African American students. *Journal of Child & Family Studies, 4* (3), 293–302.

*Taylor, R. D. (1996). Adolescent perceptions of kinship support and family management practices: Association with adolescent adjustment in African American families. *Developmental Psychology, 32* (4), 687–695.

Villas-Boas, A. (1998). The effects of parental involvement in homework on student achievement in Portugal and Luxembourg. *Childhood Education, 74* (6), 367–371.

Wallerstein, J. S., & Lewis, J. (1998). The long-term impact of divorce on children: A first report from a 25-year study. *Family and Conciliation Courts Review, 36,* 368–383.

*Williams, V. (1999). The influence of parenting practices on ethnic identity and social and academic outcomes. Doctoral dissertation. Florida Atlantic University in Boca Raton, Florida.

*Yan, W. (1999). Successful African American students. *Journal of Negro Education, 68* (1), 5–22.

Zakrisson, I., & Ekehammer, B. (1998). Social attitudes and education: Self-selection or socialization? *Scandinavian Journal of Psychology, 39* (2), 117–122.

Zdzinski, S. F. (1996). Parental involvement, selected student attributes, and learning outcomes in instrumental music. *Journal of Research in Music Education, 44* (1), 34–48.

*Zellman, G. L., & Waterman, J. M. (1998). Understanding the impact of parental school involvement on children's educational outcomes. *Journal of Educational Research, 91* (6), 370–380.

Chapter 6

Amano, I. (1990). *Education and Examination in Modern Japan.* Tokyo: University of Tokyo Press.

Benjamin, G. (1997). *Japanese Lessons*. New York: NYU press.

Bennett, W. J. (1998). *The Death of Outrage*. New York: Free Press.

Borruel, T. W. (2002). The ten p's of parent communication. A strategy for staff development. *Child Care Information Exchange, 143* (1), 54–57.

Bousquet, M. (2008). *How the University Works: Higher Education and the Low Wage Nation*. New York: New York University.

Bracket, E. (2009). *Pay to Play*. Chicago: Dee.

Brooks, R. B., & Goldstein. (2001). *Raising Resilient Children: Fostering Strength, Hope, and Optimism in your Child*. Lincolnwood, IL: Contemporary Books.

Brown, K. B., & Fellows, M. L. (1996). *Taxing America*. New York: New York University Press.

Byrd, D. M., & McIntyre, D. J. (1997). *Research on Education of our Nation's Teachers*. Thousand Oaks: Corwin.

Chronicle of Higher Education. (2003). *Notebook, 49* (42), 1–4.

Crane, D. R., & Heaton, T. B. (2008). *Handbook of Families & Poverty*. Los Angeles: Sage.

Davalos, D. B., Chavez, E. L., & Guardiola, R. J. (2005). Effects of perceived parental school support and family communication on delinquent behaviors in Latinos and white non-Latinos. *Cultural Diversity & Ethnic Minority Psychology, 11* (1), 57–68.

Delgado-Gaitan, C. (2004). *Involving Latino Families in Schools: Raising Student Achievement through Home–School Partnerships*. Thousand Oaks: Sage.

Domina, T. (2005). Leveling the home advantage: Assessing the effectiveness of parental involvement in elementary school. *Sociology of Education, 78* (3), 233–249.

Egan, K. (2002). *Getting It Wrong from the Beginning*. New Haven: Yale University Press.

Epstein, J. (2001). *School, Family, and Community Partnerships*. Boulder: Westview Press.

Farrell, W., Svoboda, S., & Sterba, J. P. (2008). *Does Feminism Discriminate Against Men? A Debate*. Oxford: Oxford University Press.

Gatto, J. G. (2001). *The Underground History of American Education*. New York: Oxford Village Press.

Geisler, N. L. (1983). Is man the measure: An evaluation of contemporary humanism. Grand Rapids: Baker.

Green, C. L., Walker, J. M. T., & Hoover-Dempsey, K. V. (2007). Parents' motivations for involvement in children's education: An empirical test of a theoretical model of parental involvement. *Journal of Educational Psychology, 99* (3), 532–544.

Heim, P. (1992). *Survey of TIAA-CREF Households*. New York: TIAA-CREF.

Hetherington, E. M., & Jodl, K. M. (1994). Stepfamilies as settings for child development. In A. Booth and J. Dunn (Eds.), *Stepfamilies: Who Benefits? Who Does Not?* (pp. 55–79). Hillsdale, New Jersey: Erlbaum Associates.

Hood, C. (2003). The third great reform of the Japanese education system: Success in the 1980s onwards. In Phillips, D. (Ed.), *Can the Japanese Change their Education System?* (pp. 73–85). Oxford, UK: Symposium.

Hughes, P. (1983). *Christian Ethics in Secular Society*. Grand Rapids: Baker.

Jeynes, W. (1999a). The effects of religious commitment on the academic achievement of black and Hispanic children. *Urban Education, 34* (4), 458–479.

Jeynes, W. (2002a). *Divorce, Family Structure, and the Academic Success of Children*. Binghamton, New York: Haworth Press.

Jeynes, W. (2003b). The effects of black and Hispanic twelfth graders living in intact families and being religious on their academic achievement. *Urban Education, 38* (1), 35–57.

Jeynes, W. (2005b). A meta-analysis of the relation of parental involvement to urban elementary school student academic achievement. *Urban Education, 40* (3), 237–269.

Jeynes, W. (2005f). The effects of parental involvement on the academic achievement of African American youth. *Journal of Negro Education, 74* (3), 260–274.

Jeynes, W. (2006a). Standardized tests and the true meaning of kindergarten and pre-school. *Teachers' College Record, 108* (10), 1,937–1,959.

Jeynes, W. (2007a). *American Educational History: School, Society & the Common Good.* Thousand Oaks, CA: Sage.

Jeynes, W. (2007b). The relationship between parental involvement and urban secondary school student academic achievement: A meta-analysis. *Urban Education, 42* (1), 82–110.

Jeynes, W. (2008d). What we should and should not learn from the Japanese and other East Asian education systems? *Educational Policy, 22* (6), 900–927.

Jeynes, W. (2010). The salience of the subtle aspects of parental involvement and encouraging that involvement: implications for school-based programs. *Teachers' College Record, 112* (3), 747–774.

Johnson, P. (1997). *A History of the American People.* New York: Harper Collins.

Keenleyside, H. L., & Thomas, A. F. (1937). *History of Japanese Education and Present Educational System.* Tokyo: Hokuseido Press.

Kennedy, R. (2001). *The Encouraging Parent,* New York: Three Rivers Press.

Lambro, D. (1980). *Fat City: How the Government Wastes your Taxes.* South Bend: Regnery.

Leary, D. (2008). *Why We Suck: A Feel Good Guide to Staying Fat, Loud, Lazy, and Stupid.* New York: Viking.

Malkin, M. (2009). *Culture of Corruption.* Washington, D.C.: Regnery.

Mapp, K. L., Johnson, V. R., Strickland, C. S., & Meza, C. (2010). High school family centers: Transformative spaces linking schools and families in support of student learning. In W. Jeynes (Ed.), *Family Factors and the Educational Success of Children* (pp. 336–366). New York: Routledge.

Mau, W. (1997). Parental influences on the high school students' academic achievement: A comparison of Asian immigrants, Asian Americans, and white Americans. *Psychology in the Schools, 34* (3), 267–277.

Morris, D., & McGann, E. (2007). *Outrage.* New York: HarperCollins.

Nakanishi, D. T., & Nishida, T. Y. (1999). *The Asian American Educational Experience.* New York: Routledge.

Ogbu, J. U. (1992). Adaptation to minority status and impact on school success. *Theory Into Practice, 31,* 287–295.

Ogbu, J. U. (1993). Differences in cultural frame of reference. *International Journal of Behavioral Development, 16,* 483–506.

Phillips, K. (1994). *Arrogant Capital.* Boston: Little Brown & Co.

Podell, J. (1987). *Religion in American life.* New York: H.W. Wilson.

Ravitch, D. (1974). *The Great School Wars.* New York: Basic Books.

Reynolds, D. R. (2001). Christian mission schools and Japan's to-a-dobun shoin: Comparisons and legacies. In G. Peterson, R. Hayhoe, & Y. Lu (Eds.). *Education, Culture, and Identity in Twentieth Century China.* Ann Arbor: University of Michigan, (pp. 82–108).

Romero, F. (2008). Hyperborder: The contemporary U.S.–Mexico border's future. New York: Princeton Architectural Press.

Saint Clair, L., & Jackson, B. (2006). Effect of family involvement training on the language skills of young families. *School Community Journal, 16* (1), 31–41.

Schonpflug, U. (2008). *Cultural Transmission.* New York: Cambridge University Press.

Shimizu, K. (1992). Shido: Education and selection in Japanese middle school. *Comparative Education, 28* (2), 114–125.

Sommers, C. H. (2000). *The War against Boys.* New York: Simon & Schuster.

Stevenson, H. W., & Stigler, J. W. (1992). *The Learning Gap.* New York, New York: Summit Books.

Turney, K., & Kao, G. (2009). Barriers to school involvement: Are immigrant parents Disadvantaged? *Journal of Educational Research, 102* (4), 257–271.

U.S. Department of Education. (1987). *Japanese Education Today.* Washington, D.C.: U.S. Department of Education.

U.S. Department of Education. (2002). *Digest of Education Statistics 2001.* Washington, D.C.: Department of Education.

U.S. Department of Education. (2007). *Digest of Education Statistics 2006.* Washington, D.C.: Department of Education.

Vasquez, O. A. (2004). A participatory perspective on parental involvement. In J. Mora, & D. R. Diaz (Eds.), *Latino Social Policy: A Participatory Research Model* (pp. 57–87). New York: Haworth.

Wallerstein, J. S., & Blakeslee, S. (1989). *Second Chances: Men, Women, and Children a Decade after Divorce.* New York: Ticknor and Fields.

Wartman, K., & Savage, M. (2008). *Parental Involvement in Higher Education: Understanding the Relationship among Students, Parents & the Institution.* Wiley: San Francisco.

Wentzel, K. R. (2002). Are effective teachers like good parents? Teaching styles and student adjustment in early adolescence. *Child Development, 73* (1), 287–301.

White, M. (1987). *The Japanese Educational Challenge: A Commitment to Children.* New York: Free Press.

Chapter 7

Aeby, V. G., Thyer, B. A., & Carpenter-Abey, T. (1999). Comparing outcomes of an alternative school program offered with and without intensive family involvement. U.S. Department of Education, Washington, D.C.

Borruel, T. W. (2002). The ten p's of parent communication. A strategy for staff development. *Child Care Information Exchange, 143* (1), 54–57.

Bronstein, P., Stoll, M. F., Clauson, J., Abrams, C. L., & Briones, M. (1994). Fathering after separation or divorce: Factors predicting children's adjustment. *Family Relations, 43* (4), 469–479.

Fan, X., & Chen, M. (2001). Parental involvement and students' academic achievement: A meta-analysis. *Educational Psychology Review, 13* (1), 1–22.

Gatto, J. G. (2001). *The Underground History of American Education.* New York: Oxford Village Press.

Green, L. R., Blasik, K., Hartshorn, K., & Shatten-Jones, E. (2000). Closing the achievement gap in science: A program to encourage minority and female students to participate and succeed. *ERS Spectrum, 18,* 3–13.

Green, S. R. (2001). Closing the achievement gap: Lessons learned and challenges ahead. *Teaching and Change, 8,* 215–224.

Griffith, J. (1996). Relation of parental involvement, empowerment, and school traits to student academic performance. *Journal of Educational Research, 90* (1), 33–41.

Griffith, J. (1997). Linkages to school structure and socio-environmental characteristics to parental satisfaction with public education and student academic achievement. *Journal of Applied Social Psychology, 27* (2), 156–186.

Hampton, F. M., Mumford, D. A., & Bond, L. (1998). Parental involvement in inner city schools: The project FAST extended family approach to success. *Urban Education, 33* (3), 410–427.

Haycock, K. (2001). Closing the achievement gap. *Educational Leadership, 58* (6), 6–11.

Hoover-Dempsey, K. V., Walker, J. M., & Jones, K. P. (2002). Teachers involving parents (TIP): Results from an in-service teacher education program for enhancing parental involvement. *Teacher and Teacher Education, 18* (7), 843–867.

Jeynes, W. (1999a). The effects of religious commitment on the academic achievement of black and Hispanic children. *Urban Education, 34* (4), 458–479.

Jeynes, W. (2002a). *Divorce, Family Structure, and the Academic Success of Children.* Binghamton, New York: Haworth Press.

Jeynes, W. (2003a). A meta-analysis: the effects of parental involvement on minority children's academic achievement. *Education & Urban Society,* 35 *(2), 202–218.*

Jeynes, W. (2003b). The effects of black and Hispanic twelfth graders living in intact families and being religious on their academic achievement. *Urban Education, 38* (1), 35–57.

Jeynes, W. (2005b). A meta-analysis of the relation of parental involvement to urban elementary school student academic achievement. *Urban Education, 40,* (3), 237–269.

Jeynes, W. (2006b). The impact of parental remarriage on children: A meta-analysis. *Marriage and Family Review, 40* (4), 75–102.

Jeynes, W. (2007b). The relationship between parental involvement and urban secondary school student academic achievement: A meta-analysis. *Urban Education, 42* (1), 82–110.

Jeynes, W. (2010). The salience of the subtle aspects of parental involvement and encouraging that involvement: implications for school-based programs. *Teachers' College Record, 112* (3), 747–774.

Koskinen, P. S., Blum, I. H., Bisson, S. A., Phillips, S. M., & Creamer, T. S. (2000). Book access, shared reading and audio models: the literacy learning of linguistically diverse students in school and at home. *Journal of Educational Psychology, 92* (1), 23–336.

Mattingly, D. J., Prislin, R., McKenzie, T. L., Rodriguez, J. L., & Kayzar, B. (2002). Evaluating evaluations: The case of parental involvement programs. *Review of Educational Research, 72* (4), 549–576.

Mau, W. (1997). Parental influences on the high school students' academic achievement: A comparison of Asian immigrants, Asian Americans, and white Americans. *Psychology in the Schools, 34* (3), 267–277.

May, R. (1970). *Love and Will.* New York: Norton.

McLanahan, S., & Sandefur, G. (1994). *Growing Up with a Single Parent: What Hurts, What Helps.* Cambridge: Harvard University Press.

Miedel, W. T., & Reynolds, A. J. (1999). Parent involvement in early intervention for disadvantaged children: Does it matter? *Journal of School Psychology, 37* (4), 379–402.

Muller, C. (1998). Gender differences in parental involvement and adolescents' mathematics achievement. *Sociology of Education, 71* (4), 336–356.

Pagitt, D., & Jones, T. (2007). *An Emergent Manifesto of Hope.* Grand Rapids: Baker.

Pestalozzi, J. (1801). *Leonard and Gertrude.* Philadelphia: Groff.

Pestalozzi, J. (1916). How a child is led to God through maternal love. In J. A. Green (Ed.), *Pestalozzi's Educational Writings.* London: Edward Arnold.

Pong, S., Dronkers, J., & Hampden-Thompson, G. (2003). Family policies and children's school achievement in single- versus two-parent families. *Journal of Marriage & the Family, 65,* 681–699.

Rodgers, K. B., & Rose, H. A. (2002). Risk and resiliency factors among adolescents who experience marital transitions. *Journal of Marriage & the Family, 64,* 1,024–1,037.

Sanders, M. G. (1998). The effects of school, family, and community support on the academic achievement of African American adolescents. *Urban Education, 33* (3), 385–409.

Shaver, A. V., & Walls, R. T. (1998). Effect of Title I parent involvement on student reading and mathematics achievement. *Journal of Research & Development in Education,* 31(2), 90–97.

Slavin, R., & Madden, N. (2006). Reducing the gap: Success for All and the achievement of African American students. *Journal of Negro Education, 75* (3), 389–400.

Villas-Boas, A. (1998). The effects of parental involvement in homework on student achievement in Portugal and Luxembourg. *Childhood Education, 74* (6), 367–371.

Wise, J. H. (1972). *Parent participation reading clinic: A research demonstration project: Final report.* Washington, D.C.: Children's Hospital of the District of Columbia.

Chapter 8

Amato, P. R., & Keith, B. (1991). Parental divorce and adult well-being: A meta-analysis. *Journal of Marriage & the Family, 53* (1), 43–58.

Ballantine, J. H. (1999). Getting involved in our children's education. *Childhood Education, 75* (3), 170–171.

Bandura, A. (1977). *Social Learning Theory.* Englewood Cliffs, NJ: Prentice Hall.

Bauch, P. A., & Goldring, E. B. (1995). Parent involvement and school responsiveness. Facilitating the home–school connection in school of choice. *Educational Evaluation & Policy Analysis, 17,* 1–21.

Bengston, V. L. (2005). *Sourcebook of Family Theory & Research.* Thousand Oaks: Sage.

Berrick, J. D. (1995). *Faces of Poverty.* New York: Oxford University Press.

Bogenschneider, K. (1997). Parental involvement in adolescent schooling: A proximal process with transcontextual validity. *Journal of Marriage & the Family, 59* (3), 718–733.

Bronstein, P., Stoll, M. F., Clauson, J., Abrams, C. L., & Briones, M. (1994). Fathering after separation or divorce: Factors predicting children's adjustment. *Family Relations,* 43(4), 469–479.

Christian, K., Morrison, F. J., & Bryant, F. B. (1998). Predicting kindergarten academic skills: Interactions among child care, maternal education, and family literacy environments. *Early Childhood Research Quarterly, 13* (3), 501–521.

Cohen, G. A. (2000). *If You're Egalitarian, How Come You're So Rich?* Cambridge: Harvard University Press.

Crane, J. (1996). Effects of home environment, SES, and maternal test scores on mathematics achievement. *Journal of Educational Research, 89* (5), 305–314.

Crouter, A. C., Helms-Erickson, H., Updegraff, K., & McHale, S. M. (1999). Conditions underlying parents' knowledge about children's daily lives in middle childhood. Between- and within-family comparisons. *Child Development, 70* (1), 246–259.

Davis-Kean, P. E. (2005). The influence of parent education and family income on child achievement: The indirect role of parent expectations and the home environment. *Journal of Family Psychology, 19* (2), 294–304.

Deslandes, R., Royer, E., Turcott, D., & Bertrand, R. (1997). School achievement at the secondary level: Influence of parenting style and parent involvement in schooling. *McGill Journal of Education, 32* (3), 191–207.

Dewey, J. (1902). *The Child and the Curriculum.* Chicago: University of Chicago Press.

Dewey, J. (1915). *The School and Society.* Chicago: University of Chicago Press.

Dewey, J. (1920). *Reconstruction in Philosophy.* New York: Holt.

Dewey, J. (1990). *The School and Society/The Child and the Curriculum.* Chicago: University of Chicago Press.

Directorate, The (1999). *Handbook of International Economic Statistics.* Washington, D.C.: The Directorate.

Eavey, C. B. (1964). *History of Christian Education.* Chicago: Moody Press.

Edwards, J., & Crain, M. (2007). *Ending Poverty in America.* New York: New Press.

Egan, K. (2002). *Getting It Wrong from the Beginning.* New Haven: Yale University Press.

Farley, R. (1996). *The New American Reality.* New York: Russell Sage.

Freud, S. (1938). *The Basic Writings of Sigmund Freud.* New York: Modern Library.

Frost, J. (2005). *Supernanny: How to Get the Best from your Children.* New York: Hyperion.

Geller, H. S. (1993). *Two Years after the Embargo.* Washington, D.C.: American Council for an Energy Efficient Economy.

Gortmaker, S. L., Must, A., Perrin, J. M., Sobol, A. M., et al. (1993). Social and economic consequences of overweight in adolescence and young adulthood. *New England Journal of Medicine, 329* (14), 1,008–1,012.

Grayson, P. J. (1999). Who goes to university and why? *Education Canada, 39* (2), 37–39.

Griffith, J. (1996). Relation of parental involvement, empowerment, and school traits to student academic performance. *Journal of Educational Research, 90* (1), 33–41.

Grolnick, W. S., Benjet, C., Kurowski, C. O., & Apostoleris, P. H. (1997). Predictors of parental involvement in children's schooling. *Journal of Educational Psychology, 89* (3), 538–548.

Hahnel, R. (2005). *Economic Justice and Democracy.* New York: Routledge.

Hamburg, D. A. (1992). *Today's Children: Creating a Future for a Generation in Crisis.* New York: Times Books.

Hampton, F. M., Mumford, D. M., & Bond, L. 1998). Parent involvement in inner-city schools: The Project FAST extended family approach to success. *Urban Education, 33* (3), 410–427.

Hara, S. R. (1998). Parent involvement: The key to improved student achievement. *School Community Journal, 8* (2), 9–19.

Heal, G., & Chilinisky, G. (1991). *Oil and the International Economy.* New York: Oxford University Press.

Hetherington, E. M., & Jodl, K. M. (1994). Stepfamilies as settings for child development. In A. Booth and J. Dunn (Eds.), *Stepfamilies: Who Benefits? Who Does Not?* (pp. 55–79). Hillsdale, New Jersey: Erlbaum Associates.

Hetherington, E. M., Stanley-Hagan, M., & Anderson, E. R. (1989). Marital Transitions: A Child's Perspective. *American Psychologist, 44*, 303–12.

Hock, R. R. (2005). *Forty Studies that Changed Psychology.* Upper Saddleback River, NJ: Prentice Hall.

Hoge, D. R., Smit, E., & Crist, J. T. (1997). Four family process factors predicting academic achievement for sixth and seventh grade. *Educational Research Quarterly, 21* (2), 27–42.

Jencks, C. (1992). *Rethinking Social Policy: Race, Poverty & the Underclass.* Cambridge, MA: Harvard University.

Jeynes, W. H. (2002a). *Divorce, Family Structure, and the Academic Success of Children.* Binghamton, New York: Haworth Press.

Jeynes, W. (2003a). A meta-analysis: the effects of parental involvement on minority children's academic achievement. *Education & Urban Society, 35* (2), 202–218.

Jeynes, W. (2005b). A meta-analysis of the relation of parental involvement to urban elementary school student academic achievement. *Urban Education, 40*, (3), 237–269.

Jeynes, W. (2007a). *American Educational History: School, Society & the Common Good.* Thousand Oaks, CA: Sage.

Jeynes, W. (2007b). The relationship between parental involvement and urban secondary school student academic achievement: A meta-analysis. *Urban Education, 42* (1), 82–110.

Jeynes, W. (2010). The salience of the subtle aspects of parental involvement and encouraging that involvement: implications for school-based programs. *Teachers' College Record, 112* (3), 747–774.

Krivy, L. (1978). *Falling Off the Ivory Tower: Common Sense Commentaries on Schools and Schooling.* Lahaska, PA: New Hope Publishers.

Lamb, M. (1997). *The Role of the Father in Child Development.* New York: Wiley.

Lawson, D. E., & Lean, A. E. (Eds.), (1964). *John Dewey and the World View.* Carbondale: Southern Illinois University Press.

Learsy, R. J. (2005). *Over a Barrel.* Nashville: Nelson Current.

Legutko, R. S. (1998). Family effect on rural high school students' postsecondary decisions. *Rural Educator, 20* (2), 11–14.

Mack, D. (1997). *The Assault on Parenthood: How our Culture Undermines the Family.* New York: Simon & Schuster.

Mau, W. (1997). Parental influences on the high school students' academic achievement: A comparison of Asian immigrants, Asian Americans, and white Americans. *Psychology in the Schools, 34* (3), 267–277.

McBride, B. A., & Lin, H. (1996). Parental involvement in prekindergarten at-risk programs: Multiple perspectives. *Journal of Education for Students Placed at Risk, 1* (4), 349–372.

McClellan, E. B., & Reese, W. J. (1988). *The Social History of American Education.* Urbana: University of Illinois Press.

McDonald, L. G., & Robinson, P. (2009). *A Colossal Failure of Common Sense.* New York: Crown.

McLanahan, S., & Sandefur, G. (1994). *Growing Up with a Single Parent: What Hurts, What Helps.* Cambridge: Harvard University Press.

Melody, M. E., & Peterson, L. M. (1999). *Teaching America about Sex.* New York: New York University Press.

Morgan, L. A., Kitson, G. C., & Kitson, J. T. (1992). The economic fallout from divorce: Issues for the 1990s. *Journal of Family and Economic Issues, 13* (4), 435–444.

Muller, C. (1998). Gender differences in parental involvement and adolescents' mathematics achievement. *Sociology of Education, 71* (4), 336–356.

Mulroy, M. T., Goldman, J., & Wales, C. (1998). Affluent parents of young children: Neglected parent education audience. *Journal of Extension, 36* (1), 15–30.

National Commission on Excellence in Education. (1983). *A Nation at Risk.* Washington, D.C.: National Commission on Excellence in Education.

Nurmi, J., & Onatsu-Arvibani, T. P. (1997). Family background and problems at school in society: The role of family compositional, emotional atmosphere, and parental education. *European Journal of Psychology of Education, 13* (2), 315–330.

Peressini, D. D. (1998). The portrayal of parents in the school mathematics reform literature: Locating the context for parental involvement. *Journal for Research in Mathematics Education, 29* (5), 55–582.

Portes, A., & MacLeod, D. (1996). Educational progress of children and immigrants: the roles of class, ethnicity, and school context. *Sociology of Education, 69* (4), 255–275.

Riley, R. W. (1996). Promoting family involvement in learning. *Research and Practice, 27* (1), 3–4.

Ryan, K., & Cooper, J. M. (Eds.). (1992). *Readings in Education.* Boston: Houghton Mifflin.

Salkind, N. J. (2006). *Encyclopedia of Human Development.* Thousand Oaks, CA: Sage Publications.

Sanders, M. G. (1998). The effects of school, family, and community support on the academic achievement of African American adolescents. *Urban Education, 33* (3), 385–409.

Shaver, A. V., & Walls, R. T. (1998). Effect of Title I parent involvement on student reading and mathematics achievement. *Journal of Research and Development in Education, 31*, 90–97.

Singh, K., Bickley, P. G., Trivette P., Keith, T. Z., Keith, P. B., & Anderson, E. (1995). The effects of four components of parental involvement on eighth grade student achievement. *School Psychology Review, 24* (2), 299–317.

Smith, H. L. (2009). *Taking Back the Tower: Simple Solutions to Saving Higher Education.* Westport, CT: Praeger.

Stevenson, H. W., & Stigler, J. W. (1992). *The Learning Gap.* New York: Summit Books.

Stotsky, S. (1999), *Losing Our Language.* New York: Free Press.

Unger, D. G., McLeod, L. E., Brown, M. B., & Tressell, P. A. (2000). The role of family support in interparental conflict and adolescent academic achievement. *Journal of Child and Family Studies, 9* (2), 191–202.

U.S. Census Bureau. (2001). *Census 2000.* Washington, D.C.: U.S. Census Bureau.

U.S. Census Bureau. (2006). *Statistical Abstracts of the United States.* Washington, D.C.: U.S. Census Bureau.

U.S. Department of Health & Human Services. (1998). *Statistical Abstract of the United States.* Washington, D.C.: U.S. Department of Health & Human Services.

U.S. Department of Justice. (1999). *Age-specific arrest rate and race-specific arrest rates for selected offenses, 1965–1998.* Washington, D.C.: U.S. Department of Justice.

Villas-Boas, A. (1998). The effects of parental involvement in homework on student achievement in Portugal and Luxembourg. *Childhood Education, 74* (6), 367–371.

Wallerstein, J. S., & Blakeslee, S. (2003). *What About the Kids?* New York: Hyperion.

Wallerstein, J. S., & Lewis, J. (1998). The long-term impact of divorce on children: A first report from a 25-year study. *Family and Conciliation Courts Review, 36* (3), 368–383.

Wilson, W. (1996). *When Work Disappears.* Chicago: University of Chicago Press.

Wirtz, W. (1977). *On Further Examination.* New York: College Entrance Examination Board.

Zakrisson, I., & Ekehammer, B. (1998). Social attitudes and education: Self-selection or socialization? *Scandinavian Journal of Psychology, 39* (2), 117–122.

Zdzinski, S. F. (1996). Parental involvement, selected student attributes, and learning outcomes in instrumental music. *Journal of Research in Music Eucation. 44* (1), 34–48.

Chapter 9

Allison, P. D., & Furstenberg, F. F. (1989). How marital dissolution affects children—variations by age and sex. *Developmental Psychology, 25,* 540–549.

Amato, P. R., & Ochitree, G. (1987). Child and adolescent competence in intact, one-parent, and stepfamilies, an Australian study, *Journal of Divorce, 10* (1), 75–96.

Anderson, E. R., & Rice, A M. (1992). Sibling relationships during remarriage. *Monographs of the Society for Research in Child Development, 57,* 149–177.

Bane, M. J., & Jargowsky, P. (1988). The links between government policy and family structure: what matters and what doesn't." In A. J. Cherlin (Ed.), *The Changing American Family and Public Policy* (pp. 219–255), Washington, D.C.: Urban Institute Press.

Bauch, P. A., & Goldring, E. B. (1995). Parent involvement and school responsiveness. Facilitating the home-school connection in school of choice. *Educational Evaluation & Policy Analysis, 17,* 1–21.

Bogenschneider, K. (1997). Parental involvement in adolescent schooling: A proximal process with transcontextual validity. *Journal of Marriage and the Family, 59* (3), 718–733.

Booth, A., & Dunn, J. (1994). Preface. In A. Booth & J. Dunn (Eds.), *Stepfamilies: Who Benefits? Who Does Not?* (pp. ix–x). Hillsdale: Erlbaum.

Bronstein, P., Stoll, M. F., Clauson, J., Abrams, C. L., & Briones, M. (1994). Fathering after separation or divorce: Factors predicting children's adjustment. *Family Relations, 43* (4), 469–479.

Cherlin, A. J. (1992). *Marriage, Divorce, and Remarriage.* Cambridge: Harvard University Press.

Christian, K., Morrison, F. J., & Bryant, F. B. (1998). Predicting kindergarten academic skills: Interactions among child care, maternal education, and family literacy environments. *Early Childhood Research Quarterly, 13* (3), 501–521.

Deslandes, R., Royer, E., Turcott, D., & Bertrand, R. (1997). School achievement at the secondary level: Influence of parenting style and parent involvement in schooling. *McGill Journal of Education, 32* (3), 191–207.

Emery, R. E. (1988). *Marriage, Divorce, and Children's Adjustment.* Newbury Park, CA: Sage Publications.

Furstenberg, F. F. Jr. (1988). Good dads and bad dads: Two faces of fatherhood. In A.

J. Cherlin (Ed.), *The Changing American Family and Public Policy* (pp. 193–218). Washington, D.C.: Urban Institute Press.

Ganong, L. H., & Coleman, M. (1994). *Remarried Family Relationships*. Thousand Oaks: Sage Publications.

Griffith, J. (1996). Relation of parental involvement, empowerment, and school traits to student academic performance. *Journal of Educational Research, 90* (1), 33–41.

Hampton, F. M., Mumford, D. M., & Bond, L. 1998). Parent involvement in inner-city schools: The Project FAST extended family approach to success. *Urban Education, 33* (3), 410–427.

Hara, S. R. (1998). Parent involvement: The key to improved student achievement. *School Community Journal, 8* (2), 9–19.

Hetherington, E. M. (1989). Coping with family transitions: Winners, losers, and survivors. *Child Development, 60* (1), 1–14.

Hetherington, E. M. (1992). Coping with marital transitions: A family systems perspective. *Monographs of the Society for Research in Child Development, 57* (2/3), 1–14.

Hetherington, E. M., & Clingempeel, W. G. (1992). Coping with marital transitions: A family systems perspective. *Monographs of the Society for Research in Child Development, 57*.

Hetherington, E. M., & Jodl, K. M. (1994). Stepfamilies as settings for child development. In A. Booth and J. Dunn (Eds.), *Stepfamilies: Who Benefits? Who Does Not?* (pp. 55–79). Hillsdale, New Jersey: Erlbaum Associates.

Hetherington, E. M., Stanley-Hagan, M., & Anderson, E. R. (1989). Marital transitions: A child's perspective. *American Psychologist, 44* (2), 303–312.

Jeynes, W. H. (1998). Examining the effects of divorce on the academic achievement of children: How should we control for SES? *Journal of Divorce and Remarriage, 29* (3/4), 1–21.

Jeynes, W. (2000b) The effects of several of the most common family structures on the academic achievement of eighth graders. *Marriage and Family Review, 30* (1), 73–97.

Jeynes, W. (2002a). *Divorce, Family Structure, and the Academic Success of Children*. Binghamton, New York: Haworth Press.

Jeynes, W. (2002b). Does widowhood or remarriage have the greater impact on the academic achievement of children? *Omega: Journal of Death and Dying, 44* (3), 319–343.

Jeynes, W. (2002c). The challenge of controlling for SES in social science and education research. *Educational Psychology Review, 14* (2), 205–221.

Jeynes, W. (2006b). The impact of parental remarriage on children: A meta-analysis. *Marriage and Family Review, 40* (4), 75–102.

Jeynes, W. (2007a). *American Educational History: School, Society & the Common Good*. Thousand Oaks, CA: Sage.

Mau, W. (1997). Parental influences on the high school students' academic achievement: A comparison of Asian immigrants, Asian Americans, and white Americans. *Psychology in the Schools, 34* (3), 267–277.

McBride, B. A., & Lin, H. (1996). Parental involvement in prekindergarten at-risk programs: Multiple perspectives. *Journal of Education for Students Placed at Risk, 1* (4), 349–372.

McLanahan, S., & Sandefur, G. (1994). *Growing Up with a Single Parent: What Hurts, What Helps*. Cambridge: Harvard University Press.

Mechanic, D., & Hansell, S. (1989). Divorce, family conflict, and adolescents' well-being. *Journal of Health and Social Behavior, 30* (1), 105–116.

Muller, C. (1998). Gender differences in parental involvement and adolescents' mathematics achievement. *Sociology of Education, 71* (4), 336–356.

Neighbors, B., Forehand, R., & Armistead, L. (1992). Is parental divorce a critical stressor for young adolescents? Grade point average as a case in point. *Adolescence, 27,* 639–646.

Nurmi, J., & Onatsu-Arvibani, T. P. (1997). Family background and problems at school in society: The role of family compositional, emotional atmosphere, and parental education. *European Journal of Psychology of Education, 13* (2), 315–330.

Peressini, D. D. (1998). The portrayal of parents in the school mathematics reform literature: Locating the context for parental involvement. *Journal for Research in Mathematics Education, 29* (5), 55–582.

Popenoe, D. (1994). The evolution of marriage and the problem of stepfamilies: A biosocial perspective. In A. Booth & J. Dunn (Eds.) *Stepfamilies: Who Benefits? Who Does Not?* (pp. 55–79). Hillsdale, New Jersey: Erlbaum Associates.

Riley, R. W. (1996). Promoting family involvement in learning. *Research and Practice, 27* (1), 3–4.

Sanders, M. G. (1998). The effects of school, family, and community support on the academic achievement of African American adolescents. *Urban Education, 33* (3), 385–409.

Shaver, A. V., & Walls, R. T. (1998). Effect of Title I parent involvement on student reading and mathematics achievement. *Journal of Research and Development in Education, 31,* 90–97.

Singh, K., Bickley, P. G., Trivette P., Keith, T. Z., Keith, P. B., & Anderson, E. (1995). The effects of four components of parental involvement on eighth grade student achievement. *School Psychology Review, 24* (2), 299–317.

Thomson, E., Hanson, T. L., & McLanahan, S. S. (1994). Family structure and child well-being: Economic resources vs. parental behaviors. *Social Forces, 73,* 221–242.

Villas-Boas, A. (1998). The effects of parental involvement in homework on student achievement in Portugal and Luxembourg. *Childhood Education, 74* (6), 367–371.

Wallerstein, J. S., & Blakeslee, S. (1989). *Second Chances: Men, Women, and Children a Decade after Divorce.* New York: Ticknor and Fields.

Wallerstein, J. S., Corbin, S. B., & Lewis, J. M. (1988). Children of divorce: A 10-year study. In E. M. Hetherington & J. D. Arasteh (Eds.), *Impact of Divorce, Single Parenting, and Step-Parenting on Children* (pp. 197–216). Hillsdale, New Jersey: Erlbaum Associates.

Wallerstein, J. S., & Lewis, J. (1998). The long-term impact of divorce on children: A first report from a 25-year study. *Family and Conciliation Courts Review, 36,* 368–383.

Walsh, W. M. (1992). Twenty major issues in remarriage families. *Journal of Counseling and Development, 70,* 709–715.

Wertlieb, D. (1997). Children whose parents divorce: Life trajectories and turning points. In I. H. Gotlib & B. Wheaton (Eds.), *Stress and Adversity over the Life Course* (pp. 179–196). Cambridge: Cambridge University Press.

Zdzinski, S. F. (1996). Parental involvement, selected student attributes, and learning outcomes in instrumental music. *Journal of Research in Music Education, 44* (1), 34–48.

Zellman, G. L., & Waterman, J. M. (1998). Understanding the impact of parental school involvement on children's educational outcomes. *Journal of Educational Research, 91* (6), 370–380.

Zill, N. (1994). Understanding why children in stepfamilies have more learning and behavior problems than children in nuclear families. In A. Booth & J. Dunn (Eds.), *Stepfamilies: Who Benefits? Who Does Not?* (pp. 109–137). Hillsdale: Erlbaum.

Zill, N., & Nord, C. W. (1994). *Running in Place.* Washington, D.C.: Child Trends.

Chapter 10

Battelle, J. (2005). *The Search.* New York: Portfolio.

Baumrind, D. (1971). Current patterns of parental authority. *Developmental Psychology, 4* (1), 1–103.

Beckwith, F., & Geisler, N. L. (1991). *Matters of Life and Death.* Grand Rapids, MI: Baker Books.

Bossidy, L., Charon, R., & Burch, C. (2004). *Confronting Reality.* New York: Crown.

Brazelton, T. B. (1992). *Touchpoints: Your Child's Emotional and Behavioral Development,* Reading, MA: Addison-Wesley.

Bronfenbrenner, U. (1979). *The Ecology of Human Development.* Cambridge, MA: Harvard University Press.

Brooks, R. B., & Goldstein, S. (2001). *Raising Resilient Children: Fostering Strength, Hope, and Optimism in Your Child.* Lincolnwood, IL: Contemporary Books.

Brown, B. B. Bakken, J. P. Nguyen, J., & Von Bank, H. G. (2007). Sharing information about peer relations: Parents and adolescent opinions and behaviors in Hmong and African American families. In B. B. Brown, & N. S. Mounts (Eds.), *Linking Parents and Family to Adolescent Peer Relations: Ethnic and Cultural Considerations* (pp. 67–82). San Francisco: Jossey Bass.

Bunnell, D., & Brate, A. (2000). *The Cisco Connection.* New York: Wiley.

Casanova, P., Garcia-Linares, C., de la Torre, M., & Carpio, d. (2005). Influence of family and socio-demographic variables on students with low academic achievement. *Educational Psychology, 25* (4), 423–435.

Cross, T., & Slater, R. B. (2000). The alarming decline in the academic performance of African–American men. *Journal of Blacks in Higher Education, 27,* 82–87.

Davis-Kean, P. E. (2005). The influence of parent education and family income on child achievement: The indirect role of parent expectations and the home environment. *Journal of Family Psychology, 19* (2), 294–304.

Delgado-Gaitan, C. (2004). *Involving Latino Families in Schools: Raising Student Achievement through Home–School Partnerships.* Thousand Oaks: Sage.

Dupuis, A. M. (1966) *Philosophy of Education in Historical Perspective.* Chicago: Rand McNally.

Egan, K. (2002). *Getting It Wrong from the Beginning.* New Haven: Yale University Press.

Farrelly, L. (2009). Baby in the womb. *Ehow.com.* Retrieved on December 4, 2009 at www. ehow.com/about_5393861_emotional-development-baby-womb.html.

Feinberg, L. (1995). A new center for the SAT. *College Board Review, 174,* 8–13, 31–32.

Gates, B. (1995). *The Road Ahead.* New York: Viking.

Gatto, J. G. (2001). *The Underground History of American Education.* New York: Oxford Village Press.

Giarelli, J. R. (1995). The social frontier, 1934–1943. Retrospect and prospect. In M. E.

James (Ed.), *School Reconstruction through Education: The Philosophy, History, and Curricula of a Radical Idea* (pp. 27–42). Norwood, NJ: Ablex.

Gillam, S. (2008). *Steve Jobs: Apple & Ipod Wizard*. Edina, MN: ABDO Publishing.

Goldberg, J. (2008). Exit stage right. *National Review, 60* (22). December 1. 8–12.

Hara, S. R. (1998). Parent involvement: The key to improved student achievement. *School Community Journal, 8* (2), 9–19.

Henderson, A. T., & Mapp, K. L. (2002). *A New Wave of Evidence: The Impact of School, Family, and Community Connections on Student Achievement*. Austin, TX: Southwest Educational Development Laboratory.

Hoover-Dempsey, K. V., Walker, J. M., & Jones, K. P. (2002). Teachers involving parents (TIP): Results from an in-service teacher education program for enhancing parental involvement. *Teacher and Teacher Education*, 18 (7), 843–867.

Imbimbo, A. (2009). *Steve Jobs: The Brilliant Mind behind Apple*. Pleasantville, NY: Gareth Stevens.

Jarvis, J. (2009). *What Would Google Do?* New York: Collins Business.

Jeynes, W. (1999a). The effects of religious commitment on the academic achievement of black and Hispanic children. *Urban Education, 34* (4), 458–479.

Jeynes, W. (2002a). *Divorce, Family Structure, and the Academic Success of Children*. Binghamton, New York: Haworth Press.

Jeynes, W. (2002b). The challenge of controlling for SES in social science and education research. *Educational Psychology Review, 14* (2), 205–221.

Jeynes, W. (2003a). A meta-analysis: the effects of parental involvement on minority children's academic achievement. *Education & Urban Society, 35* (2), 202–218.

Jeynes, W. (2003b). The effects of black and Hispanic twelfth graders living in intact families and being religious on their academic achievement. *Urban Education, 38* (1), 35–57.

Jeynes, W. (2005b). A meta-analysis of the relation of parental involvement to urban elementary school student academic achievement. *Urban Education, 40*, (3), 237–269.

Jeynes, W. (2005f). The effects of parental involvement on the academic achievement of African American Youth. *Journal of Negro Education, 74* (3), 260–274.

Jeynes, W. (2006a). Standardized tests and the true meaning of kindergarten and pre-school. *Teachers' College Record, 108* (10), 1,937–1,959.

Jeynes, W. (2006b). The impact of parental remarriage on children: A meta-analysis. *Marriage and Family Review, 40* (4), 75–102.

Jeynes, W. (2007a). *American Educational History: School, Society & the Common Good*. Thousand Oaks, CA: Sage.

Jeynes, W. (2007b). The relationship between parental involvement and urban secondary school student academic achievement: A meta-analysis. *Urban Education, 42* (1), 82–110.

Jeynes, W. (2008a). Effects of parental involvement on experiences of discrimination and bullying. *Marriage & Family Review, 43* (3/4), 255–268.

Jeynes, W. (2008b). Factors that reduce or eliminate the achievement gap. Speech given at Harvard University Conference on the Achievement Gap in Cambridge, Massachusetts, February.

Jeynes, W. (2009). *A Call to Character Education and Prayer in the Schools*. Westport, CT: Praeger.

Jeynes, W. (2010). The salience of the subtle aspects of parental involvement and encouraging that involvement: implications for school-based programs. *Teachers' College Record, 112* (3), 747–774.

Jeynes, W., Henderson, A., Hoover-Dempsey, K., & Epstein, J. (2005). Research and evaluation of family involvement in education: What lies ahead? Symposium sponsored by Harvard University. American Educational Research Association Conference.

Johnson, R. V. (1994). *Mayo Clinic Complete Book of Pregnancy and Baby's First Year.* New York: W. Morrow & Co.

Johnson, P. (1997). *A History of the American People.* New York: Harper Collins.

Kay, P., & Fitzgerald, M. (1997). Parents + teachers + action research = real involvement. *Teaching Exceptional Children, 30* (1), 8–14.

Kennedy, R. (2001). *The Encouraging Parent,* New York: Three Rivers Press.

Koenig, H. (1999). *The Healing Power of Faith.* New York: Simon & Schuster.

Lamb, M. (1997). *The Role of the Father in Child Development.* New York: Wiley.

Leary, D. (2008). *Why We Suck: A Feel Good Guide to Staying Fat, Loud, Lazy, and Stupid.* New York: Viking.

Mapp, K. L., Johnson, V. R., Strickland, C. S., & Meza, C. (2010). High school family centers: Transformative spaces linking schools and families in support of student learning. In W. Jeynes (Ed.), *Family Factors and the Educational Success of Children* (pp. 336–366). New York: Routledge.

McLanahan, S., & Sandefur, G. (1994). *Growing Up with a Single Parent: What Hurts, What Helps.* Cambridge: Harvard University Press.

Meyer, C. (2003). *It's Alive.* NewYork: Crown.

Myers, D. G. (2000). *The American Paradox.* New Haven: Yale University Press.

Noll, M. A. (2002). *The Old Religion in a New World.* Grand Rapids: Eerdmanns.

Post, S. G. (2006). *Why Good Things Happen to Good People.* New York: Broadway.

Potter, C., & Carpenter, J. (2008). Something in it for dads. Getting fathers involved in Sure Start. *Early Child Development & Care, 18* (7/8), 761–772.

Rasinski, T. V. (1995). Fast Start: Parental involvement reaching program for primary grade students. In W. M. Linek, E. G. Strutevant, & L. C. Botha (Eds.), *Generations of Literacy: The Seventeenth Year Book of the College Reading Association.* Pittsburgh, KS: College Reading Association. (pp. 301–312).

Ratelle, C. F., Larose, S., & Guay, F. (2005). Perceptions of parental involvement and support as predictors of college students persistence in science curriculum. *Journal of Family Psychology, 19* (2), 286–293.

Salkind, N. J. (2006). *Encyclopedia of Human Development.* Thousand Oaks, CA: Sage Publications.

Saracho, O. N. (1986). Play and young children's learning: In B. Spodek (Ed.), *Today's Kindergarten* (pp.91–109). New York: Teacher's College Press.

Slater, L., & Henderson, J. H. (2003). *The Complete Guide to Mental Health for Women.* Boston: Beacon.

Snyder, C. R., & Lopez, S. J. (2009). *Oxford Handbook of Positive Psychology.* Oxford: Oxford University Press.

Stross, R. E. (2008). *Planet Google.* New York: Free Press.

Swindoll, C. R. (1990). *Sanctity of Life: The Inescapable Issue.* Dallas: Word Publishing.

Tallack, P. (2006). *In the Womb.* Washington, D.C: National Geographic Society.

Van Luijk, H. (2004). Integrity in the private, the public, and corporate domain. In G. G. Brenkert (Ed.), *Corporate Integrity and Accountability* (pp. 38–54). Thousand Oaks: Sage Publications.

Vaughan, C. C. (1996). *How Life Begins: The Science of Life in the Womb.* New York: Time Books.

Wallace, J. (1995). Red teachers can't save us: Radical educators and liberal journalists in the 1930s. In M. E. James (Ed.), *School Reconstruction through Education: The Philosophy, History, and Curricula of a Radical Idea* (pp. 43–56). Norwood, NJ: Ablex.

Wempe, J., & Donaldson, T. (2004). The practicality of pluralism: Redrawing the simple picture of bipolarism and compliance in business ethics. In G. G. Brenkert (Ed.), *Corporate Integrity and Accountability.* (pp. 24–37). Thousand Oaks, CA: Sage Publications.

Wirtz, W. (1977). *On Further Examination.* New York: College Entrance Examination Board.

Yoffle, D. B. (1997). *Competing in the Age of Digital Convergence.* Boston: Harvard University.

Young, J. W. (1995). Recentering the SAT score scale. *College & University, 70* (2), 60–6.

Chapter 11

Afifi, T. D., & Olson, L. (2005). The chilling effect in families and the pressure to conceal secrets. *Communication Monographs, 72* (2), 192–196.

Baker, A. (2001). Improving parent involvement programs and practice: Parent perceptions. In S. Redding & L. G. Thomas (Eds.). *The Community of the School* (pp. 127–154). Lincoln, IL: Academic Development Institute.

Bauch, P., & Goldring, E. B. (1995). Parental involvement and school responsiveness: Facilitating the home–school connection in schools of choice. *Educational Evaluation & Policy Analysis, 17* (1), 1–21.

Baumrind, D. (1971). Current patterns of parental authority. *Developmental Psychology, 4* (1), 1–103.

Boyer, E. (1995). *The Basic School.* Princeton: Carnegie Foundation.

Borruel, T. W. (2002). The ten p's of parent communication. A strategy for staff development. *Child Care Information Exchange, 143* (1), 54–57.

Braden, J. P. (1999). School psychology for high risk populations: Gleanings from the Chicago Longitudinal Study. *Journal of School Psychology, 37* (4), 457–463.

Brooks, R. B., & Goldstein, S. (2001). *Raising Resilient Children: Fostering Strength, Hope, and Optimism in Your Child.* Lincolnwood, IL: Contemporary Books.

Bryant, S. (1996). School districts hope parents stay involved. *Houston Chronicle* November 18, p. A17.

Bunnell, D., & Brate, A. (2000). *The Cisco Connection.* New York: Wiley.

Davalos, D. B., Chavez, E. L., & Guardiola, R. J. (2005). Effects of perceived parental school support and family communication on delinquent behaviors in Latinos and white non-Latinos. *Cultural Diversity & Ethnic Minority Psychology, 11* (1), 57–68.

Davis-Kean, P. E. (2005). The influence of parent education and family income on child achievement: The indirect role of parent expectations and the home environment. *Journal of Family Psychology, 19* (2), 294–304.

Dewey, J. (1902). *The Child and the Curriculum.* Chicago: University of Chicago Press.

Dewey, J. (1910). *The Influence of Darwin on Philosophy.* New York: Holt.

Dewey, J. (1915). *The School and Society.* Chicago: University of Chicago Press.

Dobson, J. (1970). *Dare to Discipline.* Wheaton, IL: Tyndale.

Egan, K. (2002). *Getting It Wrong from the Beginning.* New Haven: Yale University Press.

Eavey, C. B. (1964). *History of Christian Education*. Chicago: Moody Press.

Englund, M. M., Luckner, A. E., Whaley, G. J., & Egeland, B. (2004). Children's achievement in early elementary school: Longitudinal effects of parental involvement, expectations and quality of assistance. *Journal of Educational Psychology, 96* (4), 723–730.

Epstein, J. (2001). *School, Family, and Community Partnerships*. Boulder: Westview Press.

Fan, X., & Chen, M. (2001). Parental involvement and students' academic achievement: A meta-analysis. *Educational Psychology Review, 13* (1), 1–22.

Ford, M. S., Follmer, R., & Litz, K. (1998). School–family partnerships: Parents, children, and teachers benefit. *Teaching Children, 4* (6), 310–312.

Gatto, J. G. (2001). *The Underground History of American Education*. New York: Oxford Village Press.

Gillam, S. (2008). *Steve Jobs: Apple & Ipod Wizard*. Edina, MN: ABDO Publishing.

Griffith, J. (1996). Relation of parental involvement, empowerment, and school traits to student academic performance. *Journal of Educational Research, 90* (1), 33–41.

Hampton, F. M., Mumford, D. M., & Bond, L. 1998). Parent involvement in inner-city schools: The Project FAST extended family approach to success. *Urban Education, 33* (3), 410–427.

Henderson, A. T., & Mapp, K. L. (2002). *A New Wave of Evidence: The Impact of School, Family, and Community Connections on Student Achievement*. Austin, TX: Southwest Educational Development Laboratory.

Hoover-Dempsey, K. V. (2005, April). Research and evaluation of family involvement in education: What lies ahead? Symposium sponsored by Harvard University at the annual conference of the American Educational research Association in Montreal, Canada.

Hoover-Dempsey, K. V. Walker, J. M., & Jones, K. P. (2002). Teachers involving parents (TIP): Results from an in-service teacher education program for enhancing parental involvement. *Teacher and Teacher Education, 18* (7), 843–867.

Imbimbo, A. (2009). *Steve Jobs: The Brilliant Mind behind Apple*. Pleasantville, NY: Gareth Stevens.

Jarvis, J. (2009). *What Would Google Do?* New York: Collins Business.

Jeynes, W. (1999a). The effects of religious commitment on the academic achievement of black and Hispanic children. *Urban Education, 34* (4), 458–479.

Jeynes, W. (2002a). *Divorce, Family Structure, and the Academic Success of Children*. Binghamton, New York: Haworth Press.

Jeynes, W. (2002b). Does widowhood or remarriage have the greater impact on the academic achievement of children? *Omega: Journal of Death and Dying, 44* (3), 3 19–343.

Jeynes, W. (2003a). A meta-analysis: the effects of parental involvement on minority children's academic achievement. *Education & Urban Society, 35* (2), 202–218.

Jeynes, W. (2003b). The effects of black and Hispanic twelfth graders living in intact families and being religious on their academic achievement. *Urban Education, 38* (1), 35–57.

Jeynes, W. (2005b). A meta-analysis of the relation of parental involvement to urban elementary school student academic achievement. *Urban Education, 40,* (3), 237–269.

Jeynes, W. (2005f). The effects of parental involvement on the academic achievement of African American youth. *Journal of Negro Education, 74* (3), 260–274.

Jeynes, W. (2006a). Standardized tests and the true meaning of kindergarten and pre-school. *Teachers' College Record, 108* (10), 1,937–1,959.

Jeynes, W. (2006b). The impact of parental remarriage on children: A meta-analysis. *Marriage & Family Review, 40* (4), 75–102.

Jeynes, W. (2007b). The relationship between parental involvement and urban secondary school student academic achievement: A meta-analysis. *Urban Education, 42* (1), 82–110.

Jeynes, W. (2010). The salience of the subtle aspects of parental involvement and encouraging that involvement: implications for school-based programs. *Teachers' College Record, 112* (3), 747–774.

Kay, P., & Fitzgerald, M. (1997). Parents + teachers + action research = real involvement. *Teaching Exceptional Children, 30* (1), 8–14.

Keith, P. B., & Lichtman, M. V. (1994). Does parental involvement influence the academic achievement of Mexican-American eighth-graders? Results from the National Education Longitudinal Study. *School Psychology Quarterly, 9* (4), 256–273.

Lindle, J. C. (1990). Five reasons to prepare your staff for parental involvement. *School Adminstrator, 47* (6), 19–22, 24.

Mattingly, D. J., Prislin, R., McKenzie, T. L., Rodriguez, J. L., & Kayzar, B. (2002). Evaluating evaluations: The case of parental involvement programs. *Review of Educational Research, 72* (4), 549–576.

McLanahan, S., & Sandefur, G. (1994). *Growing Up with a Single Parent: What Hurts, What Helps.* Cambridge: Harvard University Press.

Meyer, C. (2003). *It's Alive.* New York: Crown.

Peressini, D. D. (1998). The portrayal of parents in the school mathematics reform literature: Locating the context for parental involvement. *Journal for Research in Mathematics Education,* 29 (5), 55–582.

Pestalozzi, J. (1916). "How a child is led to God through maternal love," in J. A. Green (Ed.), *Pestalozzi's Educational Writings.* London: Edward Arnold.

Sanders, M. G., & Epstein, J. (2000). The National Network of Partnership Schools. *Journal of Education for Students Placed at Risk, 5* (1/2), 61–76.

Schwartz, S. S. (1996). *Focus on First Graders.* El Paso, Texas: El Paso Independent School District.

Shaver, A. V., & Walls, R. T. (1998). Effect of Title I parent involvement on student reading and mathematics achievement. *Journal of Research and Development in Education,* 31 (2), 90–97.

Slaughter-Defoe, D. T. (1991). Parental educational choice: Some African American dilemmas. *Journal of Negro Education, 60* (3), 354–360.

Slavin, R. (2002). Mounting evidence supports the achievement effects of Success for All. *Phi Delta Kappan, 83* (6), 479–482.

Spera, C. (2005). A review of the relationship between parental involvement and student motivation. *Educational Psychology Review, 17,* 125–146.

Tyack, D. (1974). *The One Best System: A History of American Urban Education.* Cambridge: Harvard University Press.

U.S. Census Bureau. (2004). *Statistical Abstract of the United States.* Washington, D.C.: United States.

U.S. Department of Education. (2002). *Digest of Education Statistics.* Washington, D.C.: Department of Education.

Wallace, T., & Walberg, H. (1993). Parent programs for learning: A research Synthesis.

In F. Smit, W. van Esch & H. Walberg (Eds.), *Parental Involvement In Education* (pp. 151–155) Nimegen, The Netherlands: ITS.

Wallerstein, J. S., & Blakeslee, S. (1989). *Second Chances: Men, Women, and Children a Decade After Divorce.* New York: Ticknor and Fields.

Yoffle, D. B. (1997). *Competing in the Age of Digital Convergence.* Boston: Harvard University.

Index